Help the

Ascended Masters

Stop War

Spiritualizing the World, vol 2

Help the

Ascended Masters

Stop War

KIM MICHAELS

Copyright © 2015 Kim Michaels. All rights reserved. No part of this book may be used, reproduced, translated, electronically stored or transmitted by any means except by written permission from the publisher. A reviewer may quote brief passages in a review.

MORE TO LIFE PUBLISHING

www.morepublish.com

For foreign and translation rights,

contact info@ morepublish.com

ISBN: 978-87-93297-10-4

The information and insights in this book should not be considered as a form of therapy, advice, direction, diagnosis, and/or treatment of any kind. This information is not a substitute for medical, psychological, or other professional advice, counseling and care. All matters pertaining to your individual health should be supervised by a physician or appropriate health-care practitioner. No guarantee is made by the author or the publisher that the practices described in this book will yield successful results for anyone at any time. They are presented for informational purposes only, as the practice and proof rests with the individual.

For more information: *www.ascendedmasterlight.com and www.transcendencetoolbox.com*

CONTENTS

Introduction 9
1 | How Spiritual People Can Help Stop War 13
2 | Awaken People to the Potential to Stop War 35
3 | The Non-Physical Causes of War 55
4 | Exposing the Non-Physical Causes of War 75
5 | How War Can Actually be Removed 95
6 | Awaken People to the Need for Judgment 121
7 | Fear as a Cause of War 141
8 | Shattering the Illusion of Fear 163
9 | The Warrior Mentality 183
10 | Shattering the Warrior Mentality 201
11 | Material Gain through War 221
12 | Judging War for Profit 245
13 | Exposing the False Money System 265
14 | War and the Quest for Power 285
15 | Judging the Insatiable Quest for Power 309
16 | How Ideas Are Used to Justify War 329
17 | Judging Fanaticism 353
18 | The Need to Clean Up the Astral Plane 373
19 | Clearing the Astral Plane 397
20 | Deceptions in the Mental Realm 415
21 | Clearing the Mental Realm 443
22 | Illusions of Identity 463

23 | Clearing the Identity Octave 485
24 | Protecting Yourself from the Fallen Beings 505
25 | Protection from Dark Forces 515

INTRODUCTION

This book belongs to the series *Spiritualizing the World*. The books in this series are given by the ascended masters as workbooks that provide the knowledge and practical tools we need in order to make a contribution to solving concrete world problems. This book obviously contains the knowledge and the tools we need in order to deal with the problem of war. These books do not contain foundational knowledge about ascended masters and their teachings. In order to make the most efficient use of this book, you need to have a general knowledge of the following topics:

- You need to know who the ascended masters are, how they give their teachings and how you can make the best use of them on a personal and planetary level. You can find extensive teachings on this in the books: *How You Can Help Change the World* and *The Power of Self*.

- You need to know how the earth functions as a cosmic schoolroom. You need to know your own role and the authority you have as a spiritual being in embodiment. You need to know the role of the ascended masters and how only we who are in embodiment can give them the authority to use their unlimited power to affect change on earth. You can find more on these topics in the first book in this series: *How You Can Help Change the World*.

- You need to know how to use the practical tools given by the ascended masters. You can find more on this topic in: *How You Can Help Change the World* and on the website: *www.transcendencetoolbox.com*.

- You need to know about the existence and methods of the dark forces who are ultimately responsible for creating war on earth. You can find foundational teachings on this in: *Cosmology of Evil*.

How to use this book

There is no one way of using the teachings and tools in this book. However, if you want to make a significant contribution to stopping war, it is suggested that you start by following this program:

- You read one of the chapters in the book completely in order to increase your understanding of the topic.

- You give the invocation associated with that chapter once a day for nine days while studying the same chapter again.

The reasoning behind this program is that the chapters in the book form a progression. As you give an invocation for one chapter, you are also clearing your own consciousness from certain energies and illusions. This makes it easier for you to absorb and apply the teachings from the next chapter.

You can, of course, also read the book all the way through and then select one or more invocation(s) that you give several times. It is always more powerful to give an invocation once a day for nine or 33 days.

If you feel burdened

The purpose of this book is not to merely give you intellectual knowledge. The real purpose is that you give the invocations, whereby you give the ascended masters the authority to remove the dark forces and energies that promote war. These forces will not be happy that you contribute to the process of removing them from the earth. They may therefore seek to direct energy at you that can make you feel burdened in various ways. Their purpose is to make you stop (or prevent you from starting) your efforts.

If you feel burdened, please read the last chapter in the book and use the invocation associated with that chapter to make the calls for the protection of yourself and all people around you. As stated in that chapter, most people can quickly come to a point where they are no longer vulnerable to the attacks from the forces of war.

The dark forces will always seek to inflate any condition in our personal lives that makes us vulnerable. If you have particular issues, it may be helpful to use other tools that address those issues in a more direct manner. The ascended masters have given many invocations and decrees that can help you deal with specific topics, and you can find most of them on *www.transcendencetoolbox.com*. Some tools are found in the other books by Kim Michaels, and you can see them on *www.morepublish.com*.

As stated in this book, it is important that a certain number of people give the invocations and transcend the consciousness behind war. It is highly recommended that you talk to other people about this book, including using social media. As Mother Mary states, if enough people use this book and its invocations, it will be possible for the ascended masters to remove war from earth within the foreseeable future. *Isn't that a message worth spreading?*

1 | HOW SPIRITUAL PEOPLE CAN HELP STOP WAR

I am the Ascended Master Mother Mary! For the purpose of this book, I will assume that you know what an ascended master is. You have a basic knowledge of who we are. You have a basic knowledge of the dynamic on earth, meaning the relationship between human beings and ascended masters. You understand the Law of Free Will and that we, the ascended masters, do have the power to change every condition on earth, to remove all imperfections, all darkness, all evil and all war. We have the power to do this, but we do not have the authority because free will reigns supreme. That means the free will of human beings in embodiment must be allowed to outplay itself until people have had enough and do indeed change.

The force that does not respect free will

I will also assume that you understand the basic dynamic that there is a force on this earth that does not respect free will, the free will of human beings. This force attempts to manipulate human beings in all ways possible, based on deceit, based on raw force, based on any scheme you can imagine. Because free will reigns supreme, we of the ascended masters cannot step in and override the efforts of these deceptive or dark forces. We are not allowed to do this, even though they are violating the free will of human beings. This is because even though the dark forces are manipulating and deceiving human beings, they are not truly violating the Law of Free Will. You cannot be manipulated or deceived, unless you make a choice to allow this to happen because you are not willing to take full responsibility for your own life or your own situation. It is, therefore, the lack of willingness to take full responsibility that has created the dark force and that allows it to remain on earth.

I know very well that, when I talk about the dark force, there are many spiritual people who will immediately reject this, or at least be very reluctant to look at it. This is, in fact, one of the main reasons why this dark force remains on earth.

Taking responsibility for yourself—and the whole

When you look at humankind, you can clearly see that there are many who are very far from the point where they are able and willing to take responsibility for their lives. These people will not change the earth. They will not change the basic dynamic that will allow the ascended masters to step in and remove major problems, such as war. Who can bring about a change on earth? Only those who have risen to a higher level of consciousness where they are beginning to take responsibility for themselves. There are, unfortunately, many of these people who have not yet reached the point where they are open to the teachings we give in books such as this one. They have started to take responsibility for themselves as individuals, but they have not come to the point where they are willing to look beyond themselves and their own situation. They have, sort of, isolated and insulated themselves from the world and from the things that are going on in the world. They do not really want to look at certain problems, such as the problem of war.

They want to believe that, as long as they sit there in their ashrams or their communities or even in their individual homes and focus on the positive, focus only on positive vibrations, then they are making a contribution to improving the world. My beloved, they *are* making a contribution. I am not disputing this, but they are not making the maximum contribution that they could be making if they would step up to a higher sense of responsibility.

You will not truly change the earth by only focusing on yourself and raising your own consciousness. This is because of the nature of free will and the nature of energy. We have given many teachings on the fact that humankind has created a downward energy spiral where people are feeding fear-based energy, such as anger and hatred, into a vortex that has become so strong that it can overpower individual people. This you cannot change by only changing your own consciousness.

Those who are the spiritual people on earth cannot change the basic dynamic on earth only by focusing on raising their own consciousness. It is necessary to look beyond yourself and to take responsibility for the planet as a whole, for humanity as a whole. If you will not do this, then you will continue to make a contribution by producing love-based vibrations, but this contribution will not reach a level where it will have a decisive impact on the future of this planet. It will not reach a level that will allow the ascended masters to step in and remove major problems, such as war.

How you can and cannot remove war

The energy vortexes that drive war are so powerful that even if all of the spiritual and religious people on earth raised their own consciousness, it would not be enough to consume these energy vortexes. If all of the people on earth shifted into sending out only positive vibrations, even this would not be enough to consume the vortexes of war. Only the power of the ascended masters can consume these vortexes. Human beings do not have the power to do this alone. That is why Jesus, 2,000 years ago, said: "With men this is impossible, but not with God, for with God all things are possible."

Human beings alone cannot remove war from planet earth. Only by working with the ascended masters can war be removed. We need you to give us the authority to use the power that we have been given by God. How do you give us the authority? Not by sitting in your own ivory tower and focusing on yourself and raising your own consciousness. You give us the authority only by looking beyond yourself, taking an honest and open look at what is happening on this planet, understanding the dynamic of why war was created and how it can continue. Then you make the appropriate calls that will give us the authority and the energy to multiply so that we can step in and remove war and other major problems.

Looking at darkness without giving it power

There are so many wonderful people in spiritual, mystical and New Age movements. There are so many wonderful people in religious movements. They have the best of intentions, but they have come to believe that they do not need to look at anything dark or evil. Some have even come to believe that if they look at darkness they reinforce it, they give it power. It is important that you understand why this is not the case, or rather, it is important that you understand how to look at darkness without giving it power.

As I said, there are many spiritual people who are focusing on raising their own consciousness while refusing to look at anything dark or evil, while refusing to look at any problems. There is also a certain segment of spiritual people who have passed this point. They have become willing to look at the darkness, but they have not yet transcended some of the matrices of their own egos.

As they look at the darkness, they go into a spiral of anger. They have what they themselves call "righteous indignation," but it is not *righteous* in the sense that it is based on non-attachment. They are very much attached to producing a specific result, such as defeating the dark forces or removing them from the earth. Through this attachment, that leads to anger, you *will* give power to dark forces. It is very true, as many of the, shall we say, *gentle* spiritual people have realized, that if you engage in a fight against darkness that is based on anger, then you will give power to darkness. This is, of course, not the only way to look at darkness.

You can step up to a higher way where you have transcended anger, and therefore, you can look at the darkness with non-attachment. You can realize that you, as a human being, do not have to fight darkness. You allow the ascended masters to do the work, and you allow us to do it our way based on our higher vision. Your job is to have enough information so that you know how to make precise calls for specific situations. You make those calls, and then you allow us to decide how to do the actual work.

There has never been a war in heaven

My beloved, there are images in the collective consciousness of this planet, starting with the Bible but also with some of the Eastern scriptures, of how, supposedly, angels fight the devil and his forces. There are the images from the *Book of Revelation* of how there was a war in heaven where Michael and his angels fought the dragon, and the dragon prevailed not and was cast down into the earth. These are images that were given at a time when the collective consciousness was even lower than it is today.

There has never been a war in heaven. We have explained how the origin of dark forces did not occur in heaven but in a previous sphere that was not yet ascended. Archangel Michael has never fought the devil as you see fighting today on earth and have seen it throughout history. We do not need to *fight* the devil and the dark forces. We only need to bring our light, and the light itself either consumes or judges the dark forces. We do not engage the dark forces at *their* level. We do not engage in a dualistic struggle. Once you begin to understand this, you can also step up to that level where you are aware of the darkness but you are neutral.

Overcoming the fear of looking at darkness

There are many well-meaning spiritual people who are focusing on raising their own consciousness, while thinking they should not focus on the darkness because it gives power to the darkness. They think they are being loving, they think they are focusing on love. If you are not willing to look at the darkness, there can be only one explanation. You are *afraid* to look at the darkness. Fear and love are incompatible emotions. You cannot be fully loving while having fear in your subconscious mind, in your energy field, in your four lower bodies. I know that many of these people, if they were to read this (which they are not likely to do) would say that they are entirely loving, that they are always focusing on the positive, always being loving and kind.

Those of you who are open to a higher teaching can, perhaps, begin to see that human beings have a very unique ability. They have the ability to compartmentalize their minds. They have an ability to create two or more divisions in their minds and to switch between them without being consciously aware of the switch. When they are in one compartment of the mind, or one personality as you might call it, they are acting as that personality. Then they switch to another personality, and now they are acting like that personality without seeing the discrepancy or the contradiction between the two. This is what allows people to believe that they are fully loving while having unrecognized vortexes of fear in their subconscious minds.

I said that there are some spiritual people who have started to awaken from this state. They have been willing to look at the dark forces, but they have been caught in a spiral of anger. Fear is a paralyzing emotion. When you are completely trapped in fear, you cannot move, you cannot do anything. There are people who are trapped in fear and who know they are living in fear. They are conscious of their fear. There are also people who are trapped by fear and they are not conscious. Some of these people are spiritual and religious people who think that, by being loving and kind, they are doing all they need to do to improve things on earth. You will not truly improve things on earth without looking at and overcoming your own fear.

Overcoming anger against darkness

As you begin to overcome fear, it is possible that you need to go through a phase where you have a certain amount of anger. When you have been trapped in the paralyzing state of fear, it is often necessary to have anger as the drive to get you to start moving. It is sometimes better that people are moving in any direction than when they are standing still. We hope that our students can see that anger should be a very short phase on your spiritual path. It is absolutely necessary that you move out of anger as quickly as possible. Even though you are moving, you are not moving in a direction that will allow you to have the maximum impact on the future of this planet. You will not improve things on earth as long as you allow vortexes of anger in your energy field.

You need to be willing to look at this and use the many tools we have given for overcoming such matrices [See *www.transcendencetoolbox.com*]. We have given many invocations, many teachings, including books on forgiveness and clearing your chakras [See *www.morepublish.com*], that will allow you to quickly move through this phase and overcome the anger. You can begin to look at darkness without engaging in these angry or hateful feelings or without having an attachment to a specific outcome where you feel that some epic goal must be attained.

Dare to follow your inner knowing

How do you have the greatest impact on the future of this planet? Why do you want to have the greatest impact? May I ask you to consider one of the most peculiar mechanisms that you are exposed to as you grow up almost anywhere on earth? Why are you a spiritual person? Many will say they have grown up in a spiritual or religious environment. They have been exposed to certain spiritual teachings and ideas. *That* is not why you are a truly spiritual person who is open to the teachings of the ascended masters.

You can be a spiritual person only because you sense and know something inside yourself. You sense and know something that is beyond what you have been told from without, perhaps even in direct contradiction to what you were told as you were growing up. You are daring to follow your inner knowing, rather than the outer programming that you have received.

The peculiar mechanism that I am talking about is that most people have been brought up in an environment that strongly discourages them from listening to and following their inner knowing, their intuitive sense of what is right and what is their goal in life. There are today millions of spiritual people on earth who have come into this embodiment with the higher knowing that they have reached a level on the spiritual path where they have the potential to serve in various capacities for bringing about positive change on this planet.

When I say they have the awareness, I mean that they had this awareness before they came into embodiment. This does not mean you have this awareness now or that you had it during your childhood. One reason is that you have a certain forgetfulness that happens to most people as they come into the density of the body and the outer mind. Another important reason is the programming from society and the environment that encourages you to override your intuitive knowing. In order to become a spiritual person who is open to reading this book, you have learned to override the programming and again tune in to your inner knowing. You may not have fully overcome the programming. You may not have fully unlocked your inner knowing or dared to listen to it. If you are one of the people who believe you only need to focus on the positive, then you have not overcome the programming from the world. The entire idea that you can be a spiritual person and make a contribution to improving the world without looking at anything negative or evil is indeed a programming created by the dark forces in order to prevent the spiritual people from fulfilling their highest potential. The idea that when you look at dark forces, you need to go into anger, even righteous indignation, and attempt to fight these forces is also created by the dark forces for the purpose of preventing spiritual people from fulfilling their highest potential. The dark forces do not want to lose the grip they have on humanity and this planet. This you need to acknowledge consciously.

Explaining the senselessness of war

May I ask you to just cast a glance back at human history? Look at the many wars that have taken place on this planet. There are hundreds if not thousands of wars in which thousands, tens of thousands, millions of people have been killed. When you look at this in history, can you honestly believe that such a phenomenon could come about for any kind of rational, human reason?

I know there are historians who point to various factors, be they economic, political or sociological, as the cause of war. Can you honestly believe that a phenomenon as senseless as war could be caused by sensible, rational reasons? Do you really believe that all the fighting you have seen in the world, and see today, happens by people who are completely rational and who think that going out and indiscriminately murdering men, women and children serves some rational purpose? I am not here asking you to contemplate the cause of war because we will go into that later. I am just asking you to ask yourself whether war can be explained in completely rational terms.

When you look at some of the things that are happening in the world today, such as the things going on in Africa or in Syria or other parts of the Middle East, can you not see that there is a certain element of fanaticism that drives some of these people who are going out and killing or raping women or children? Can you honestly say that fanaticism is rational? I think you will agree that it cannot be rational. These people are not in a rational frame of mind.

I then ask you to consider how it is possible for human beings to be in a non-rational frame of mind where they are not open to any kind of rational arguments? They are driven by motives that they do not fully understand, and they have not contemplated the consequences of their actions. Reach back to my earlier statement that human beings have the ability to compartmentalize their lives. Do you understand, my beloved, that there are many examples from history of people who have gone to war and killed and then come home and lived a seemingly normal life?

Take one of the generally recognized examples of fanaticism, namely the Nazi concentration camps. Do you realize that some of the leaders of these concentration camps would go to work during the day and oversee the killing of millions of people, including children, and then at night, they would come home to their families and be exemplary parents to their own children? They would see no discrepancy or contradiction between the personality they had during the day, that allowed them to kill children without reflecting upon it, and then the personality they went into at night of adoring their own children. When you look at this, can you not see that there must be an explanation here that defies the common knowledge prompted by the thought systems of this world, be they materialistic, scientific or religious in origin? When you acknowledge this, then you need to look for an explanation that goes beyond the normal. The explanation is that there is a dark force on this planet, which has the ability to take over the minds of individual human beings, even groups of human beings. It is this force that blinds people to the fact that they have two or more incompatible personalities or action patterns in their minds. It is this force that causes people to go into the fanatical state of mind where they are willing to kill without reflecting upon the fact that they are killing other human beings.

Human beings cannot kill other human beings

We have said before that a human being cannot kill another human being. This is because the human body has a certain programming in the brain and nervous system. This programming forms what we might call the outer mind or the carnal mind. It is programmed, much like what you see in animals, to secure the survival of both the individual and the race. This means that human beings are programmed *not* to kill others of their own species. This is not a programming that is rational or reflective in any way. There is a programming that causes you to know that it is not right to kill other human beings. This programming is in the physical body, the brain and the nervous system.

It takes quite a lot to override this programming and get people into a state of mind where they indiscriminately kill human beings without consciously acknowledging what they are doing. Only a force that is more powerful than the individual, or even more powerful than certain groups of people, can override the programming not to kill. Surely, there are many explanations for why people have felt it was justified to kill certain other groups of people. These we will talk about later, but for now, I want you to consider, if you have not already, that the only explanation for the fanatical killing that you see and have seen, is that there is a force – let us call it a *dark* force – that overrides the free will of human beings and overrides even the deepest programming not to kill.

Giving the masters the authority to remove war

If there is ever going to be a state where war has been removed from planet earth, then it can come about only because the dark force that promotes war has been removed from planet earth. The removal of this dark force cannot be produced by human beings. You do *not* have the power. The removal of this dark force can be accomplished very easily by the ascended masters. We *do* have the power.

We could remove the dark forces on earth instantly, if we had enough authority from human beings. What *you* have is the authority, and by giving *us* the authority – and by giving us a certain amount of energy we can multiply – then you and we together *can* remove the forces of war from planet earth. This cannot be done by you being positive and thinking "It's all good." When you look at the atrocities that are being committed, even as I speak, you cannot honestly say that all is good on this planet.

Therefore, I am asking you to awaken yourself to the reality that change needs to happen and that change is not going to be brought about by you staying in fear where you think being loving and kind is enough. Neither is change going to happen by you staying in anger where you think you have to be judgmental of dark forces, where you think you have to fight them, either physically or in some spiritual battle. If you use our invocations and decrees from a state of anger, then they will not have the necessary effect. They may indeed, in the long run, open you up to the very dark forces that you think you are fighting. I am asking you to consider stepping up to a higher level of responsibility.

Awareness without attachment

Those who think "It's all good" have taken responsibility for themselves, but they have not taken responsibility beyond themselves, even though they think they are serving to save the world. Those who are in anger have started to take responsibility for the planet as a whole and for the existence of dark forces, but they have not actually taken the higher sense of responsibility. That is because they think they have to fight the dark forces.

The higher form of responsibility that I am talking about is where you realize the dynamic I have explained. You, as a human being in embodiment, have the authority to allow the ascended masters to remove the dark forces. You do not have the authority to go out and fight these dark forces. When a human being in embodiment begins to fight anything, you are only serving to produce energy that sustains the dark forces. The higher sense of responsibility is where you realize that you do not have the power or the responsibility for fighting or removing dark forces. Your responsibility is to educate yourself to the existence of dark forces, to their methods, to how they are manipulating and using human beings, and then you do two things:

- The Omega aspect is that you may share this with other people in an appropriate, non-attached manner.

- The Alpha aspect is that you give the calls to the ascended masters, also in a non-attached manner, that allows us to step in.

This is your highest responsibility. It is awareness without attachment that is the highest way to fulfill your reason for coming into embodiment. You came here because you had a true desire to help raise this planet to a higher level. Before you came, you were in the etheric realm looking down on the physical octave from that elevated perspective. At that level, you did not have an attachment. You had a true desire, but it was a non-attached desire.

Transcending fear and anger

What has happened to many people is that because you are now in embodiment, because you have seen or even personally experienced the atrocities that take place on this planet, you go into a state of mind of being attached. You may still have some memory and awareness of your desire to make a difference, but you become attached. You do this in an attached way with great emotional involvement, in terms of fear, anger or other feelings. You may call it "righteous indignation" if you like, but it is still a fear-based emotion. You will not fulfill your highest potential and responsibility until you transcend that emotion.

How will you transcend fear and anger? By realizing that there is nothing to fear because we of the ascended masters do have the power to remove all darkness and evil from the earth. There is no reason to be angry because, if you give us the authority and the energy, then we *will* step in and do the work.

Anger often comes because you have started to move out of the paralysis of fear, but you still feel disempowered to produce the results you think you need to produce. Anger is overcome when you, first of all, consider whether the results you think need to be produced are the highest possible results. Then, when you have a realistic assessment of the goal, you can begin to see that by working with the ascended masters, it is indeed possible to achieve the goal. Therefore, you do not need to feel frustrated or disempowered.

How you can help the ascended masters

I said that we of the ascended masters have the power to remove all darkness instantly. This was to give you the realistic assessment of our power. Of course, that power must and will be expressed within the context of the Law of Free Will. It would never be possible that there would be an instant shift in the consciousness of seven billion people on earth so that we could remove war instantly.

Removing war is a process because it is not a matter of producing the outer result of removing war. The real, underlying dynamic is to raise people's state of consciousness. War will not be removed from this earth until a critical mass of people have transcended the consciousness that made war possible. This is a process that will not happen instantly.

It cannot be forced on people from without. It must happen gradually by people raising their consciousness and having these intuitive breakthroughs and shifts in their consciousness where they gradually transcend the consciousness they are in right now. You may say: "But then, what is the purpose?" What am I talking about? What is it that you are supposed to do for the ascended masters?

I have told you that the dark forces do not respect the free will of human beings. They have used various means, which we will talk about later, to overpower people's minds so that they are not exercising their free will. I said that this has been possible because people have not been willing to take responsibility for themselves, and that is why the dark forces could even come to this planet.

This we will also talk more about later, but the basic dynamic is that you, as a spiritual person who has started to awaken from the collective state of mind, have the right and the authority to call for the ascended masters to reduce the power of the dark forces. By reducing the power of these dark forces, they will no longer be able to blind people. This means that people will now gradually move into a state where they can see things that they could not see while they were overpowered by the dark forces. People can now begin to actually exercise their free will freely. They can exercise their free will from a state of seeing rather than a state of blindness.

This still does not mean that a shift will happen instantly. It will require a process of people gradually raising their awareness and shifting their consciousness. Once the energy that overpowers people is reduced in strength, they will have the freedom to rethink many of the conditions on earth that they now take for granted or cannot see at all. It is not a matter of you helping us to force people. We of the ascended masters have ultimate respect for free will, and that is what we are asking you to attain as well.

You are in embodiment, and we understand that this is more difficult for you because you are threatened by other people who can attack you physically. We are still asking you to work towards an absolute respect for other people's free will. You realize that we of the ascended masters never seek to force people, even for their own good. You may say: "Well, obviously it is for everybody's good to remove war from the earth." We of the ascended masters agree that it is, but this does not mean that we would ever override people's free will and force them in order to achieve this goal. We seek to achieve the goal by freeing people's will so that they can freely make the choice to transcend the consciousness that makes war possible.

Do you begin to see the dynamic here? War is possible because there is a force that overrides peoples' basic programming and their free will. People do not have a free choice to stop war, to stop killing. Even people in seemingly peaceful nations do not have a free choice to say that their country should not engage in wars and they should not engage in many other activities that actually support war or the entire culture and consciousness of war, even the industry of war.

You cannot remove war alone

What we of the ascended masters seek to achieve with this book is to awaken a critical mass of the spiritual people so that you will have a correct understanding of what it will take to remove war from this planet. This will then empower you to make the most efficient possible contribution to removing war. In order to give you the tools to make this contribution, we will present you with a series of invocations that will truly give you, along with the many other tools we have given, the power to give us the power to step in on earth. You alone cannot remove war. It is not your task and responsibility to do it alone. Your task is to work with us so that we *together* can have the maximum impact on this planet. By acknowledging that it is not you alone who must do something, you can overcome the paralysis that so many people feel.

Consider that you have grown up on a planet and in a society where many people consider war inevitable. When you look back at the last few hundred years, you will see that there has been a gradual shift happening in many of the more developed nations. If you go back a few hundred years, you will see that many people thought war was not only inevitable but even desirable. There was a certain honor associated with being a solider and going to war and defeating the enemy. Many young men were brought up to want to go to war, want to do heroic deeds.

Even in the first world war and the second world war, this was the case. Even in more recent wars, you have seen people volunteer to go out and do something that they felt had ultimate importance. You have also seen many nations where there has been a shift where most people have begun to feel that war is not honorable and war is not desirable. War is something that ideally should be avoided, yet these people do not see how it could be avoided. Again, you have an example of the compartmentalization of people's minds.

There are many people who feel that they themselves do not support war, and they would not go to war and they would not kill another human being. At the same time, they have another compartment of their minds where they have given up and think that war is inevitable, that it cannot be removed from the earth. It is a matter of trying to avoid it and staying away from it. This is what has caused many spiritual people to go into the sense that: "If I just focus on myself, and if I am loving and kind, then I am doing all that I can do to improve planet earth." This is the paralysis that we seek to awaken you from so that you can fulfill the potential for which you came into this embodiment.

You decided that you wanted to make a decisive contribution to removing war from this planet. Millions of spiritual people did this before coming into this lifetime. This is because we of the ascended masters know that there is a realistic potential that we can remove war from this planet within the foreseeable future. Cosmic cycles are right that this can be achieved. It will not be easy; it will take time, but it is a possible and realistic goal. You know this in your heart if you are open to this book.

I am asking you to acknowledge that you have an outer programming that makes it seem like war is inevitable. After all, there is always some other people that you cannot control who are willing to start a war. When you look at what is going on in Africa or the Middle East, how can you not feel disempowered? How can you not feel the impossibility of stopping this?

Empowerment with the ascended masters

I am asking you to recognize that you are not disempowered when you work with the ascended masters. There *is* a possibility of stopping war because these people are completely overpowered by the dark forces. If you remove the power that the dark forces have over people, then the people will awaken. They will awaken to the basic programming in the human body and mind, but also to the fact that they too are spiritual beings who have a higher goal and a higher vision of their lives. There is hardly any person who could not be awakened. There are some that it would be very difficult to awaken, but then we of the ascended masters have the authority to remove them from the earth when enough other people have transcended a certain level of consciousness.

There is nothing that cannot be changed and overcome. There is nothing that is impossible because free will reigns supreme. Why is war still on earth? Because too many people are using their free will to accept war as desirable or as inevitable. When a critical mass of people use their free will to transcend the level of consciousness that makes war seem desirable or inevitable, then we of the ascended masters *can* and *will* remove war from this planet. If you find in your heart that this is a goal that resonates with you, then follow me as I reveal to you how the goal can be achieved.

Mother Mary I AM, the Ascended Master Mother Mary I AM!

2 | AWAKEN PEOPLE TO THE POTENTIAL TO STOP WAR

In the name of the I AM THAT I AM, Jesus Christ, I call upon Mother Mary and the Divine Director to awaken people from the illusion that war is too big of an issue for us to do anything about. Awaken people to the reality that we are spiritual beings and that we can co-create a new future by working with the ascended masters. I especially call for …

[Make your own calls here.]

Part 1

1. Mother Mary, awaken people to the existence of the ascended masters. Awaken people to the Law of Free Will and that the ascended masters have the power to remove war, but that we who are in embodiment must give you the authority to do so.

O blessed Mary, Mother mine,
there is no greater love than thine,
as we are one in heart and mind,
my place in hierarchy I find.

**O Mother Mary, generate,
the song that does accelerate,
the earth into a higher state,
all matter does now scintillate.**

2. Mother Mary, awaken people to the existence of a force that does not respect our free will but attempts to manipulate us into creating and sustaining war.

I came to earth from heaven sent,
as I am in embodiment,
I use Divine authority,
commanding you to set earth free.

**O Mother Mary, generate,
the song that does accelerate,
the earth into a higher state,
all matter does now scintillate.**

3. Mother Mary, awaken people from the tendency to reject, or be reluctant to look at, the existence of a dark force. Help people see that this is what keeps the dark force in power on earth.

I call now in God's sacred name,
for you to use your Mother Flame,
to burn all fear-based energy,
restoring sacred harmony.

> **O Mother Mary, generate,**
> **the song that does accelerate,**
> **the earth into a higher state,**
> **all matter does now scintillate.**

4. Mother Mary, awaken people to the fact that the only way to stop war is to allow the ascended masters to remove the dark force. Help people see that only those who are willing to take responsibility for themselves can bring about this shift.

> Your sacred name I hereby praise,
> collective consciousness you raise,
> no more of fear and doubt and shame,
> consume it with your Mother Flame.

> **O Mother Mary, generate,**
> **the song that does accelerate,**
> **the earth into a higher state,**
> **all matter does now scintillate.**

5. Mother Mary, awaken people from the tendency to isolate themselves and from their unwillingness to look for a deeper, spiritual understanding of war. Help them see that focusing on the positive and sending out good vibrations is not enough to stop war.

> All darkness from the earth you purge,
> your light moves as a mighty surge,
> no force of darkness can now stop,
> the spiral that goes only up.

**O Mother Mary, generate,
the song that does accelerate,
the earth into a higher state,
all matter does now scintillate.**

6. Mother Mary, awaken people to the reality that we will not truly change the earth by only focusing on ourselves and raising our own consciousness. It is necessary to look beyond ourselves and take responsibility for the planet, for humanity as a whole.

All elemental life you bless,
removing from them man-made stress,
the nature spirits are now free,
outpicturing Divine decree.

**O Mother Mary, generate,
the song that does accelerate,
the earth into a higher state,
all matter does now scintillate.**

7. Mother Mary, awaken people to the realty that the energy vortexes that drive war are so powerful that even if all of the spiritual and religious people on earth raised their own consciousness, it would not be enough to consume these vortexes.

I raise my voice and take my stand,
a stop to war I do command,
no more shall warring scar the earth,
a golden age is given birth.

**O Mother Mary, generate,
the song that does accelerate,
the earth into a higher state,
all matter does now scintillate.**

8. Mother Mary, awaken people to the reality that only the power of the ascended masters can consume these vortexes. Only the ascended masters have that power.

As Mother Earth is free at last,
disasters belong to the past,
your Mother Light is so intense,
that matter is now far less dense.

**O Mother Mary, generate,
the song that does accelerate,
the earth into a higher state,
all matter does now scintillate.**

9. Mother Mary, awaken people to the reality that we alone cannot remove war from planet earth. Only by working with the ascended masters can war be removed.

In Mother Light the earth is pure,
the upward spiral will endure,
prosperity is now the norm,
God's vision manifest as form.

**O Mother Mary, generate,
the song that does accelerate,
the earth into a higher state,
all matter does now scintillate.**

Part 2

1. Divine Director, awaken people to the need for us to give the ascended masters the authority to act on earth. We do this only by understanding the dynamic of why war was created and how it can continue.

> Divine Director, I now see,
> the world is unreality,
> in my heart I now truly feel,
> the Spirit is all that is real.
>
> **Divine Director, send the light,**
> **from blindness clear my inner sight,**
> **my vision free, my vision clear,**
> **your guidance is forever here.**

2. Divine Director, awaken people from the illusion that they do not need to look at anything dark or evil. Help them see how to look at darkness without giving it power.

> Divine Director, vision give,
> in clarity I want to live,
> I now behold my plan Divine,
> the plan that is uniquely mine.
>
> **Divine Director, send the light,**
> **from blindness clear my inner sight,**
> **my vision free, my vision clear,**
> **your guidance is forever here.**

3. Divine Director, awaken people from the tendency that they are willing to look at darkness but are then deceived into reacting with anger. Help them see that wanting to defeat the dark forces does give power to darkness.

> Divine Director, show in me,
> the ego games, and set me free,
> help me escape the ego's cage,
> to help bring in the golden age.
>
> **Divine Director, send the light,**
> **from blindness clear my inner sight,**
> **my vision free, my vision clear,**
> **your guidance is forever here.**

4. Divine Director, awaken people to the Middle Way where you look at darkness with non-attachment. You look at darkness in order to make precise calls for the ascended masters to remove it.

> Divine Director, I'm with you,
> my vision one, no longer two,
> as karma's veil you do disperse,
> I see a whole new universe.
>
> **Divine Director, send the light,**
> **from blindness clear my inner sight,**
> **my vision free, my vision clear,**
> **your guidance is forever here.**

5. Divine Director, awaken people to the reality that we do not have to fight darkness. We allow the ascended masters to do the work based on your higher vision.

Divine Director, I go up,
electric light now fills my cup,
consume in me all shadows old,
bestow on me a vision bold.

**Divine Director, send the light,
from blindness clear my inner sight,
my vision free, my vision clear,
your guidance is forever here.**

6. Divine Director, awaken people from their fear of looking at the darkness on earth. Help them see that we will not truly improve things on earth without looking at and overcoming our own fear.

Divine Director, heart of gold,
my sacred labor I unfold,
o blessed Guru, I now see,
where my own plan is taking me.

**Divine Director, send the light,
from blindness clear my inner sight,
my vision free, my vision clear,
your guidance is forever here.**

7. Divine Director, awaken people to their inner knowing, their inner ability to know and experience the reality of the spiritual realm, the ascended masters and why we are here on earth.

Divine Director, by your grace,
in grander scheme I find my place,
my individual flame I see,
uniqueness God has given me.

> Divine Director, send the light,
> from blindness clear my inner sight,
> my vision free, my vision clear,
> your guidance is forever here.

8. Divine Director, awaken people to the fact that we have been brought up in an environment that strongly discourages us from listening to and following our inner knowing, our intuitive sense of what is right and what is our goal in life.

> Divine Director, vision one,
> I see that I AM God's own Sun,
> with your direction so Divine,
> I am now letting my light shine.

> Divine Director, send the light,
> from blindness clear my inner sight,
> my vision free, my vision clear,
> your guidance is forever here.

9. Divine Director, awaken people from the forgetfulness that happens as we take embodiment. Help people see their reason for taking embodiment at this time.

> Divine Director, what a gift,
> to be a part of Spirit's lift,
> to raise mankind out of the night,
> to bask in Spirit's loving sight.

> Divine Director, send the light,
> from blindness clear my inner sight,
> my vision free, my vision clear,
> your guidance is forever here.

Part 3

1. Mother Mary, awaken people to the fact that the idea that one can be a spiritual person and make a contribution to improving the world without looking at anything negative or evil is a programming created by the dark forces in order to prevent the spiritual people from fulfilling their highest potential.

> O blessed Mary, Mother mine,
> there is no greater love than thine,
> as we are one in heart and mind,
> my place in hierarchy I find.
>
> **O Mother Mary, generate,**
> **the song that does accelerate,**
> **the earth into a higher state,**
> **all matter does now scintillate.**

2. Mother Mary, awaken people to the reality that the dark forces do not want to lose the grip they have on humanity and this planet. Help people acknowledge this consciously.

> I came to earth from heaven sent,
> as I am in embodiment,
> I use Divine authority,
> commanding you to set earth free.
>
> **O Mother Mary, generate,**
> **the song that does accelerate,**
> **the earth into a higher state,**
> **all matter does now scintillate.**

3. Mother Mary, awaken people to the reality that a phenomenon as senseless as war cannot be caused by sensible, rational reasons. War always involves an element of fanaticism that is not rational.

> I call now in God's sacred name,
> for you to use your Mother Flame,
> to burn all fear-based energy,
> restoring sacred harmony.
>
> **O Mother Mary, generate,**
> **the song that does accelerate,**
> **the earth into a higher state,**
> **all matter does now scintillate.**

4. Mother Mary, awaken people to the reality that fanaticism allows people to compartmentalize their lives so they see no discrepancy between their normal beliefs and the act of killing others.

> Your sacred name I hereby praise,
> collective consciousness you raise,
> no more of fear and doubt and shame,
> consume it with your Mother Flame.
>
> **O Mother Mary, generate,**
> **the song that does accelerate,**
> **the earth into a higher state,**
> **all matter does now scintillate.**

5. Mother Mary, awaken people to the reality that the only way to explain this irrational fanaticism is the existence of a dark force, which has the ability to take over the minds of individual human beings, even groups of human beings.

> All darkness from the earth you purge,
> your light moves as a mighty surge,
> no force of darkness can now stop,
> the spiral that goes only up.

> **O Mother Mary, generate,**
> **the song that does accelerate,**
> **the earth into a higher state,**
> **all matter does now scintillate.**

6. Mother Mary, awaken people to the reality that only the existence of a dark force can explain the senselessness and irrationality of war. We can remove war only by looking at this force and making the calls for the ascended masters to deal with it.

> All elemental life you bless,
> removing from them man-made stress,
> the nature spirits are now free,
> outpicturing Divine decree.

> **O Mother Mary, generate,**
> **the song that does accelerate,**
> **the earth into a higher state,**
> **all matter does now scintillate.**

2 | Awaken People to the Potential to Stop War

7. Mother Mary, awaken people to the reality that the only explanation for the fanatical killing on earth is that there is a dark force that overrides our free will and the deepest programming not to kill.

> I raise my voice and take my stand,
> a stop to war I do command,
> no more shall warring scar the earth,
> a golden age is given birth.
>
> **O Mother Mary, generate,**
> **the song that does accelerate,**
> **the earth into a higher state,**
> **all matter does now scintillate.**

8. Mother Mary, awaken people to the reality that the only way to stop war is to remove this force from the earth. We human beings have the authority to call for this and the ascended masters have the power to make it a reality.

> As Mother Earth is free at last,
> disasters belong to the past,
> your Mother Light is so intense,
> that matter is now far less dense.
>
> **O Mother Mary, generate,**
> **the song that does accelerate,**
> **the earth into a higher state,**
> **all matter does now scintillate.**

9. Mother Mary, awaken people to the reality that by giving the ascended masters the authority and the energy to multiply, we together can remove war from the earth.

In Mother Light the earth is pure,
the upward spiral will endure,
prosperity is now the norm,
God's vision manifest as form.

**O Mother Mary, generate,
the song that does accelerate,
the earth into a higher state,
all matter does now scintillate.**

Part 4

1. Divine Director, awaken people to the reality that change needs to happen and that change is not going to be brought about by people staying in fear where they think being loving and kind is enough. Neither is change going to happen by people staying in anger where they think they have to be judgmental of or fight dark forces.

Divine Director, I now see,
the world is unreality,
in my heart I now truly feel,
the Spirit is all that is real.

**Divine Director, send the light,
from blindness clear my inner sight,
my vision free, my vision clear,
your guidance is forever here.**

2. Divine Director, awaken people to the higher sense of responsibility where we realize that we do not have the power or the responsibility for fighting dark forces. Our responsibility is to educate ourselves to the existence of dark forces and then share this knowledge and make the calls to the masters.

> Divine Director, vision give,
> in clarity I want to live,
> I now behold my plan Divine,
> the plan that is uniquely mine.
>
> **Divine Director, send the light,**
> **from blindness clear my inner sight,**
> **my vision free, my vision clear,**
> **your guidance is forever here.**

3. Divine Director, awaken people to our reason for coming into embodiment, our true, non-attached desire to help raise this planet to a higher level. Help people transcend fear and anger.

> Divine Director, show in me,
> the ego games, and set me free,
> help me escape the ego's cage,
> to help bring in the golden age.
>
> **Divine Director, send the light,**
> **from blindness clear my inner sight,**
> **my vision free, my vision clear,**
> **your guidance is forever here.**

4. Divine Director, awaken people to the fact that stopping war is not a goal in itself. The real, underlying dynamic is to raise people's state of consciousness. War will not be removed from this earth until a critical mass of people have transcended the consciousness that made war possible.

> Divine Director, I'm with you,
> my vision one, no longer two,
> as karma's veil you do disperse,
> I see a whole new universe.
>
> **Divine Director, send the light,**
> **from blindness clear my inner sight,**
> **my vision free, my vision clear,**
> **your guidance is forever here.**

5. Divine Director, awaken people to the fact that as spiritual people, who have started to awaken from the collective state of mind, we have the right and the authority to call for the ascended masters to reduce the power of the dark forces.

> Divine Director, I go up,
> electric light now fills my cup,
> consume in me all shadows old,
> bestow on me a vision bold.
>
> **Divine Director, send the light,**
> **from blindness clear my inner sight,**
> **my vision free, my vision clear,**
> **your guidance is forever here.**

6. Divine Director, awaken people to the reality that when they are no longer blinded by dark forces, people will have a real choice to abandon the consciousness of war. The ascended masters are not seeking to force people but to free their will so that they can freely make the choice to transcend the consciousness that makes war possible.

> Divine Director, heart of gold,
> my sacred labor I unfold,
> o blessed Guru, I now see,
> where my own plan is taking me.
>
> **Divine Director, send the light,**
> **from blindness clear my inner sight,**
> **my vision free, my vision clear,**
> **your guidance is forever here.**

7. Divine Director, awaken people to the reality that there is a realistic potential that war can be removed from this planet within the foreseeable future. Cosmic cycles are aligned so that this can be achieved.

> Divine Director, by your grace,
> in grander scheme I find my place,
> my individual flame I see,
> uniqueness God has given me.
>
> **Divine Director, send the light,**
> **from blindness clear my inner sight,**
> **my vision free, my vision clear,**
> **your guidance is forever here.**

8. Divine Director, awaken people to the reality that war is not inevitable. We are not disempowered when we work with the ascended masters. By removing the power that the dark forces have over people, the people will awaken to the fact that they too are spiritual beings who have a higher goal and a higher vision of their lives.

> Divine Director, vision one,
> I see that I AM God's own Sun,
> with your direction so Divine,
> I am now letting my light shine.

> **Divine Director, send the light,**
> **from blindness clear my inner sight,**
> **my vision free, my vision clear,**
> **your guidance is forever here.**

9. Divine Director, awaken people to the reality that there is nothing that cannot be changed and overcome. There is nothing that is impossible because free will reigns supreme. When a critical mass of people transcend the level of consciousness that makes war seem desirable or inevitable, then the ascended masters can and will remove war from this planet.

> Divine Director, what a gift,
> to be a part of Spirit's lift,
> to raise mankind out of the night,
> to bask in Spirit's loving sight.

> **Divine Director, send the light,**
> **from blindness clear my inner sight,**
> **my vision free, my vision clear,**
> **your guidance is forever here.**

Sealing

In the name of the I AM THAT I AM, I accept that Archangel Michael, Astrea and Shiva form an impenetrable shield around myself and all constructive people, sealing us from all fear-based energies in all four octaves. I accept that the Light of God is consuming and transforming all fear-based energies that make up the forces behind war!

3 | THE NON-PHYSICAL CAUSES OF WAR

I am the Ascended Master Mother Mary! In my first discourse, I attempted to reach out to a broader audience, hoping to reach those who are, so to speak, sitting on the fence. They are not quite sure whether they dare to engage in a direct encounter with war and the forces behind war. I also attempted to reach those who have opened themselves to seeing a deeper understanding of what is happening on this planet but who have been trapped in anger or other fear-based emotions, thinking they have to battle dark forces. In this discourse, I will give you the more direct meat, assuming that those who are willing to read on in this book have decided that they are willing to know reality rather than the somewhat glorified picture of life that they have received while growing up on this planet.

A deeper understanding behind physical events

You might as well realize, if you have not already, that one of the purposes of the ascended masters and our progressive revelation is to give you the truth, the reality, the deeper understanding of what happens on this planet. You have been brought up with a very limited understanding of what truly goes on because you have only been given the physical, material perspective on life. You have even been given only a small portion of what goes on at the physical level.

What we of the ascended masters seek to help you understand is that the physical level is only the most superficial aspect of life on this planet. If you look only at the physical level, you get only the most superficial understanding and explanation for the deeper causes of the events that you see around you. Physical events are, in most cases, not caused by what happens at the physical level. Physical events are never *exclusively* caused by what happens at the physical level. There are always hidden causes that reach into the three higher octaves: the emotional, mental, and identity realms. This I would like to explain to you, focused on the concept of war.

The physical horrors of war

There are some authors who have attempted to describe in more realistic terms what they see at the physical level on a battlefield. Some have described the horrors of seeing decaying corpses. One American author, Ernest Hemingway, described a so-called "natural history" of the battlefield. Other writers have in other ways attempted to also describe the horrors of war, perhaps even in ironic terms by describing the beauty of a battlefield. What I would like to give you here is a "spiritual history" of the battlefield. I know that most of you have seen some of the modern television programs where they show decaying corpses and how forensic medicine can use various techniques to solve crimes by studying what happens to the corpses. I know that most of you are familiar with some of the physical horrors that you see on a battlefield. Yet I can assure you that very few people are prepared for the reality of seeing large numbers of dead people in various states of being blown up, lying scattered about a landscape. Truly, this is something that no one should have to see, but given that you live on a planet where war is a reality, it is something that many people have seen throughout history.

I can tell you that the ugliness and the horror that you see at the physical level is as nothing compared to what you see at the other levels. We have explained to you that there is a part of the emotional octave where there has been made room for those lifestreams who have gone into such a low state of consciousness that they cannot any longer take physical embodiment on earth. We have explained that, in this astral plane or astral pit, there are many beings who were not created as co-creators or angels. These are beings who have been created by those who have fallen into the duality consciousness.

How entities and demons are created

We have explained that you create everything out of the raw material of energy but that you give energy form through consciousness. When a self-aware being, a co-creator, focuses its attention on a given matrix long enough, there will be a certain amount of energy qualified through that matrix. Because the focus happens through the consciousness of the co-creator, the energy will eventually gain a certain rudimentary form of consciousness. This is what makes it possible to create an energy being, an entity, a spirit or even what we call a demon.

No individual co-creator is powerful enough to create a demon, but demons can be created collectively by large numbers of people focusing their attention on the same thought matrix and thereby feeding it both energy and consciousness. This thought matrix can then take on the appearance of a being that has a consciousness and a will. It has the rudimentary kind of consciousness that is somewhat similar to what you see in the animal form. Animals are conscious that they exist, although not self-aware. They do have a survival instinct and an instinct to propagate. This is what you see in these entities or demons that exist in the astral plane.

Entities and demons cannot choose

They know they exist. They know they can only continue to exist by being fed, and they know that what feeds them is energy that comes from human beings in embodiment. They also understand, although not as clearly as you can do as a self-aware being, that human beings will continue to feed them energy only when their minds are locked in a certain track. An entity or a demon is not a being that has the ability to choose: "I no longer want to be this kind of entity." It is the same as an animal who does not have the ability to choose: "I no longer want to be a giraffe. I want to be an elephant."

An entity or a demon is created out of a certain thought matrix. It cannot by itself change that matrix; it is simply not possible because it was not created with self-awareness. A demon that is created out of violence, for example, knows that it can continue to exist only by being fed energy. It can be fed energy only when human beings continue to engage in violence. Such a demon has the ability to project thoughts and feelings into the minds of human beings who are susceptible to the thought matrix that created the demon. It can, because it was created collectively, overpower the minds of individuals and, thereby, propel them into engaging in more violence. This feeds the demon so that it becomes even stronger.

This is a principle that you need to understand if you are to understand the hidden causes of war. There never has been a war on this planet, and there never will be a war on this planet, that is caused exclusively by causes at the material, physical level. I am well aware, and I will later talk more about, the fact that there are many physical causes of why people go to war, but war is never caused *exclusively* by such physical causes. There has never been, and there never will be, a war that was not to a large degree caused by demons in the astral plane who have taken over the minds of individual people. They have managed to manipulate them into taking the steps that gradually led to the outbreak of war.

The horrors of the astral plane

Once you understand that such beings exist and that they want to be fed by the energy misqualified by human beings, you can begin to understand the spiritual history of a battlefield. Let us, therefore, imagine that there has been a battle in a war. Many, many people have been killed in one day, and now their corpses, along with their blown up vehicles and tanks, are lying scattered around on the battlefield. Let us imagine that we move into this battlefield, and let us now imagine that you are equipped with a special pair of goggles.

In their initial state, these goggles reveal only what you can see with your physical eyes. You are seeing the physical horrors of the decaying and blown-up corpses. You are seeing people with blown off limbs where the blood is running into the sand. You are seeing people with holes in their bodies – small entry wounds, big exit wounds – where something has blown up inside their bodies. You are seeing the horror of this, and you are naturally shocked. Now, we adjust a setting on your goggles, and you see beyond the material level. You see what is happening on the battlefield at the level of the astral plane. If you think the physical horrors of the battlefield are ugly and repulsive, I can assure you that they are nothing compared to the ugliness you see in the astral plane. I am sure you have seen paintings from medieval times that show various creatures. Some of these painters have actually seen levels of the astral plane. Throughout the ages, many people have in various situations, whether under the influence of drugs or alcohol or in certain life-threatening situations, had their sights cleared so that they could see into the astral plane. The entities and demons you find there are so ugly and so repulsive that it almost defies description. You may have seen some of the newer movies that have come out where computers have been used to generate various creatures. Not long ago, the movies about the *Lord of The Rings* showed various creatures. Other movies have showed other creatures, including space creatures. I can assure you that even such creatures are not as ugly and repulsive as what you see in the astral plane.

Entities and demons feed off life energy

What you see on a physical battlefield when you can see beyond the physical level is a large amount of entities and demons that are literally feeding on the corpses. They are not feeding on them physically as you would see, for example, maggots and

3 | The Non-Physical Causes of War

insects feeding on the corpses. They are feeding on the energy bodies of the corpses, first of all, the emotional body. They are sucking out the life energy from those energy bodies.

You may, of course, ask yourself why human beings are not constantly having their life energies sucked out by demons and entities in the astral plane. You would be shocked to know how many people are actually having their life energies sucked out by such beings on a daily basis. Still, this is for most people nothing compared to what happens on a physical battlefield.

The reason is that there is a certain separation between the physical octave and the astral plane. There is what we might call an energy veil that provides somewhat of a protective shield that holds back the entities and demons in the astral plane from interfering with people at the physical level. This shield can, of course, be broken down by various factors. There are many such factors, but there is no factor that is more powerful at breaking down this shield than a physical battle in war. Even the loud noises of the guns and explosions serve to break down the energy shield, the energy veil, between the physical and the astral plane. Even more than this is the feelings of the soldiers who are in battle being killed, being wounded, seeing their comrades being killed and wounded.

In a large battle there can literally be opened up what you might call a wormhole or a black hole into the astral plane. You would see this almost like a maelstrom or a tornado of swirling energy that literally sucks energy from the physical level into a certain level of the astral plane. You may also see it as an open portal through which entities and demons of every persuasion can stream into the physical level or very close to it. They do not become physically visible, but they come so close to the vibration of the physical level that they have much greater access to the energy bodies of the corpses lying on the battlefield.

The energy fields of the soldiers

Depending on the condition of the soldier's energy field before the battle and depending on what happened to the energy field during the battle, these demons and entities can do a variety of things. Sometimes they only manage to insert a small hook into the energy fields, and they can then suck out the energy through what is almost like a pipeline or a hose. In other cases, bigger holes have been blown where the entities or demons can more directly reach in. Some of them have claw-like fangs where they can pull out chunks of energy. Others have suction hoses almost like the snout of an elephant, and they can suck out energy. Others manage to dig their way into the energy field and insert themselves almost like the parasites and worms you see at the physical level.

Some soldiers have been so low in the protection of their energy fields before a battle that their energy fields can be scattered into pieces when they are brutally killed. If you see a corpse that has been physically blown up and scattered, then in most cases, the energy field, the aura, of that person will also have been blown into bits and pieces. You will then see demons and entities that come out and literally eat away at these pieces of the energy field almost like you see hyenas and vultures eat away at a corpse.

The shock of realizing such forces exist

I am, of course, not giving you these images in order to shock you beyond what you can handle. I *am* giving you these images in order to shock you awake to the reality of the aggressiveness of the entities and demons in the astral plane. You know very well that at the physical level there is nothing that can hold

3 | The Non-Physical Causes of War

back the flies from laying eggs on a corpse. There is nothing that can hold back the maggots from eating away at that corpse. There is nothing that can hold back the hyenas, the vultures, from ripping open the corpse and eating the insides first. Even more, there is no force at the physical level that can hold back the entities and demons of the astral plane from having their fill when a battle has taken place and people have been physically killed.

You need to understand that these entities and demons do not have the ability to feel what you feel: compassion, empathy, pity, regret, a sense of injustice, a sense that this should not be taking place. Such feelings, they do not have. You cannot reason with them and seek to make them understand that what they are doing is wrong. They are only doing what every animal at the physical level is doing: securing their own survival and their growth by sucking out the energy that helps them grow and maintain themselves. You cannot even blame them for doing that which they were created to do.

The reason I am explaining this to you is to help you come to one of these hitting-the-concrete experiences, a moment of truth, a moment of realization. What I am seeking to give you here is the realization that war is caused by forces that have no pity and no empathy and that you cannot reason with. There is absolutely no way that you could persuade the demons and entities in the astral plane to stop doing what they are doing. *This* you need to acknowledge consciously.

I know that this will be a shocking realization for many people. I know that many people will initially feel overwhelmed, almost paralyzed, by realizing this. Naturally, when you realize that there is nothing that can stop these demons and entities, as there is nothing that can stop a charging tiger, then you might feel: "But what can I then do to protect myself from this and to stop war on the planetary level?" There is nothing you can do *directly*, but there *is* something you can do *indirectly* because we of the ascended masters do have the power to deal with these entities and demons.

What we need in order to use that power is authorization from you. I explained in my previous discourse the absolute nature of the Law of Free Will. Human beings in physical embodiment have, over thousands of years, created the demons and entities in the astral plane. We of the ascended masters cannot remove them until a critical mass of people give us the authority to do so. You can do this by giving our invocations associated with this book and many of our other invocations and decrees. You also do it by becoming aware of what is going on and, therefore, knowingly transcending the consciousness that allows war to continue on this planet.

A description of the astral plane

I now want to go on with my description of what goes on in the astral plane. The astral plane has many levels—thirty-three to be exact. Some of the lowest levels have almost no form because they are like the insides of a volcano. Everything is so hot that there is barely any form that can exist because everything is broken down into this melting pot. At the higher levels, if one can talk about "higher" levels of the astral plane, there are more and more distinct forms.

There are some levels where you have the demons and the entities I have talked about. These are the ones who simply do what they do, and they are like the vultures, the hyenas and the jackals that are feeding off already dead animals. Surely, these are ugly. They are aggressive. They are beyond reason. They

3 | The Non-Physical Causes of War

are beyond empathy. At, so to speak, higher levels of the astral plane, you find some demons that are actually more conscious of what they are doing.

They could be compared to the animals that actively hunt and kill other animals. I am hesitant to use this image because you can surely see that the vulture is ugly, but you might not see a lion or a tiger as ugly. What I want you to realize is that there is a certain level of the astral plane where you find demons and entities that simply feed off people. Then, there is a higher level where you find predatory demons that actively go out and create the situations where people are physically killed or in other ways are vulnerable to having their energies stolen.

These are demons who have a higher level of consciousness, but they still do not have self-awareness. They do not feel pity or empathy with human beings at all, and they never will be able to feel this. At this level, you find two classes of demons. One is demons that have been created as I described earlier. They have been created by self-aware beings who fed their energy and their consciousness into a matrix that eventually became a being with a survival instinct.

These have over time become more complex than the demons that passively feed on people. They have, therefore, learned to use more aggressive measures to manipulate people into committing physical actions that make them vulnerable to the astral plane. There are many such actions. Any addiction makes you vulnerable to having your energy stolen by demons in the astral plane. There is no physical action that opens up the vulnerability more than physical killing and especially the large-scale killing you see on a battlefield of war. These demons will do everything in their limited powers to manipulate people into killing or going to war; yet, they do have limited powers.

The fallen beings in the astral plane

There is, however, another class of demons that are found in the astral plane, and these are what we have, in other books, called *fallen* beings. As we have explained, there are fallen beings in all four octaves, but those that are trapped in the astral plane are what I also call demons because they have lost almost all conscious awareness of themselves as beings with self-awareness.

We can always debate whether they have a certain rudimentary form of self-awareness or whether they are so trapped that they no longer have it for practical purposes, but I do not wish here to go into an academic discussion. What I wish to point out to you is that in the higher levels of the astral plane, you do find beings that started out as either co-creators or angels in a previous sphere. They have then fallen in consciousness, and they have continued to fall in consciousness until they are now almost unconscious of themselves.

Take care to note the difference. I am not saying these beings are unconscious. Many of them have a very sophisticated consciousness and understanding of what happens in the four octaves of earth. They have great ability to manipulate human beings, but they do not have enough self-awareness to choose to do something differently. It is almost impossible to reason with such demons. You might say then that we can use the terminology "a demon" about beings that are not susceptible to reason. I know some will dispute this use of terminology, but let us use it for practical reasons here.

Fallen beings in the mental realm

My motivation for doing this is that, when we change another setting on your goggles, you will begin to see beyond the emotional level, beyond the astral plane, and into the mental octave. Here, you find fallen beings that I would not characterize as demons because they still have some self-awareness. They are not mechanically driven by a certain matrix. They are driven by a certain *reasoning*. They have a mental, intellectual reasoning for doing what they are doing.

The demons I talk about in the astral plane are not really reasoning about what they are doing or why they are doing it. They are simply doing it because they know that it works, and it gives them energy. They are not even doing it because it gives them a sense of power over human beings because most of them do not have a high enough consciousness to enjoy having power over human beings.

In the mental level, however, you do find many fallen beings who do have enough awareness to know that they can have power over human beings and who enjoy this. The beings in the mental realm are not as aggressive as those in the emotional realm. They are not seeking to overpower or force people. They are seeking to persuade people.

This difference is important for several reasons. On a more superficial level, the fallen beings in the mental realm are not nearly as ugly and repulsive as those in the astral plane. Some of them have taken on an appearance that might be very attractive to many people. You can find many fallen beings in the mental realm that appear as the professors, learned people or philosophers that you see on earth, especially in history. You can find many who have set themselves up as kings or emperors, taking on a seemingly benign but very impressive and powerful appearance.

Many of these beings in the mental realm have learned to disguise themselves as being benign and well-meaning. They come across as having only your best interests at heart, but how can they have anything at heart when they have no heart? They are all mental. It is all mind. It is all intellect. It is all relative, dualistic reasoning. When I say relative, dualistic reasoning, I mean that they always operate with a scale that has two opposites. They always divide people up into categories based on such a scale with an absolute value judgment that something is right and something is wrong. Those people who are in the category of "wrong," can justly be killed. This is the basic reasoning that you find in the mental realm: Why it is justifiable to kill human beings.

The consciousness that justifies killing

If you look at human beings in embodiment, you will see that there are people who will kill indiscriminately. At the most extreme level, you see either serial killers or dictators – even soldiers or criminals – who have passed the point where they feel they need to justify killing. They kill anyone who seems to fit in a certain category where they are labeled as a threat. You may call them psychopaths or whatever you want to call them. They are not needing to justify their killing because they have crossed the line where this no longer seems necessary to them.

You will, of course, see that most people who engage in killing are temporarily blinded by a certain state of consciousness. When they are distant from the battlefield or the scene of the crime, they may snap out of this and now realize what they did. Both of these instances can be explained by the fact that these people have had their minds taken over by demons in the astral plane. That is why they can kill without reflecting on it, at least in the moment.

You will also see, especially when you look at war, that there are people who can engage in killing, even the long-term acts of planning for war or planning for so-called defense, and they do it because they feel it is a necessary and justifiable act. These people have their minds taken over by fallen beings in the mental realm.

Fallen beings in the identity octave

Let us imagine that we switch your goggles to the highest setting, and now you are beginning to look into the lower levels of the identity octave. Here you find fallen beings who appear even more benign or more impressive than those in the mental realm. There are, however, very few people who have had their minds taken over directly by the fallen beings in the identity octave because these beings usually work through the beings in the mental realm. This means that a person who is engaging in war and feeling it is justified is, first of all, controlled directly by a being in the mental realm. The being in the mental realm is then controlled by fallen beings in the identity realm.

The beings in the mental realm are all intellectual and are reasoning. As a human being, you can engage in a reasoning process with them, but you can never convince them that you are right and that they are wrong. This you also need to understand. You need to understand, as I said about the demons in the astral plane, that you cannot fight them, reason with them or make them feel empathy. Likewise, the beings in the mental realm cannot be persuaded by any argument you can come up with. Why is that so? Because they believe firmly that you, as a human being in embodiment, are fundamentally inferior to themselves. They believe that no argument you could ever come up with would be better than their argument. Many of the beings in the mental realm, the more sophisticated fallen beings, know that any argument is just *that*—an argument. It would actually be great progress if all people on earth would realize that any argument is just an argument.

Some of the most sophisticated beings in the mental realm have realized this, but they are still firmly convinced that their argument is superior to yours because you are fundamentally inferior, or you would not be in physical embodiment—so they reason.

You can engage these beings with argumentation and seek to persuade them, but all you do is feed them your energy. You never achieve a decisive outcome. Again, you might feel overwhelmed by this, but then you need to realize that we of the ascended masters have the power to deal with the beings in the mental realm if you give us your authority. You give us the authority by making the calls but also by consciously choosing not to engage these beings and not to engage in arguments with people whose minds are taken over by the fallen beings in the mental realm.

When it comes to the fallen beings in the identity octave, again, you can attempt to reason with them, but you can never persuade them because they also believe that you are inferior to them. There is no point, as a human being in embodiment, in engaging such beings. You need to make the calls so that we of the ascended masters can deal with them.

The hidden cause of war

The fallen beings in the identity octave have a higher level of consciousness than those in the mental octave, and they

3 | The Non-Physical Causes of War

understand that nothing on earth is as it seems. There are beings in the mental realm who actually believe in the cause that they are seeking to get human beings to fight and die for. They believe it is a right cause, a worthy cause. Those in the identity realm realize that none of the causes on earth are truly valid or have any real significance. They certainly do not have the significance that they purport to have. They do not lead to the end that they claim to be leading towards, whether it be to banish the devil from the earth and make God's kingdom physically manifest or to manifest some other utopia.

The beings in the identity realm know that all of this is just camouflage. All of the epic dramas and the epic causes are just a sham. They only have one purpose, and that is to get people to engage in a struggle, to engage in battle, for the purpose of assisting the fallen beings and their battle to prove God wrong. I want you to be aware that there is an even deeper cause that has never before been articulated on earth. You can look at all of the philosophies, religions and thought systems found on earth, and you can see that none of the causes defined there are real causes. They are all camouflage for hiding the deeper cause of the fallen beings trying to prove God wrong by getting human beings to misuse their free will.

Your reaction to these teachings

I know well that I have given you more than most people can handle in one sitting. I want you to tune in to what is going on in your energy field as a result of hearing or reading these teachings. Do you feel a certain weight? Do you feel a certain sense of being overwhelmed, of being up against forces that are too big for you to handle, perhaps even too big to contemplate? Is it too overwhelming to acknowledge the reality of what I am saying? Is there a part of your mind that just wants to withdraw and run away? Is there another part that just wants to argue with what I am saying?

All of these reactions are understandable. I am not expecting that you can, by reading or hearing this teaching, instantly make the switch. I *am* expecting that you will be willing to make an effort to step beyond these feelings or thoughts. I am expecting that you will be willing to make the calls for yourself and other people to be cut free from the ignorance and denial of what is truly the causes behind war, the non-physical causes behind war. There are, as I have now explained, two main causes.

One cause is that war enables beings in the astral plane and in the mental realm to steal energy from human beings. Another is that war is the most extreme outcome of the attempt of certain fallen beings to prove God wrong, to prove that free will was a mistake. Once you begin to acknowledge this, you have the foundation for stepping up to being truly helpful in bringing about peace on this planet.

Giving you the overall framework

You may think that I should have started more gently, and gradually built up to this realization. I have chosen to go the other way and start by giving you the overall picture. This makes it much easier for me to explain what I will explain in the coming discourses. Instead of starting at the lowest level and gradually taking you higher, thereby giving you a chance to get used to things gradually, I have chosen to start by giving you a framework that makes it much easier for you to put the other pieces in their right place. I know this may make you feel overwhelmed from the beginning, but I think that as you move

3 | The Non-Physical Causes of War

into the following discourses and give the invocations, you will begin to feel how things gradually fall into place. You begin to see how the disconnected pieces, that people have, all fit into a bigger context. When you look at the explanations that people have attempted to come up with for war, you can see that some of them seem to be contradicting other explanations. It can be difficult to make sense out of them and find out what is really going on.

This is because people do not have the big picture that I am attempting to give you here. They do not understand these hidden causes. They think that, when you look at the physical motivation that people supposedly have for going to war, then there must be some rationale, some rational reason behind it. When you see that there is no rational reasoning behind it, people do not know what to do, and that is when they feel ultimately discouraged.

This is one of the main reasons why so many people have felt overwhelmed and pacified when it comes to doing something about war. This is the main reason why so many people feel there is nothing they can do about war. They look at someone like Adolf Hitler, and they seek to find a rational reason for why he did what he did. When they cannot find an ultimate explanation, they don't know what to do next.

What I am attempting to give you here is the overall framework so that you can move on from this paralysis. What I am attempting to give you here is the understanding that there is no rational reason at the physical level. There is a reason in the astral plane where certain demons and entities simply want to steal people's energy. There is the even higher reason that certain fallen beings want to prove God wrong. Once you begin to see this, you realize that you do not need to explain everything rationally at the physical level. More importantly, you also realize that since the cause of war is not found at the physical level, the way to remove war is not found at the physical level either.

Removing war with the light of the masters

You have options for removing war from this planet that are beyond what you can do at the physical level. Even though there may be some things at the physical level that you, as an individual, can do nothing about, there is still *something* you can do about it at the emotional, mental and identity levels. You do this by making the calls and transcending the consciousness so that we of the ascended masters get the authority to step in and use our power to deal with the forces that are creating war at the physical level. Once you remove those non-physical forces, then much of the momentum, the reasoning and the motivation behind physical war will also vanish into thin air.

Have you ever experienced how a meadow can be heavy with dew in the morning? Have you ever experienced that when the sun comes up and gains strength, the dew disappears? I know that the dew on the meadow is beautiful, and the forces I have described in the astral, mental, and identity realms are not beautiful in comparison. They can still melt away under the rising sun of the power of the ascended masters when you give us the authority to shine our light into all four octaves of earth. This is what can remove war, and in this book, we will give you the tools to accomplish *your* end of this task. Rest assured that *we* will fulfill our end of the bargain.

4 | EXPOSING THE NON-PHYSICAL CAUSES OF WAR

In the name of the I AM THAT I AM, Jesus Christ, I call upon Mother Mary, the Divine Director and Surya to expose that the major causes of war are found in the form of dark forces in the emotional, mental and identity realms. Awaken people to the reality that we are spiritual beings and that we can co-create a new future by working with the ascended masters. I especially call for …

[Make your own calls here.]

Part 1

1. Divine Director, shatter the energy veil and expose that physical events are never exclusively caused by what happens at the physical level. There are always hidden causes that reach into the emotional, mental and identity realms.

Divine Director, I now see,
the world is unreality,
in my heart I now truly feel,
the Spirit is all that is real.

Divine Director, send the light,
from blindness clear my inner sight,
my vision free, my vision clear,
your guidance is forever here.

2. Divine Director, shatter the energy veil and expose the existence of entities and demons in the astral plane, the astral pit.

Divine Director, vision give,
in clarity I want to live,
I now behold my plan Divine,
the plan that is uniquely mine.

Divine Director, send the light,
from blindness clear my inner sight,
my vision free, my vision clear,
your guidance is forever here.

3. Divine Director, shatter the energy veil and expose that such beings know they can continue to exist only by stealing emotional energy from human beings in embodiment.

Divine Director, show in me,
the ego games, and set me free,
help me escape the ego's cage,
to help bring in the golden age.

> **Divine Director, send the light,
> from blindness clear my inner sight,
> my vision free, my vision clear,
> your guidance is forever here.**

4. Divine Director, shatter the energy veil and expose that a demon created out of violence can continue to exist only by stealing energy from human beings who engage in violence.

> Divine Director, I'm with you,
> my vision one, no longer two,
> as karma's veil you do disperse,
> I see a whole new universe.

> **Divine Director, send the light,
> from blindness clear my inner sight,
> my vision free, my vision clear,
> your guidance is forever here.**

5. Divine Director, shatter the energy veil and expose that such a demon has the ability to project thoughts and feelings into the minds of human beings who are susceptible to the thought matrix that created the demon.

> Divine Director, I go up,
> electric light now fills my cup,
> consume in me all shadows old,
> bestow on me a vision bold.

> **Divine Director, send the light,
> from blindness clear my inner sight,
> my vision free, my vision clear,
> your guidance is forever here.**

6. Divine Director, shatter the energy veil and expose that because the demon was created collectively, it can overpower the minds of individuals and propel them into engaging in more violence, which then feeds the demon so that it becomes even stronger.

> Divine Director, heart of gold,
> my sacred labor I unfold,
> o blessed Guru, I now see,
> where my own plan is taking me.

> **Divine Director, send the light,**
> **from blindness clear my inner sight,**
> **my vision free, my vision clear,**
> **your guidance is forever here.**

7. Divine Director, shatter the energy veil and expose that there never has been a war that is caused exclusively by causes at the material, physical level. A war is to a large degree caused by demons in the astral plane who have taken over the minds of individual people.

> Divine Director, by your grace,
> in grander scheme I find my place,
> my individual flame I see,
> uniqueness God has given me.

> **Divine Director, send the light,**
> **from blindness clear my inner sight,**
> **my vision free, my vision clear,**
> **your guidance is forever here.**

8. Divine Director, shatter the energy veil and expose how the demons have no empathy with human beings and will cause a war in order to make it easier for themselves to steal people's energies.

> Divine Director, vision one,
> I see that I AM God's own Sun,
> with your direction so Divine,
> I am now letting my light shine.
>
> **Divine Director, send the light,
> from blindness clear my inner sight,
> my vision free, my vision clear,
> your guidance is forever here.**

9. Divine Director, shatter the energy veil and expose how the demons seek to break down the separation between the astral and physical planes in order to steal people's energy. Nothing does this more effectively than a physical war where many people are killed on a battlefield.

> Divine Director, what a gift,
> to be a part of Spirit's lift,
> to raise mankind out of the night,
> to bask in Spirit's loving sight.
>
> **Divine Director, send the light,
> from blindness clear my inner sight,
> my vision free, my vision clear,
> your guidance is forever here.**

Part 2

1. Beloved Surya, shatter the energy veil and expose the reality of the aggressiveness of the entities and demons in the astral plane.

> Surya, cosmic being bright,
> your balance is my pure delight,
> I am in orbit round God Star,
> in perfect unity we are.
>
> **Surya, banish all extremes,**
> **Surya, shatter Serpent's schemes,**
> **Surya, balance to me bring,**
> **Surya, making my heart sing.**

2. Beloved Surya, shatter the energy veil and expose that the beings in the astral plane have no sympathy for humans and that it is impossible to reason with them.

> Surya, there is more to life,
> than human conflict, war and strife,
> your balance gives me inner peace,
> all outer conflicts do now cease.
>
> **Surya, banish all extremes,**
> **Surya, shatter Serpent's schemes,**
> **Surya, balance to me bring,**
> **Surya, making my heart sing.**

3. Beloved Surya, shatter the energy veil and expose the reality that war is caused by forces that have no pity and no empathy and that we cannot reason with them. There is no way to persuade the demons and entities in the astral plane to stop doing what they are doing.

> Surya, what a wondrous sight,
> from Sirius you send the light,
> of one mind, I now call to thee,
> for your apprentice I would be.

> **Surya, banish all extremes,**
> **Surya, shatter Serpent's schemes,**
> **Surya, balance to me bring,**
> **Surya, making my heart sing.**

4. Beloved Surya, shatter the energy veil and expose that we humans cannot deal with the forces in the astral plane but that the ascended masters have the power to remove them all from this planet.

> Surya, radiate your light,
> with balance you set all things right,
> consuming energetic dross,
> my letting go is not a loss.

> **Surya, banish all extremes,**
> **Surya, shatter Serpent's schemes,**
> **Surya, balance to me bring,**
> **Surya, making my heart sing.**

5. Beloved Surya, shatter the energy veil and expose that the ascended masters need only the authorization from those of us who are in embodiment in order to clear the astral plane from all entities, demons and misqualified energies.

> Surya, your light is alive,
> for inner balance I do strive,
> the alchemy is now begun,
> my heart transformed into a sun.

> **Surya, banish all extremes,**
> **Surya, shatter Serpent's schemes,**
> **Surya, balance to me bring,**
> **Surya, making my heart sing.**

6. Beloved Surya, shatter the energy veil and expose that there is a certain level of the astral plane where there are demons and entities that simply feed off people.

> Surya, come enlighten me,
> duality you help me see,
> extremes they cannot pull me in,
> on Middle Way I always win.

> **Surya, banish all extremes,**
> **Surya, shatter Serpent's schemes,**
> **Surya, balance to me bring,**
> **Surya, making my heart sing.**

7. Beloved Surya, shatter the energy veil and expose that there is a "higher" level of the astral plane where there are predatory demons that actively go out and create the situations where people are physically killed or in other ways are vulnerable to having their energies stolen.

> Surya, in your cosmic sphere,
> with Cuzco I your light revere,
> from your perspective o so grand,
> life finally I understand.

> **Surya, banish all extremes,**
> **Surya, shatter Serpent's schemes,**
> **Surya, balance to me bring,**
> **Surya, making my heart sing.**

8. Beloved Surya, shatter the energy veil and expose that these demons use more aggressive measures to manipulate people into committing physical actions that make them vulnerable to the astral plane.

> Surya, show me God's design,
> I see that God is all benign,
> you calm my feeling body's storm,
> I know the God beyond all form.

> **Surya, banish all extremes,**
> **Surya, shatter Serpent's schemes,**
> **Surya, balance to me bring,**
> **Surya, making my heart sing.**

9. Beloved Surya, shatter the energy veil and expose that there is no physical action that opens up the vulnerability more than the large-scale killing on a battlefield of war. These demons will do everything in their powers to manipulate people into killing or going to war.

Surya, I come from afar,
and as you show me my home star,
I see now my internal light,
a star I am in my own right.

**Surya, banish all extremes,
Surya, shatter Serpent's schemes,
Surya, balance to me bring,
Surya, making my heart sing.**

Part 3

1. Divine Director, shatter the energy veil and expose the existence of fallen beings in the astral plane that started out as either co-creators or angels in a previous sphere.

Divine Director, I now see,
the world is unreality,
in my heart I now truly feel,
the Spirit is all that is real.

**Divine Director, send the light,
from blindness clear my inner sight,
my vision free, my vision clear,
your guidance is forever here.**

2. Divine Director, shatter the energy veil and expose that these fallen beings can appear to have a sophisticated consciousness and ability to manipulate human beings, but they do not have enough self-awareness to choose to do something differently.

> Divine Director, vision give,
> in clarity I want to live,
> I now behold my plan Divine,
> the plan that is uniquely mine.
>
> **Divine Director, send the light,**
> **from blindness clear my inner sight,**
> **my vision free, my vision clear,**
> **your guidance is forever here.**

3. Divine Director, shatter the energy veil and expose that in the mental octave are fallen beings that still have some self-awareness. They have a mental, intellectual reasoning for manipulating us.

> Divine Director, show in me,
> the ego games, and set me free,
> help me escape the ego's cage,
> to help bring in the golden age.
>
> **Divine Director, send the light,**
> **from blindness clear my inner sight,**
> **my vision free, my vision clear,**
> **your guidance is forever here.**

4. Divine Director, shatter the energy veil and expose that in the mental level are fallen beings who have enough awareness to know that they can have power over human beings and who enjoy this.

> Divine Director, I'm with you,
> my vision one, no longer two,
> as karma's veil you do disperse,
> I see a whole new universe.
>
> **Divine Director, send the light,**
> **from blindness clear my inner sight,**
> **my vision free, my vision clear,**
> **your guidance is forever here.**

5. Divine Director, shatter the energy veil and expose that the beings in the mental realm are not as aggressive as those in the emotional realm. They are not seeking to overpower or force people, they are seeking to persuade people.

> Divine Director, I go up,
> electric light now fills my cup,
> consume in me all shadows old,
> bestow on me a vision bold.
>
> **Divine Director, send the light,**
> **from blindness clear my inner sight,**
> **my vision free, my vision clear,**
> **your guidance is forever here.**

6. Divine Director, shatter the energy veil and expose that the fallen beings in the mental realm have taken on an appearance as professors, learned people or philosophers. Some have set themselves up as kings or emperors, taking on a seemingly benign but very impressive and powerful appearance.

> Divine Director, heart of gold,
> my sacred labor I unfold,
> o blessed Guru, I now see,
> where my own plan is taking me.
>
> **Divine Director, send the light,**
> **from blindness clear my inner sight,**
> **my vision free, my vision clear,**
> **your guidance is forever here.**

7. Divine Director, shatter the energy veil and expose how the beings in the mental realm have created sophisticated reasonings that seek to justify why human beings kill each other and engage in war.

> Divine Director, by your grace,
> in grander scheme I find my place,
> my individual flame I see,
> uniqueness God has given me.
>
> **Divine Director, send the light,**
> **from blindness clear my inner sight,**
> **my vision free, my vision clear,**
> **your guidance is forever here.**

8. Divine Director, shatter the energy veil and expose that the beings in the mental realm have taken over the minds of many human beings, and this explains why people can engage in killing, even the long-term acts of planning for war or planning for so-called defense, and feel it is a necessary and justifiable act.

> Divine Director, vision one,
> I see that I AM God's own Sun,
> with your direction so Divine,
> I am now letting my light shine.

> **Divine Director, send the light,**
> **from blindness clear my inner sight,**
> **my vision free, my vision clear,**
> **your guidance is forever here.**

9. Divine Director, shatter the energy veil and expose that the only way for people to feel that killing and war is necessary, unavoidable or justified is when their minds have been taken over by demons in the astral or mental realms.

> Divine Director, what a gift,
> to be a part of Spirit's lift,
> to raise mankind out of the night,
> to bask in Spirit's loving sight.

> **Divine Director, send the light,**
> **from blindness clear my inner sight,**
> **my vision free, my vision clear,**
> **your guidance is forever here.**

Part 4

1. Beloved Surya, shatter the energy veil and expose that in the identity octave are fallen beings who appear even more benign or more impressive than those in the mental realm. These beings usually control people through the beings in the mental or astral realms.

> Surya, cosmic being bright,
> your balance is my pure delight,
> I am in orbit round God Star,
> in perfect unity we are.
>
> **Surya, banish all extremes,**
> **Surya, shatter Serpent's schemes,**
> **Surya, balance to me bring,**
> **Surya, making my heart sing.**

2. Beloved Surya, shatter the energy veil and expose that when a person is engaging in war and feeling it is justified, the person is controlled directly by a being in the mental realm. The being in the mental realm is then controlled by fallen beings in the identity realm.

> Surya, there is more to life,
> than human conflict, war and strife,
> your balance gives me inner peace,
> all outer conflicts do now cease.

> **Surya, banish all extremes,**
> **Surya, shatter Serpent's schemes,**
> **Surya, balance to me bring,**
> **Surya, making my heart sing.**

3. Beloved Surya, shatter the energy veil and expose that the beings in the mental and identity realms cannot be persuaded by any argument we humans can come up with. They see us as fundamentally inferior to themselves.

> Surya, what a wondrous sight,
> from Sirius you send the light,
> of one mind, I now call to thee,
> for your apprentice I would be.

> **Surya, banish all extremes,**
> **Surya, shatter Serpent's schemes,**
> **Surya, balance to me bring,**
> **Surya, making my heart sing.**

4. Beloved Surya, shatter the energy veil and expose that the fallen beings in the mental and identity realms know that any argument is just an argument and not an absolute truth. They will use any argument to make us go to war with each other.

> Surya, radiate your light,
> with balance you set all things right,
> consuming energetic dross,
> my letting go is not a loss.

> Surya, banish all extremes,
> Surya, shatter Serpent's schemes,
> Surya, balance to me bring,
> Surya, making my heart sing.

5. Beloved Surya, shatter the energy veil and expose that the fallen beings in the identity realm realize that none of the causes on earth are valid or have any real significance. They do not lead to the end that they claim to be leading towards because it is all camouflage.

> Surya, your light is alive,
> for inner balance I do strive,
> the alchemy is now begun,
> my heart transformed into a sun.

> Surya, banish all extremes,
> Surya, shatter Serpent's schemes,
> Surya, balance to me bring,
> Surya, making my heart sing.

6. Beloved Surya, shatter the energy veil and expose that the beings in the identity realm know that all of the epic dramas have only one purpose, and that is to get people to engage in war for the purpose of assisting the fallen beings in their battle to prove God wrong.

> Surya, come enlighten me,
> duality you help me see,
> extremes they cannot pull me in,
> on Middle Way I always win.

> Surya, banish all extremes,
> Surya, shatter Serpent's schemes,
> Surya, balance to me bring,
> Surya, making my heart sing.

7. Beloved Surya, shatter the energy veil and expose that all of the philosophies, religions and thought systems found on earth are based on artificial causes. They are all camouflage for hiding the deeper cause of the fallen beings trying to prove God wrong by getting human beings to misuse their free will.

> Surya, in your cosmic sphere,
> with Cuzco I your light revere,
> from your perspective o so grand,
> life finally I understand.

> Surya, banish all extremes,
> Surya, shatter Serpent's schemes,
> Surya, balance to me bring,
> Surya, making my heart sing.

8. Beloved Surya, shatter the energy veil and expose that war has no rational reason at the physical level. Since the cause of war is not found at the physical level, the way to remove war is not found at the physical level either.

> Surya, show me God's design,
> I see that God is all benign,
> you calm my feeling body's storm,
> I know the God beyond all form.

**Surya, banish all extremes,
Surya, shatter Serpent's schemes,
Surya, balance to me bring,
Surya, making my heart sing.**

9. Beloved Surya, shatter the energy veil and expose that there is something we human beings can do to remove war from this planet. We can make the calls and transcend the consciousness so that the ascended masters get the authority to remove the forces that are creating war at the physical level.

Surya, I come from afar,
and as you show me my home star,
I see now my internal light,
a star I am in my own right.

**Surya, banish all extremes,
Surya, shatter Serpent's schemes,
Surya, balance to me bring,
Surya, making my heart sing.**

Sealing

In the name of the I AM THAT I AM, I accept that Archangel Michael, Astrea and Shiva form an impenetrable shield around myself and all constructive people, sealing us from all fear-based energies in all four octaves. I accept that the Light of God is consuming and transforming all fear-based energies that make up the forces behind war!

5 | HOW WAR CAN ACTUALLY BE REMOVED

I am the Ascended Master Mother Mary! I know that for some my first two discourses have been highly shocking, perhaps even beyond what they were willing to bear. I am not seeking to reach everyone with this book and with these discourses. My purpose is to reach those who have the potential to *act,* to do something actively about the issue of war.

The effects of previous lifetimes

Why do you have this potential? Is it just something that happens? No, it is not. It is a result of a process that you have gone through. For most of you, you have not gone through this process in this lifetime. You have gone through it in previous lifetimes. Perhaps it has taken you many lifetimes to reach the level where you have the potential to be a forerunner for banishing war from this planet.

You cannot fully understand life and what is happening on this planet without understanding and accepting reincarnation. Otherwise, you will not be able to understand what is going on in your own psychology, but neither will you be able to understand why you so often see history repeating itself. You may look at many ages and see how there has been war upon war. You may see that the same old arguments have been used again and again and again to justify the killing of other people. Why are these arguments used, you might ask yourself? Why not go even further and ask yourself why these arguments can continue to appeal to people? The simple explanation is that it is the same people they are appealing to, only in different lifetimes.

People will, in this lifetime, believe what they believed in the last several lifetimes. This will go on until they reach a turning point where they begin to see that the arguments simply cannot be true. They cannot make sense. They cannot be rational. People experience over several lifetimes that the arguments do not lead to the end that they claim to lead to. You come to a point where you experience that killing other people will not bring about peace. You realize that the outer excuses that justify killing cannot be real, cannot be true.

Awakening from the mindset of war

I have said in my previous discourse that there are forces in the astral, mental and identity realms that you cannot reason with. I have also said that such forces can overpower the minds of individual human beings. If human beings in embodiment have had their minds overpowered by forces in the three other realms, then you cannot reason with these people in embodiment. It is not so that all human beings in the world have had their minds overpowered by these non-material forces, but there are those who have had their minds overpowered by them over several lifetimes. For these, it can be a matter of taking things to such an extreme that they finally begin to awaken.

Some have had to go to war time and time again and take their warring to such an extreme level that they finally woke up and realized that this cannot go on, that they cannot continue to live their lives this way—or to die and be killed this way. There are, of course, others who have always known that justification for killing is not real, and they have not gone into warring themselves. However, these people have often been the victims of war, and this can also cause you to open your mind to certain entities in the higher realms because these entities are very clever (especially some of the ones in the mental and identity realms) at making you believe that you have to fight for peace, fight for a good cause.

This may not mean physical fighting in the sense that you kill other people, but it may mean that you take certain aggressive measures. Many people have been fooled into, so to speak, fighting for causes that may seem worthy causes, but the means they have used have not been worthy means. You will probably know that back in the 1960s there was a big movement of young people who were actively working for and demonstrating for an end to war. This, for example, took place during the war fought by the United States in Vietnam where many people throughout the world demonstrated against this war.

Soldiers are not the main reason for war

There was even a song that came to be somewhat of an exponent for this so-called peace movement, and in the song, there was a line that said: "He is a universal soldier, and he really is to blame." The idea was that it was the soldiers who fought in the war who were the driving force behind war, and if you could make the soldiers refuse to fight, then those who were the leaders had no one to fight for them.

This is not necessarily untrue in the sense that most of the human beings in embodiment who have initiated wars would not have gone out and fought themselves. They were dependent on having those who were willing to be the cannon fodder and go out there and actually fight the war. Nevertheless, you should not think that the soldiers are the cause of war. You should not think that this is a viable way to bring peace to the world: to blame the soldiers and to start demonstrating against the soldiers.

What I aim to show you here is that both the soldiers who went to war thinking they were fighting for a good cause and the people demonstrating against the soldiers were blinded by the consciousness of the entities, demons and fallen beings in the three higher levels. There are fallen beings in the identity realm who are very, very clever at coming up with argumentation that seemingly justifies taking action against other people. The characteristic you will see is that they always use the us-versus-them mentality. They separate humankind into easily-defined categories. For example, there were the soldiers and those demonstrating against the soldiers.

The duality consciousness as the foundation for war

Those who were demonstrating were thinking that they were peaceful people because they were not going to war and they were not using violent methods in their protests. They were simply going out on public places and sitting down and letting themselves be arrested. Without realizing this, these people had also been affected by fallen beings in the identity realm. The entire so-called peace movement was affected by these beings and the mentality that there were other people, such as the soldiers, who were to blame for war. When you have this mentality, this us-versus-them mentality, you are not serving to actively remove war from this planet.

This may seem shocking, but it is a reality. Why is it a reality? What is war? Consider what war really is. It is the extreme outcome of a certain state of consciousness. What is the state of consciousness behind war? I have said it is the us-versus-them mentality, but what is behind the idea that there is us and there is them? Behind it is a state of consciousness that divides reality into separate compartments. This state of consciousness looks at humankind. It then looks for certain characteristics that set one group of people apart from another group of people. It uses these characteristics to define a division between the two groups. It applies a value judgment, saying one group is doing something wrong. The other group is doing something right, or it must do something right to compensate for or stop what the first group is doing.

This is what we have called the duality consciousness, which always has two opposite polarities: good and evil, right and wrong, God and the devil. It uses this to create the idea that there is an epic struggle and that some people are on the wrong side of the struggle. Those who are on the right side must take various measures to force these other people to stop what they are doing.

My beloved, science has now proven that there is no such thing as locality, as separate compartments in the universe. This has been proven through the most advanced scientific measures. Locality, the idea that the universe can be divided into separate compartments, is an illusion created by the human mind, especially by the outer senses and the mind that runs the body. It is an illusion that goes all the way up through the four levels of the material realm. For most people, it has become part of their sense of identity.

Once you go into this duality consciousness, you see yourself as a separate being. You are separated from your God, from your source. You are separated from the nature in which you live. You are separated from the other people, except, perhaps, those who belong to the group that you identify yourself with and that you think is right in some epic sense. This state of consciousness is the very foundation for war.

In its extreme form, it makes you believe that you can kill another human being without affecting yourself. You may even believe that you are affecting yourself positively or affecting some greater cause. You may even believe you are promoting or working for God's cause by killing other human beings. The idea that there is a heaven and there is a hell is an outcome of the duality consciousness. The reality is that there is only one continuum of vibrations. There are certain divisions, layers or realms in this energy continuum, but they are not separated by impenetrable barriers.

The potential for human beings to turn around

My beloved, there are so many of the ideas that people take for granted that support the illusion of separation that I could not possibly comment on all of them. I can assure you that, if you can see what I see from the ascended realm, you see that all human beings came from the same source. All were originally created as pure and innocent beings. They were all given free will, and they started life on a clean white slate. This means that their present condition is a result of choices they have made. This also means that their present condition can be undone if they make other choices that undo their previous choices. There is absolutely no being in embodiment on earth who does not have this potential.

I have said in my previous discourse that there are certain beings in the astral plane who started out as self-aware beings and who have descended into such a low state of consciousness that they have, for all practical purposes, lost the self-awareness that is necessary for them to undo their previous choices. Any being who started out as a self-aware being can be awakened to the potential to make choices that lead upward (instead of downward) in self-awareness. For some of the beings in the astral plane, it would take rather extreme measures, but we of the ascended masters are fully capable of delivering such measures. This will give even the darkest demon in the lowest level of the astral pit an opportunity to awaken and choose to engage in an upward path that will return it to its pure state of innocence.

Take care to notice that I have also said that there are entities and demons in the astral plane that were not created as self-aware beings, and therefore, they do not have the potential to choose. Such beings must simply be consumed, and again, we of the ascended masters are fully capable of doing this. We are not allowed to do this until the self-aware beings who created these unaware beings have renounced their state of consciousness or until another measure has been reached, which I will explain in this discourse.

Why is it that all of the human beings who are in embodiment on earth have the potential to turn around and that some of the beings in the astral plane have lost this potential on their own? It is simply because the Law of Free Will states that, if you have gone below the limit where you could not pull yourself out of the downward spiral, you are not allowed to embody on earth. You are not allowed to take physical embodiment.

There are beings in the astral plane who have not taken physical embodiment on earth or any other physical planet for a very, very long time.

Some of these beings started out taking embodiment on earth and sank so low in consciousness that they can no longer take physical embodiment. Others started out on different planetary systems, some of them even in previous spheres as we have explained in other books [See *Cosmology of Evil*]. They are allowed to continue to be in the astral plane associated with earth because there are people in embodiment who have not yet transcended a certain level of consciousness.

The level of consciousness of the people in physical embodiment determines what is allowed to exist in the emotional, mental and identity realms of earth. If a critical mass of people in physical embodiment shift their consciousness upwards, it will mean that we of the ascended masters now gain the authority to go into the astral plane, go into the mental realm, go into the identity octave and clean out some of the demons, the beings who are below that level of consciousness.

I have said very clearly that there are certain beings in the other realms that you cannot reason with. I have now also said that there are certain human beings that you cannot reason with. This means that, as a human being in embodiment, there is nothing you can do to make these beings change their minds voluntarily. We of the ascended masters cannot manifest ourselves in front of these beings and make them change their minds voluntarily.

This is proven by the fact that Christ stood before some of the human beings in embodiment who were completely blinded by the duality consciousness. Even though he stood there in the full light of the Christ consciousness, they did not recognize him as such. They were so blinded by duality that they did not see his light, and therefore they condemned him to death and executed him without giving it a second thought.

Throughout the ages there has always been a certain power elite whose members have been willing to execute anyone who crossed them, anyone who seemed to be a threat. This is what they did to Jesus, as they have done to many other beings who had greater light than the average human being. They may not recognize Christ as being the Christ in embodiment, but they did subconsciously feel that he had greater light, and they were threatened by this. They reasoned that it was better that one man should die than the whole population should suffer.

The limit to what you can actually do

When you look at yourself as a spiritual person who is open to the teachings of the ascended masters, you must ask yourself: "What can I really do to remove war from this planet when there are people that cannot be reasoned with and when there are forces in the three other octaves that cannot be reasoned with? What good does it do that I go out on the street and demonstrate, if the people who are sitting in their rooms making decisions about war are not susceptible to any argument that I think makes sense? What good does it do that I sit here and make the calls and invocations given by the ascended masters for invoking light when there are beings in the three other octaves and human beings in embodiment who will not respond to the increase in light?"

This is a valid question, which I will answer in this discourse. The simple answer is that there is a limit to what you can do by invoking spiritual light. This does not mean that it is not effective to invoke spiritual light, because it *is*. It only means there is a limit to what you can do. I have explained to you that everything works based on the principle of free will.

There are many people on earth, many people in embodiment, who are not completely blinded by beings in the three other realms. There are many human beings whose minds are not completely taken over by entities and demons in the astral plane or the clever beings in the mental realm or the even more clever beings in the identity octave. They have enough self-awareness that they are able to stand back and look at what is right and wrong. Most of these beings know it is wrong to kill. Most of these people would rather live peaceful lives, but they can be manipulated into supporting a war if they think there is no other way to respond to a situation that has been forced upon them by the aggression of others.

You may look at the terrorist attacks in America, for example, and you will see that most people in the West were shocked by this and would much have preferred that this event had not taken place. They would much have preferred to avoid going to war in Iraq and Afghanistan. They were still manipulated into supporting this because they were afraid that, if they did nothing, then those who had attacked the World Trade Center would simply continue to commit similar atrocities around the world. The people felt that they had to do something to stop these terrorists from continuing to attack what they saw as innocent people.

These many human beings, the majority (although not a wide majority) of human beings, have already reached a level of awareness where they would prefer to avoid war. This is a shift, and it should be acknowledged that this is an important shift. If you go back just a few hundred years, you will see that, in many parts of the world, young men were brought up to see it as honorable to go to war. There were cultures where it was considered that young men had to go into some form of battle in order to prove their manhood and earn respect. There were cultures that were entirely based upon having young men be educated to become warriors of some kind. There were people who were eager to go to war and prove themselves, who thought it was a matter of honor and prestige to go to war and prove your valor in battle.

This is still so in some areas of the world, but certainly very large areas of the world have gone through a shift where this desire to win honor in battle is no longer there or is no longer as prominent or dominating. I am bringing this up because I want you to see that there has been a forward progression in the collective consciousness. What has brought about this progression? It is an increase in the light, the amount and the intensity of light, that is available not only in the physical octave but in the three higher octaves of earth.

Invoking light to choose an alternative to war

Imagine that you are in a dark room. In the room is a labyrinth, and there are many obstacles, many blind turns. People are walking around in this dark room, and they must fumble their way along the walls and try to find their way out of the maze. Now imagine that you increase the level of light very gradually. Suddenly, people can begin to see what is in the room, and now it is much easier for them to navigate. If you increase the light even more, then people can begin to see that there is an exit to the room. By following a certain path through the maze, you can reach the exit.

This does not mean that all people in the room will instantly choose to move towards the exit. There may be some who still want to explore what is in the maze because they think some hidden treasure is there somewhere. It does mean that all people who can now see the exit door have an option they did not have before. They have a choice, a *real* choice. Why is it that so many people on earth have chosen to transcend a culture that saw war as a way to gain honor? It is because the spiritual light has been increased in the four octaves of earth and more people have begun to see that there is a higher state of consciousness than the warring consciousness that they were in just a few lifetimes ago.

The principle that I want you to grasp here is that everything revolves around free will but that people's will is no more free than what they can see. You cannot choose what you cannot see, what you cannot grasp, what you cannot envision, what you cannot understand, what you cannot accept. Your vision determines the options you can see, and as long you cannot grasp an option, you cannot really choose it, even if it is theoretically there for you.

The exit door was still there when the room was completely dark, and maybe a few people fumbled their way to it by chance. People did not even know what it was when they found the door because they did not have enough vision to understand that there was something outside the room and that they could exit the darkness. There *is* a way to help remove war by invoking spiritual light through our decrees and invocations. By increasing the light in the four octaves of earth, you are making it easier for people to see an alternative to the consciousness that generates war.

Humankind's evolution throughout time

This is extremely important. This is how humankind progresses, in general. There is an ongoing progression on this planet that has been taking place for all of recorded history.

5 | How War Can Actually be Removed

You will recall that, according to science, the history of humankind started only a few thousand years ago when people lived at the caveman stage, which is seen as being only a step up from the apes. This is a very limited view of history because the history of intelligent life on earth is much, much older, as we have explained in other books.

The deeper reality is that, in previous ages, there were civilizations that were far more sophisticated than what you see on earth today and they had developed far more sophisticated weapons. These weapons were so powerful that, when used, they were able to create widespread earth changes that reduced those civilizations to rubble. This caused humankind to have to start over again at a very low level of development.

What you see as a scientific evolution is not the beginning of humankind, but it is the beginning of the upward spiral that you are currently in. Your civilization is not the highest civilization ever to appear on earth, but it is the highest to appear in the upward cycle that started with the caveman stage.

The cause for the upward movement

You need to realize that, due to the choices of the few, an upward spiral has been created and sustained now for a long time. This has not been a smooth process; there have been ups and downs. There certainly have been periods when there has been more warring, more atrocities and more control by a small elite than what you see right now. The general tendency has been an upward movement.

The cause of this upward movement is very simple. A small number of people have become instruments, they have become open doors, for bringing spiritual light into the four octaves of earth. This has caused other people to respond by choosing a higher state of consciousness, once they could see the alternative to their present level of consciousness. This is the ongoing progression of earth.

You now need to understand that, in this ongoing progression, there are certain cycles. You are most likely aware of the concept of spiritual ages. You have no doubt heard about the Age of Pisces, that was the last 2,000 years, and you have heard about the Age of Aquarius, which is the cycle that the earth is now moving into. You now need to understand that, as there is a changing from one cycle to another, there is an interim phase. When Jesus appeared in physical embodiment 2,000 years ago, he said: "For judgment, I am come." He also made the seemingly contradictory statement: "I judge no man, but if I judge, my judgment is true, for it is not I, but the Father within me who is doing it." So how do you balance these two statements?

Christ judgment and dualistic judgment

The deeper reality is that the Christ in embodiment does not judge based on the duality consciousness, the consciousness of separation, that divides humankind into separate groups and applies a value judgment to them. Certainly, you see human beings who judge others, and those were the ones that Jesus warned by saying: "With whatever measure you measure out to others, it shall be measured out to you also." You shall be judged as you judge others, because you are judged through your own state of consciousness.

The Judgment of Christ is different because the Christ consciousness is the consciousness of Oneness. The alternative to duality is open to all people, meaning that Jesus was the example of what all people can attain by striving for the

Christ consciousness. The Christ consciousness is when you know that all life is one. Human beings cannot be divided into separate compartments. You cannot apply a value judgment saying some are good and some are evil, and therefore the evil deserved to be killed by the good.

There is a higher form of judgment where you judge based on the awareness that all life is one. This is an essential recognition and discernment for those who are open to this book. If you are to be effective in helping remove war, you must contemplate the difference between dualistic judgment and the judgment of Oneness. What is the difference? One obvious difference is that when you judge from the consciousness of duality, you think that those other people, those *bad* people, are completely separate from you. If they are destroyed or killed, it will not affect you.

The reality of the Christ consciousness is that all people are part of the one Body of God on earth. What affects some human beings will affect the whole, and therefore, it will effect *you* as well. Another effect is that, in the consciousness of duality, you want those separate people to either be destroyed, so they cannot do what you label as evil, or you want them to be punished for doing what you judge to be bad. In the Christ consciousness there is no desire whatsoever to destroy any part of life. There is only a desire to raise up all life. There is also no desire whatsoever to punish other forms of life because you know that if you punish others, you are punishing yourself.

Transcending the consciousness of the Piscean cycle

What I want you to see here is that the earth is right now going through this interim period between Pisces and Aquarius. There is an extraordinary opportunity for transcending the old state of consciousness and embracing the new. For each 2,000 year period, there is a certain state of consciousness that humankind is meant to transcend. This is part of the consciousness that generates war. What humankind had the potential to transcend in the Age of Pisces was the very consciousness that generates war, the idea that the ends can justify the means and that it is justifiable to kill other people in order to achieve some abstract goal defined by an abstract idea.

Do you see that the justification used by Pontius Pilate to kill Jesus was an abstract idea? The abstract idea was used to justify the killing of a physical human being. This consciousness needs to be transcended by humankind before they can make the transition into the Aquarian Age.

When I say that it needs to be transcended, you need to understand that there is a somewhat flexible process that takes place. On the one hand, there does come a point – and we have passed the point – where you will say that we have moved from the Piscean to the Aquarian Age. Saint Germain has announced this. This change has taken place, but there are many human beings who have not moved from the Piscean consciousness to the Aquarian consciousness.

Some are very unwilling to let go of the Piscean Age and the consciousness that they were meant to transcend. This explains why you have seen so many wars and the increasing severity of wars in the past hundred years. Humankind was meant to transcend the consciousness of Pisces much earlier. Had people done so, it would not have been necessary to have the very severe wars that you have seen in the past hundred years. When people do not transcend a certain level of consciousness, they begin to act out that consciousness in more and more extreme forms. At the same time, there is an increase of light that challenges or exposes that consciousness.

The purpose is very simple: to make the consciousness so visible that people have a better opportunity to transcend it by seeing the negative effects of the old consciousness and seeing the alternative. This has worked for many people, but it has not worked for all. It has not yet worked for the critical mass that is necessary for humankind as a whole to make the shift to the Aquarian consciousness.

Calling forth judgment during the transition phase

The importance of this transition period between two ages is that it is a period where certain measures can come into play that normally do not apply. There is a general underlying upward movement. During the past 2,000 years, it was not lawful for you to bring about the judgment of other people, nor was it lawful for you to bring about the judgment of non-material forces in the three other realms. This is not lawful in the biggest part of a particular cycle. When we move into the transition phase – and when not enough people on the planet have made the switch to the new state of consciousness – then it does become lawful for those who are in embodiment to call forth actively the judgment of not only human beings in embodiment but especially the non-material forces in the three other realms.

The tool that I wish to give you here and in the rest of the book is that it is possible and lawful for you to call forth the active judgment, the Judgment of Christ, upon forces and even certain human beings so that they get an extraordinary opportunity to choose. Take note of what I am saying. Everything happens within the Law of Free Will. If you violate the free will of other people, you will make karma for doing so. Do you understand my concern here as a spiritual teacher, as a spiritual being?

The potential for these tools to be misused

We have given you many decrees and invocations that invoke spiritual light. It is very difficult to abuse these tools. It is very difficult to make karma by invoking spiritual light. You can do so if you continue to misuse the light so that you continue to misqualify light and then use our invocations to simply clean up after yourself without changing your consciousness. If you keep doing this for an extended period of time, you will eventually begin to make karma, but it is difficult to force other people by invoking spiritual light.

However, the tools that we will give you in this book, where you will actively invoke the judgment, can be misused. You can give these invocations and decrees with a state of dualistic judgment, of feeling negative, fear-based feelings against other human beings, and this will make karma for yourself. That is why I begin this book by giving you an understanding. It is also why I am giving you a warning in this discourse. This is not to scare you away from using the tools, but it is to make you aware that you need to use these tools with as neutral of a state of mind as you can possibly obtain.

Confronting people with a choice

Take note of what I said: The consciousness of Christ is the consciousness of oneness. It does not want to destroy, and it does not want to punish other human beings. Christ only wants to raise up all. How do you raise up other beings with free will? By making it easier for them to choose the light over darkness. How do you make this easier for them? By showing them the light!

It is entirely possible to increase the light in the room, and there are still some who refuse to see it but focus on the darkness. This is perfectly acceptable for most of a planetary 2,000 year cycle. When you come to this transition period where humankind as a whole needs to make the switch into a higher state of consciousness, then there comes that point where it is no longer acceptable for people to ignore the light.

The majority of the people have started to acknowledge the light. It is not within the Law of Free Will that a small minority can hold back the transition into the next spiritual cycle. This does not mean that this minority is *forced* to go into the new cycle, but it does mean that there comes a point where they have to make a choice between the new and the old. Will they go into the new cycle? Will they go into the light? Will they let go of the old, or will they cling to the old?

This is not something you can do as a human being in embodiment, but we of the ascended masters have the authority to confront people with the necessity to make a choice. For people who are in physical embodiment, this choice can mean the difference between whether they are allowed to embody again on earth or whether this will be their last physical embodiment on this planet.

Confronting beings in the other planes

Some of the beings who are now in the astral plane, and can no longer embody here, did take physical embodiment in the past. The reason they are no longer allowed to take physical embodiment is that they were exposed to this Judgment of Christ.

They did choose the darkness over the light, and they have not changed that choice. They are not allowed to take embodiment because the planet has moved on from the consciousness that they will not let go of.

For beings in the astral plane, the situation is somewhat different than for people in embodiment. They can also be confronted with the Judgment of Christ where they must make a choice. Will they start the upward spiral that can lead them back to oneness, or will they take another step down into separation? For some of them, it will mean they will go to an even lower level of the astral plane. For others, it will mean that they will go so low that they can no longer go lower in the astral plane on earth.

Some of these lifestreams may go to other planets that are even lower than earth, but there are not that many of these left in the physical universe. Others will be confronted with what we have called the second death. This is the final judgment where the lifestream must either choose the upward spiral or it will be dissolved in what we call the Lake of Sacred Fire. All of the negative momentums that this lifestream has gathered over a very long period of time will be dissolved instantly.

The same, of course, applies to the self-aware beings in the mental and identity realms. Those in the identity realm who will not choose to go upwards may descend into the mental realm. Those in the mental may descend into the astral. There are some in each realm who have reached the end of their opportunity and may be confronted with the initiation of the final judgment that may lead to the dissolution of the lifestream.

Why the judgment is initiated

Do you understand why this process is initiated? It is initiated because of two facts. One is the fact that all life is one, all life is interconnected. The other is free will. Free will can be taken into such extremes by one individual that it works against the forward progression, the choices, of the whole. There must be a certain balance, and this is simply how the process has been defined. This process was not invented or created specifically for earth. It was initiated on other planets. It has proven itself over and over and over again on many different planets in the physical universe and in previous spheres. It is a process that works. It is a very slow process, a very gradual process.

I fully understand that many people will feel impatient and say: "Why does life have such patience with those who over and over again have chosen a self-destructive spiral and have chosen to destroy others?" It is, again, because all life is one. We who have attained oneness with the Christ mind always seek to raise up all life, and we seek to give opportunity after opportunity. You may look at the astral plane, and look at the darkness that I have described, and you may say: "What is the purpose of allowing this to go on? Why don't the ascended masters just wipe this out once and for all and just clear it?"

The choice to rise lower or higher

The reason is that any experience has the potential to become the final experience for a given number of lifestreams. They come to the point where they say: "This is as far down into separation as I am willing to go. I cannot continue this downward spiral. I want something more, I want to turn around." We are not defining how low lifestreams are allowed to go.

They are defining it themselves. There is this concept floating around that God created hell, but God never created hell. It was individual lifestreams with free will who created their own hell. They are deciding how hellish it has to become before they have had enough and turn around.

We of the ascended masters are allowing this, but we are not allowing it for a given planet when it goes too far, compared to the consciousness of the majority on that planet. That is why you have the concept of the judgment that says: "The majority has now moved on to a higher state of consciousness. You have ignored this movement now for a long time, but there is no longer time in the evolutionary cycles of earth to ignore this, you must make a choice. Will you enter the upward spiral along with the majority, or will you deny the upward spiral?"

If the lifestream makes the choice to deny, then it can no longer be allowed to remain either in physical embodiment or in one of the other octaves. It may not be allowed to remain with earth, or it may not be allowed to remain in existence if it has denied this so many times. I will not put a number on how many times a lifestream can deny the upward choice because this varies from lifestream to lifestream. It varies based on a set of factors that are so complex that I do not wish to go into them here.

What I do wish you to see is that, because the earth is now in a transition phase, you have the authority to call forth the judgment. I do wish you to understand here that even Jesus himself made certain statements that have been misinterpreted by Christians to mean that he thought the end of the world was coming. There was talk about the "end times," but end times is not the same as the end of the world.

My beloved, the world will not end. What will end is a certain cycle, a certain time, where people can ignore the light.

Then, the end time comes, the day of judgment arrives, when they can no longer refuse to make the choice between light and darkness. They must choose either to go upward in the light or to go downward in the darkness and therefore not remain with earth.

This is how a planet progresses. It progresses in two ways: By those who choose to open themselves to the light and therefore bring more light to the planet, and by the judgment of those who will not open themselves to the light so that they are removed and that their darkness can no longer weigh down the planet and form a magnetic pull on the human beings in embodiment.

Using the Judgment of Christ constructively

The Judgment of Christ that I am talking about is not the same as the judgment of the duality consciousness. We are not, in any way, encouraging you to start looking at other people, dividing them up based on the us-versus-them mentality and then saying that these other people are bad and deserve to be judged by the ascended masters. We are encouraging you to transcend this state of consciousness and enter, if you can, the Christ consciousness. We know that some of you are not quite ready to enter the Christ consciousness, and that is why I am asking you to enter a consciousness where you are as neutral as possible towards other people.

I know very well that the invocations we are giving you in this book can be used to judge specific people, specific groups of people, who are waging war and continue to wage war. I am not saying you should not use the invocations for this purpose. I am strongly encouraging you *not* to feel anger, hatred, or other negative feelings towards the people that you mention in these invocations. Do not allow yourself to feel a desire to destroy these people or to see them punished. If you do this, you will make karma for yourself, and that is not my desire for you.

You may say that we should not release these invocations then, but we judged – based on the Judgment of Christ – that a sufficient number of people are ready to use them constructively. They can have a major positive impact on accelerating the transition from the Piscean state of consciousness into the Aquarian state of consciousness. As I said, the state of consciousness that humankind was meant to overcome in the Piscean age was the state where you were willing to kill a physical being because of an abstract idea, and this is the major cause of war at a certain level right now. As I have said, there are forces, there are beings, in the identity octave who are seeking to prove God wrong. Proving God wrong is an abstract idea. These beings are willing to kill physical human beings, and thereby deprive them of the opportunity to be in physical embodiment, because of their abstract idea.

What we need to do here is to transcend the level where so many people can be deceived by this consciousness and believe that the ends of furthering an abstract idea can justify the means of killing physical people. We need to get to the point where a vast majority among humankind recognize that it is never justified to kill physical people because of an abstract idea. The reason being that physical life is a precious opportunity for growth.

My beloved, I have once again given you a mouthful, as they say. I have given you more in one sitting than you are probably prepared to handle. I will rest, or rather let *you* rest, for now. I have no need for rest, and I will return in due time and give you further teachings on these topics.

I once again want to impress upon you that there is *something* you can do. This does not mean that you are the doer, but you become the open door whereby we of the ascended masters can be the doer through you and through the calls you make. To this end, I seal you in my deepest love. Mother Mary I AM!

6 | AWAKEN PEOPLE TO THE NEED FOR JUDGMENT

In the name of the I AM THAT I AM, Jesus Christ, I call upon Mother Mary, Surya and Alpha to awaken people to the need for us to call forth the judgment of the demons and fallen beings who create war. Awaken people to the reality that we are spiritual beings and that we can co-create a new future by working with the ascended masters. I especially call for …

[Make your own calls here.]

Part 1

1. Beloved Surya, awaken people from the illusion of the us-versus-them mentality, created by the entities, demons and fallen beings in the three higher levels. Cut people free from the argumentation that seemingly justifies taking action against others based on separating humankind into easily-defined categories.

Surya, cosmic being bright,
your balance is my pure delight,
I am in orbit round God Star,
in perfect unity we are.

**Surya, banish all extremes,
Surya, shatter Serpent's schemes,
Surya, balance to me bring,
Surya, making my heart sing.**

2. Beloved Surya, awaken people to the reality that when you have the us-versus-them mentality, you are not serving to actively remove war from this planet.

Surya, there is more to life,
than human conflict, war and strife,
your balance gives me inner peace,
all outer conflicts do now cease.

**Surya, banish all extremes,
Surya, shatter Serpent's schemes,
Surya, balance to me bring,
Surya, making my heart sing.**

3. Beloved Surya, awaken people to the reality that war is the extreme outcome of a state of consciousness that divides reality into separate compartments. It defines a division between groups of people, applies a value judgment, saying one group is doing something wrong and the other group must stop this.

Surya, what a wondrous sight,
from Sirius you send the light,
of one mind, I now call to thee,
for your apprentice I would be.

Surya, banish all extremes,
Surya, shatter Serpent's schemes,
Surya, balance to me bring,
Surya, making my heart sing.

4. Beloved Surya, awaken people to the reality that the duality consciousness always has two opposite polarities and uses this to create the idea that there is an epic struggle and that some people are on the wrong side of the struggle. Those who are on the right side must force others for a greater good.

Surya, radiate your light,
with balance you set all things right,
consuming energetic dross,
my letting go is not a loss.

Surya, banish all extremes,
Surya, shatter Serpent's schemes,
Surya, balance to me bring,
Surya, making my heart sing.

5. Beloved Surya, awaken people from the illusion that we can kill other human beings without affecting ourselves, even the illusion that we are working for God's cause by killing other human beings.

Surya, your light is alive,
for inner balance I do strive,
the alchemy is now begun,
my heart transformed into a sun.

Surya, banish all extremes,
Surya, shatter Serpent's schemes,
Surya, balance to me bring,
Surya, making my heart sing.

6. Beloved Surya, awaken people to the reality that all human beings came from the same source. All were originally created as pure and innocent beings. We were all given free will, and our present condition can be undone if we make choices that undo our previous choices.

Surya, come enlighten me,
duality you help me see,
extremes they cannot pull me in,
on Middle Way I always win.

Surya, banish all extremes,
Surya, shatter Serpent's schemes,
Surya, balance to me bring,
Surya, making my heart sing.

7. Beloved Surya, awaken people to the reality that the entities and demons in the astral plane were not created as self-aware beings and they do not have the potential to choose. Such beings must be consumed, and the ascended masters are fully capable of doing this when we give them the authority.

> Surya, in your cosmic sphere,
> with Cuzco I your light revere,
> from your perspective o so grand,
> life finally I understand.
>
> **Surya, banish all extremes,**
> **Surya, shatter Serpent's schemes,**
> **Surya, balance to me bring,**
> **Surya, making my heart sing.**

8. Beloved Surya, awaken people to the reality that the level of consciousness of the people in physical embodiment determines what is allowed to exist in the emotional, mental and identity realms of earth. If a critical mass of people in physical embodiment shift their consciousness upwards, the ascended masters gain the authority to clean out the demons who are below that level of consciousness.

> Surya, show me God's design,
> I see that God is all benign,
> you calm my feeling body's storm,
> I know the God beyond all form.
>
> **Surya, banish all extremes,**
> **Surya, shatter Serpent's schemes,**
> **Surya, balance to me bring,**
> **Surya, making my heart sing.**

9. Beloved Surya, awaken people to the reality that there is a limit to what we can do by invoking spiritual light. The entities, demons and fallen beings in the three higher octaves may not respond to the light, and thus we have the authority to actively call for their judgment.

Surya, I come from afar,
and as you show me my home star,
I see now my internal light,
a star I am in my own right.

**Surya, banish all extremes,
Surya, shatter Serpent's schemes,
Surya, balance to me bring,
Surya, making my heart sing.**

Part 2

1. Beloved Alpha, awaken people to the reality that here has been a shift in the collective consciousness, meaning most people no longer see it as honorable to go to war and seek prestige by killing other people.

Beloved Alpha, God's great plan,
in Central Sun it all began,
what wondrous vision of a world,
the cosmic spheres were then unfurled.

**Beloved Alpha, in your light,
I now see God with inner sight,
as man I will no longer live,
my life to God I fully give.**

2. Beloved Alpha, awaken people to the reality of spiritual cycles. Help them see that we are now moving into a new cycle, which means we can call forth the judgment of Christ for the beings who will not make the shift in consciousness.

> Beloved Alpha, serve the All,
> this is Creator's timeless call,
> from out Creator's perfect whole,
> sprang lifestreams with a sacred goal.
>
> **Beloved Alpha, in your light,**
> **I now see God with inner sight,**
> **as man I will no longer live,**
> **my life to God I fully give.**

3. Beloved Alpha, awaken people to the reality that the judgment of Christ is based on the consciousness of Oneness. The Christ consciousness knows that all life is one, that human beings cannot be divided into separate compartments, that we cannot apply a value judgment saying some people are evil and deserve to be killed by the good.

> Beloved Alpha, all was one,
> as we were sent from Central Sun,
> to you we shall in time return,
> for cosmic union we do yearn.
>
> **Beloved Alpha, in your light,**
> **I now see God with inner sight,**
> **as man I will no longer live,**
> **my life to God I fully give.**

4. Beloved Alpha, awaken people to the reality that to the Christ consciousness, all people are part of the one Body of God on earth. What affects some human beings will affect the whole, and therefore, it will effect us as well.

Beloved Alpha, I now see,
you with Omega form the key,
it was from your polarity,
that I received identity.

Beloved Alpha, in your light,
I now see God with inner sight,
as man I will no longer live,
my life to God I fully give.

5. Beloved Alpha, awaken people to the reality that in the Christ consciousness there is no desire to destroy other people. There is also no desire to punish other people because if we punish others, we are punishing ourselves.

Beloved Alpha, cosmic gate,
the nexus of your figure-eight,
I sprang from Cosmic Cube so bright,
I am at heart a spark of light.

Beloved Alpha, in your light,
I now see God with inner sight,
as man I will no longer live,
my life to God I fully give.

6. Beloved Alpha, awaken people to the reality that the earth is going through an interim period between Pisces and Aquarius. Humankind is meant to transcend the consciousness that generates war, the idea that the ends can justify the means and that it is justifiable to kill other people in order to achieve some abstract goal defined by an abstract idea.

6 | Awaken People to the Need for Judgment

Beloved Alpha, from your womb,
I did descend to matter's tomb,
but buried I will be no more,
my inner vision you restore.

**Beloved Alpha, in your light,
I now see God with inner sight,
as man I will no longer live,
my life to God I fully give.**

7. Beloved Alpha, awaken people from the illusion that an abstract idea can justify the killing of a physical human being. Help people see that if we do not transcend this consciousness, the wars will only continue to become more severe until we finally awaken.

Beloved Alpha, I now know,
the love you did on me bestow,
a co-creator, I will bring,
the light to make all matter sing.

**Beloved Alpha, in your light,
I now see God with inner sight,
as man I will no longer live,
my life to God I fully give.**

8. Beloved Alpha, awaken people to the reality that when a planet moves into the transition phase, it becomes lawful for those who are in embodiment to call forth the judgment of human beings in embodiment and the non-material forces in the three other realms.

Beloved Alpha, on this earth,
a new age we are giving birth,
for we are here to bring the love,
that you are sending from Above.

Beloved Alpha, in your light,
I now see God with inner sight,
as man I will no longer live,
my life to God I fully give.

9. Beloved Alpha, awaken people to the reality that by calling forth the judgment of Christ upon certain forces and human beings, they receive an extraordinary opportunity to choose between light and darkness.

Beloved Alpha, you and me,
we form a true polarity,
as up Above, so here below,
with life's own river I do flow.

Beloved Alpha, in your light,
I now see God with inner sight,
as man I will no longer live,
my life to God I fully give.

Part 3

1. Beloved Surya, awaken the spiritual people to the opportunity to call for the judgment of Christ and the need to do so from a completely neutral state of mind.

> Surya, cosmic being bright,
> your balance is my pure delight,
> I am in orbit round God Star,
> in perfect unity we are.
>
> **Surya, banish all extremes,**
> **Surya, shatter Serpent's schemes,**
> **Surya, balance to me bring,**
> **Surya, making my heart sing.**

2. Beloved Surya, awaken the spiritual people to the awareness that the Christ consciousness wants to raise up all life. We raise up other beings with free will by making it easier for them to choose the light over darkness. We show them the light!

> Surya, there is more to life,
> than human conflict, war and strife,
> your balance gives me inner peace,
> all outer conflicts do now cease.
>
> **Surya, banish all extremes,**
> **Surya, shatter Serpent's schemes,**
> **Surya, balance to me bring,**
> **Surya, making my heart sing.**

3. Beloved Surya, awaken the spiritual people to the reality that because a majority of the people have started to acknowledge the light, it is not within the Law of Free Will that a small minority can hold back the transition into the next spiritual cycle. There comes a point where beings have to make a choice between the new and the old.

Surya, what a wondrous sight,
from Sirius you send the light,
of one mind, I now call to thee,
for your apprentice I would be.

**Surya, banish all extremes,
Surya, shatter Serpent's schemes,
Surya, balance to me bring,
Surya, making my heart sing.**

4. Beloved Surya, awaken the spiritual people to the awareness that the ascended masters have the authority to confront beings with the necessity to make a choice. What we can do is to call upon the ascended masters to execute this judgment of Christ for both people in embodiment and beings in the three higher realms.

Surya, radiate your light,
with balance you set all things right,
consuming energetic dross,
my letting go is not a loss.

**Surya, banish all extremes,
Surya, shatter Serpent's schemes,
Surya, balance to me bring,
Surya, making my heart sing.**

5. Beloved Surya, awaken the spiritual people to the absolute need to call forth the judgment of Christ for the beings in the astral plane who are mindlessly seeking to control human beings into going to war again and again.

Surya, your light is alive,
for inner balance I do strive,
the alchemy is now begun,
my heart transformed into a sun.

**Surya, banish all extremes,
Surya, shatter Serpent's schemes,
Surya, balance to me bring,
Surya, making my heart sing.**

6. Beloved Surya, awaken the spiritual people to the awareness that for some of the beings in the astral, mental and identity realms, the next logical step is the final judgment, leading to the second death in which all of the negative momentums of a lifestream are dissolved.

Surya, come enlighten me,
duality you help me see,
extremes they cannot pull me in,
on Middle Way I always win.

**Surya, banish all extremes,
Surya, shatter Serpent's schemes,
Surya, balance to me bring,
Surya, making my heart sing.**

7. Beloved Surya, awaken the spiritual people to the awareness that free will can be taken into such extremes by one individual that it works against the forward progression and the choices of the whole. There must be a certain balance, and the process defined by the ascended masters has proven itself on many different planets.

Surya, in your cosmic sphere,
with Cuzco I your light revere,
from your perspective o so grand,
life finally I understand.

Surya, banish all extremes,
Surya, shatter Serpent's schemes,
Surya, balance to me bring,
Surya, making my heart sing.

8. Beloved Surya, awaken the spiritual people to the reality that God never created hell. It was individual lifestreams with free will who created their own hell. They are deciding how hellish it has to become before they have had enough and turn around.

Surya, show me God's design,
I see that God is all benign,
you calm my feeling body's storm,
I know the God beyond all form.

Surya, banish all extremes,
Surya, shatter Serpent's schemes,
Surya, balance to me bring,
Surya, making my heart sing.

9. Beloved Surya, awaken the spiritual people to the awareness that even though lifestreams are allowed to create their own hell, there is a limit to how far this can go for a given planet. It is time for us to decide that the hell of war shall no longer be allowed on earth.

Surya, I come from afar,
and as you show me my home star,
I see now my internal light,
a star I am in my own right.

**Surya, banish all extremes,
Surya, shatter Serpent's schemes,
Surya, balance to me bring,
Surya, making my heart sing.**

Part 4

1. Beloved Alpha, I call forth the judgment of Christ upon all human beings in physical embodiment who believe in and act upon the concept that it is justifiable to kill a physical human being in order to defend or promote an abstract idea.

Beloved Alpha, God's great plan,
in Central Sun it all began,
what wondrous vision of a world,
the cosmic spheres were then unfurled.

**Beloved Alpha, in your light,
I now see God with inner sight,
as man I will no longer live,
my life to God I fully give.**

2. Beloved Alpha, I call forth the judgment of Christ upon all entities, demons and fallen beings in the astral plane who are controlling the minds of human beings, seeking to make them kill others in order to defend or promote an abstract idea.

Beloved Alpha, serve the All,
this is Creator's timeless call,
from out Creator's perfect whole,
sprang lifestreams with a sacred goal.

**Beloved Alpha, in your light,
I now see God with inner sight,
as man I will no longer live,
my life to God I fully give.**

3. Beloved Alpha, I call forth the judgment of Christ upon all entities, demons and fallen beings in the mental octave who are controlling the minds of human beings, seeking to make them kill others in order to defend or promote an abstract idea.

Beloved Alpha, all was one,
as we were sent from Central Sun,
to you we shall in time return,
for cosmic union we do yearn.

**Beloved Alpha, in your light,
I now see God with inner sight,
as man I will no longer live,
my life to God I fully give.**

4. Beloved Alpha, I call forth the judgment of Christ upon all entities, demons and fallen beings in the identity octave who are controlling the minds of human beings, seeking to make them kill others in order to defend or promote an abstract idea.

> Beloved Alpha, I now see,
> you with Omega form the key,
> it was from your polarity,
> that I received identity.
>
> **Beloved Alpha, in your light,**
> **I now see God with inner sight,**
> **as man I will no longer live,**
> **my life to God I fully give.**

5. Beloved Alpha, I call forth the judgment of Christ upon all beings in and out of embodiment who will not let go of this idea. I call for them to be removed from all four octaves of planet earth so that their darkness can no longer weigh down the planet and form a magnetic pull on the human beings in embodiment.

> Beloved Alpha, cosmic gate,
> the nexus of your figure-eight,
> I sprang from Cosmic Cube so bright,
> I am at heart a spark of light.
>
> **Beloved Alpha, in your light,**
> **I now see God with inner sight,**
> **as man I will no longer live,**
> **my life to God I fully give.**

6. Beloved Alpha, I call forth the judgment of Christ upon all beings in the identity octave who are seeking to prove God wrong.

> Beloved Alpha, from your womb,
> I did descend to matter's tomb,
> but buried I will be no more,
> my inner vision you restore.
>
> **Beloved Alpha, in your light,**
> **I now see God with inner sight,**
> **as man I will no longer live,**
> **my life to God I fully give.**

7. Beloved Alpha, I call forth the judgment of Christ upon all beings in the identity octave who are willing to kill physical human beings, and thereby deprive them of the opportunity to be in physical embodiment, because of their abstract idea.

> Beloved Alpha, I now know,
> the love you did on me bestow,
> a co-creator, I will bring,
> the light to make all matter sing.
>
> **Beloved Alpha, in your light,**
> **I now see God with inner sight,**
> **as man I will no longer live,**
> **my life to God I fully give.**

8. Beloved Alpha, help all people rise above the consciousness of dividing humankind based on the us-versus-them mentality. Help all people rise above the dualistic extreme and find the balance of the Christ consciousness that knows all life is One.

Beloved Alpha, on this earth,
a new age we are giving birth,
for we are here to bring the love,
that you are sending from Above.

**Beloved Alpha, in your light,
I now see God with inner sight,
as man I will no longer live,
my life to God I fully give.**

9. Beloved Alpha, help all people rise to the balanced awareness that the ends of furthering an idea can never justify the means of killing physical people. Help people see that it is never justified to kill physical people because of an abstract idea.

Beloved Alpha, you and me,
we form a true polarity,
as up Above, so here below,
with life's own river I do flow.

**Beloved Alpha, in your light,
I now see God with inner sight,
as man I will no longer live,
my life to God I fully give.**

Sealing

In the name of the I AM THAT I AM, I accept that Archangel Michael, Astrea and Shiva form an impenetrable shield around myself and all constructive people, sealing us from all fear-based energies in all four octaves. I accept that the Light of God is consuming and transforming all fear-based energies that make up the forces behind war!

7 | FEAR AS A CAUSE OF WAR

I am the Ascended Master Mother Mary! I come to discourse with you on one of the causes of war that I desire people in embodiment to be aware of and to make calls on. Before I go into it, I would like to briefly summarize what I have talked about in my previous discourses.

The masters want to raise up all lifestreams

I know that when you are in embodiment, it is almost impossible that you are not affected by the dualistic consciousness. This consciousness hangs as a heavy cloud, as an almost impenetrable veil, as a fog around this planet. It affects the minds of almost all people who are in physical embodiment, blinding them to the deeper reality of oneness.

This dualistic consciousness may cause you to look upon my previous discourse and wonder if it is really true that we of the ascended masters want to raise up all lifestreams. Is it really true that we want to raise up even the demons and the fallen beings in the lowest levels of hell, of the astral plane? Is it really true that we want to raise up lifestreams such as Hitler, Stalin or Mao, who perpetrated mass killings of other people or even their own people? Are we really seeking to save or raise up every lifestream?

The answer is: "Yes!" We are not in the duality consciousness so we see the oneness of all life. We see how all life is interconnected and how each lifestream is part of the Body of God for a given planet and even for the universe as a whole. We see that there is a loss to the whole when a lifestream goes through the second death. The potential for that lifestream reaching its ascension will not be fulfilled.

We also see that even the lifestreams that most people would consider beyond help, or might even consider evil, are only deceived and blinded by the duality consciousness. Of course, we also see that those people who judge others as being evil are, likewise, blinded by the duality consciousness, and we are not trapped by that judgment. So yes, we will do everything we can to raise up any lifestream.

The struggle is inside your mind

In some cases a lifestream has gone into a self-reinforcing, downward spiral. When you are in such a spiral, you are struggling against something. You are perceiving that this something – against which you *think* you have to struggle – is outside yourself. We see the reality that the struggle is inside your own mind. What you are really struggling against is not a reality outside yourself but a *perception* of reality. This requires a delicate understanding.

When two nations go to war, there is a struggle between them. You cannot simply say that they have no enemy, they have only made up the enemy in their minds. There is, of course, an outer enemy that is attacking them or resisting them, but this is because both sides are caught in the duality consciousness. Yes, there is an outer enemy, but what they are fighting is not really the outer enemy. Both sides are fighting the mental images, the perception, of the other group of people. This perception is entirely dualistic, and it covers over the fact that both sides are part of the one Body of God. This is how it needs to be understood: You are fighting a *perception*.

When you begin to understand this, you realize that your only real way to stop war is to free people from the dualistic perception. If a lifestream has gone into a downward, self-reinforcing spiral, that lifestream is unreachable for a spiritual teacher. We cannot simply appear to such a lifestream and give that lifestream a spiritual teaching that will suddenly convert it and help it see the errors of its ways, so to speak.

The turning point in a downward spiral

When you have gone into a self-reinforcing, downward spiral, the spiral has to reach some kind of extreme point where you have had enough of the struggle and the fighting. You open your mind to the possibility that there is an alternative. Then, you can begin to see that the alternative is that, instead of struggling against outer enemies, you begin to look at yourself, your own mind, your own perception. You begin to look at the beam in your own eye, instead of the splinter in the eyes of your brother. You begin to realize that, if your life is to change, *you* have to change. Your mind has to change.

The question is: "How far down in consciousness does the lifestream have to go before it reaches this turning point?" We do in some cases allow forces to outplay themselves because it is necessary for all of the lifestreams involved to have that extreme experience. As soon as people have reached the turning point and are now open to any kind of higher teaching, then we of the ascended masters are there with a teaching that can appeal to them at their current level of consciousness. This does not mean that we can give all lifestreams a higher spiritual teaching. We cannot start talking about non-duality to a lifestream that has gone very far into a downward spiral and has just turned around. Such a lifestream is not ready to even contemplate the ideas I am giving you in this book, but it is ready to contemplate *something*.

Raw fear as a cause of war

Based on this, I will now go into the cause of war that I wish to discuss in this discourse, and that cause revolves around what we might call "raw fear." The first fear I would like to talk about here is the fear that you will physically be attacked by others. This is a feeling, but it is very tied to a potential or even a real physical threat.

You live on a planet where war is a common occurrence. There have been many situations in history where one group of people have been faced with an enemy who had built a physical army and who were threatening them. In many cases, there has been a real physical threat that has given rise to this fear. It has sometimes become so intense and taken over people's minds to the point that they have attacked first because they were so sure that their enemy would attack them.

There are also examples where one side has been afraid of the other side and has built up their army to avoid an attack from that side. The second side has then used this as an excuse for building up their own army because they feared that the first side would attack them. You have seen situations where two groups of people have actually gone to war based entirely on their perception that they would be attacked by the others. Once you have entered a spiral of fear, you are simply looking for something outside of yourself that can validate the fear.

My beloved, did you take note of what I just said? If you go into these situations I have described, where two groups of people have feared an attack from the other, you will see that, in all cases, they would say that their fear was based on the reality of the outer threat, the actions of the other people. They would say that the physical situation came first, and the fear came second.

It may seem like this in the actual situation, but when you know about reincarnation, when you understand that life has been happening on this planet for a very long time, then you see that it is never so that the physical conditions come before what is happening in the three higher octaves. Fear never actually springs from the physical condition. Fear happens at a higher level of manifestation than material conditions.

Spiritual energies come before material conditions

The stream of energy that upholds the entire material universe comes from the spiritual realm, flows first into the identity, then into the mental, then into the emotional and then into the physical. When the energy flows into the identity level, it is given a certain matrix, a certain form. It then flows into the mental, but the mental cannot override the matrix set at the higher level of the identity body. Likewise with the emotional and the physical. Even though there may be an actual physical enemy that seems to be threatening you, your fear came before the enemy, or the enemy would not have arisen. Or perhaps you would not have seen the other group of people as an enemy. In all of the situations I am talking about, a group of people had, over several lifetimes, built up fear in their emotional bodies. It was this fear that actually precipitated the outer enemy. Of course, once people are trapped in fear, they cannot see this. They would deny it if one explained it to them.

You can go to the Middle East today, and you can see that there is great fear between Jews and Arabs. Each would say that it is the other group that has caused the fear. Each group would deny that the fear, their own fear, came before the other group. They would say: "But the other people have always been there." No, they have not always been there. They have only been there as long as you can remember, and you do not remember a time when you were not trapped in fear.

Forgetting who you are in duality

Once you become blinded by the duality consciousness, you no longer remember how it was when you were not blinded by duality. This is one of the reasons it is so difficult to extricate yourself from duality once you have stepped into it. It is the veil, the energy veil, evil itself, that blinds you. The lowest kind of fear that precipitates war is the fear of being attacked by a physical enemy. Of course, this very physical fear has an emotional parallel. It is what in individuals is called paranoia where you see people who fear an outer enemy that is not there.

You will see in psychological institutions around the world that there are people who are so trapped in this paranoia that they cannot function normally. They are so afraid of something that they cannot carry on their normal lives. Some people are afraid of the sky falling. Some people are afraid that somebody will steal what they have or that somebody wants to kill them. Again, such a fear (over lifetimes) can precipitate the outer condition.

Why is it so that you need to precipitate a physical condition as a result of what you have allowed to build up in your three higher bodies? You are a spiritual being. One of your tasks in the physical octave is to realize and acknowledge that you are spiritual being who cannot be trapped in or even permanently altered by what you experience in the material world.

You came from a higher world. Your I AM Presence is beyond the material realm with its four octaves and cannot be affected by what happens to you in the material world. We have explained that the Conscious You is a spiritual being and cannot be altered by what you experience or do in the material realm. Your task is to be here and be a co-creator and acknowledge that you are a co-creator and not let anything change you.

When you go into duality, you forget this. You forget who you are. You forget you are a spiritual being. Then you go into the state of paranoia of fearing some condition. The question now is how you can be free from the fear? The answer is that you can be free from the fear only by experiencing the condition you fear. Then, you realize that the condition was not as serious as what you feared.

Becoming free from fear

When I said that you can be free only by experiencing the condition, it is, of course, possible that you can become free by realizing that your fear was an illusion, was a product of your perception. This does not happen to the vast majority of lifestreams until they have experienced the physical conditions that they fear. Once they have experienced such a physical condition a sufficient number of times, then they realize that it was not as bad as what they feared.

They begin to see that reality is never as bad as their own inner feeling and expectation. Then, they can take the next step and begin to realize that this must be because what happens in the psyche is more important to their life experience than what happens at the physical level. They can begin to realize that they are actually psychological beings.

If they are psychological beings, that means they are not physical beings. Why then do they have this extreme fear of physical conditions, if these physical conditions cannot really touch them? Then, they can gradually begin climbing to the point where they can take responsibility for themselves and get out of the paranoia at the emotional level.

World history has seen examples of especially some dictators who have had such extreme paranoia that they have taken their nations to war entirely because they feared the attack of some enemy. They have also in some cases started campaigns to eradicate other groups of people out of paranoia, a completely irrational fear. I am sure you can mention examples by yourself.

The outcome of raw fear at the mental level

When we go up to the mental level, we see that the extreme outcome of raw fear is the desire for revenge, the desire to punish other people. This is where you have an idea, and it can often be a very sophisticated idea. It can be based on a political ideology or even a religious teaching. Even the teachings of Christianity have been perverted to justify revenge and punishment. Even though Jesus told you to turn the other check, to not resist evil and to forgive seventy times seven, there are people who have managed to take his teachings and pervert them to the point where they felt that their version of Christianity justified them seeking revenge and seeking to punish other people or even groups of people.

The idea that someone deserves to be punished is always based on some epic concept of a battle that is going on. There is an ideal condition that *should* be manifest on earth, and it is not manifest. The reason it is not manifest is that there are these other people who are opposing this ideal condition. It is justifiable that these people are punished for opposing what you see as the ideal condition. This may be from the very personal level where you feel that you have been wronged by one other individual. You seek revenge against that person or you seek to punish that person. It may also be taken to a larger scale. For example, there are people who believe that all of those who do not belong to their religion will go to hell and suffer for all eternity. There are other people who have believed that these other groups of people who have done something wrong, deserve to be punished.

The irony is that you have even seen religious people who believe that they have been wronged by another group of people. They have desired revenge against this other group of people, but they have had a religious teaching which told them: "Thou shalt not kill." They have used other aspects of that religious teaching to reason, to build the perception, that these people had wronged God and God's plan for the world. Therefore, they deserve to be punished. Surely, God would punish them in hell, but while they were still here on earth, someone needed to help God punish these people. The people then felt that God had justified what was simply their own desire for revenge against others.

Having enough of the struggle

The human ego truly does not like to have its perception of life challenged or disturbed. It does not like to have its plans for control shattered. When people have gone into the downward self-reinforcing spiral, this spiral needs to come to some extreme where they have had enough of the struggle. What makes the spiral come to an extreme? It is that two groups of people struggle against each other. They see each other as enemies.

How do we of the ascended masters see two groups of people who are struggling against each other? We see them as substitute teachers for each other. We would like to give each group a higher spiritual teaching, but we cannot because they are blinded to us. We therefore desire them to, as quickly as possible, get to the bottom of their self-reinforcing spiral so they can be turned around.

We, of course, cannot do this because we do not struggle against them and we do not give them false teachings. We allow them to struggle against each other. Thereby, they become substitute teachers for each other. Your enemy is really doing you a favor. Why, then, do you seek revenge? Why do you seek to punish your enemy?

Why do you not seek to use your enemy as a motivation for looking at yourself so you can transcend the consciousness that precipitated the enemy? If you do not transcend that consciousness, you will just attract another enemy in this or in a coming lifetime. I realize that people blinded by duality do not grasp this line of reasoning, but *you* do. Therefore, you can make the calls for the consuming of the entities, the demons and the fallen beings who are precipitating these spirals.

The outcome of raw fear at the identity level

When you go to the identity level, what do you see as the outcome of fear? You actually see that there are people who are so consumed by hatred against other people that they are ready to kill them as soon as they get the opportunity to do so. Hatred is one aspect of fear-based emotions.

There is a form of hatred that is, of course, entirely emotional. It has no reason. It has no justification. It just hates. There are demons and entities that are created out of the hatred that has been expressed on this planet for a very long time. You cannot reason with these beings. They have no reasoning ability. They simply hate human beings. Some of them even hate life. They hate anything that changes, anything that grows in a positive direction, and they are programmed to destroy it.

There are also human beings who have become so blinded by the beings in the higher octaves, even by those in the identity realm, that they are almost completely driven by hatred. Their entire attention is geared towards hating another group of people or, perhaps, only one individual. Their minds are completely focused on how wrong the other person is or the other group is. They might even be completely focused on how they can destroy this enemy that is doing such terrible things.

This can happen at the personal level where people are in a so-called love relationship. It ends and one or both partners go into the state of hating the other partner, camouflaging it, perhaps, even with some seemingly benign motivation of having to expose what the ex-partner is doing as being so wrong in an epic way. It may also be on a larger scale where you define that this other race, such as the Jews, are threatening your country or even civilization. Therefore, they deserve to be exterminated. You may go and look at these examples of mass killings found throughout history and you will discover that even though there may have been reasons for this, there was also an element of pure hatred.

Hate as a driving force behind war

What do people really hate? Do they hate the other group of people? Nay, my beloved, they hate something in themselves, in their own psychology. Because they are not willing to look at their own psychology, they are entirely focusing their attention outside themselves. In order to keep their attention focused outside themselves, so that it does not accidentally stray into looking at themselves, they project that these other people have done something so terrible that they must be exterminated or punished. All of their attention is directed towards destroying the other group of people so that there is no attention left over for looking at themselves and asking some critical questions.

You will see how this was the case for the Germans during World War II. Those who were trapped in the perception filter created by the Nazi war machine were so blinded that they did not ask critical questions, such as: "Why do we need to kill the Jews? What good will it do? How will it positively affect Germany?" They were convinced they did not need to ask such questions, let alone ask questions as to whether or not it was right according to their professed religion.

People can be blinded by this hatred and do things that are atrocious without reflecting upon it. When suddenly the bubble bursts, then people have an opportunity to ask the questions. Some do; some do not. Germany as a nation has been willing to at least look at its past and ask some critical questions.

7 | Fear as a Cause of War

The need for nations to question their past

Stalin's Russia was also driven by hatred. When you look at Stalin himself, you see a person who had extreme paranoia and who would suspect anyone and was willing to kill anyone based on suspicion alone. Behind that, you also saw a hatred of human beings. What you see today is that Russia as a nation has not been willing to ask questions about its past. Russia has not even started seriously transcending the consciousness of the Stalinist era and the Soviet era. You see the same in China where Chairman Mao, the "Great Chairman Mao" as they still call him, was also driven by a hatred against human beings. This caused him to kill even more people than Hitler and Stalin combined. China has not even begun to question this reign of terror, as it truly was.

You see the need to make calls for nations to be willing to question their past, for it is the only way they can begin to transcend the past and the state of consciousness that precipitated the events of the past. It will surely precipitate even worse events in the future, if it is not transcended.

When you look at people, such as Hitler, Stalin, Mao and others, can you not see that, even though they may have had outer so-called rational reasons for doing what they did, there was an element of irrationality there? There cannot be a truly rational reason for killing your own people. If you are a dictator who has attained absolute power in your country and you have a desire to extend that power to the rest of the world, you need people to fight for you. Therefore, it is not ultimately rational to kill the people who could potentially fight for you.

What drives these dictators to do this? It is that their minds are entirely taken over by demons, by entities and by fallen beings in the emotional, mental, and identity realms. You may think that what I am telling you here contradicts everything you have been taught as you were growing up. You may think that what I am saying is irrational, unrealistic and cannot explain anything about the world and how it really works. You may think that there are physical, material causes behind war and that I should be addressing these. My beloved, take an honest look at Hitler, Stalin, Mao and other dictators. Then, ask yourself: "What material reason could there be for killing millions of your own people? What material explanation is there for killing on such a scale?"

You have two options here, my beloved. Either you agree with the reasoning of Hitler that the Jews were a threat to Germany and, therefore, should be exterminated in order to further the interests of Germany. Or you take the other option of agreeing with me that there is no rational reason for killing the Jews or so many Soviet citizens or Chinese citizens. If there is no rational reason, there can be no material reason. There was no gain here.

What did these three dictators gain from killing so many millions of people? They thought they gained something, but what did they gain physically? It only took up resources that could have been used for their expansive quest. When you begin to acknowledge that there cannot be a physical, material reason, there cannot be a rational reason, then you must seek other explanations. You must take the approach expressed by the author of the Sherlock Holmes mysteries: When you have excluded the impossible, whatever remains must be the truth, no matter how improbable it seems to you.

It is impossible to find a rational or material explanation for killing on such a scale. What remains is my explanation of non-material causes, non-material beings in the three higher realms. It may seem improbable to you, but if you apply the principle given by science, you might shift your perspective.

7 | Fear as a Cause of War

The principle of science is that, even if an explanation seems improbable, one should consider whether it can explain something that other explanations cannot explain. If you cannot find a material, rational explanation for mass killing, then you should consider what my explanation can add to the mixture. I will, of course, give more teachings in coming discourses, but in this discourse, I want you to consider that mass killing of millions of people must carry with it an element of hatred against human beings, hatred against life itself.

The explanation behind extreme hatred

Where does such hatred come from? Which lifestream, which kind of mind, which kind of consciousness, can have such extreme hatred against life and, specifically against human beings? You may think that Hitler had a rationale. You may think he aimed at creating an ideal society and that he thought extermination of the Jews was one part of this plan. You *can* say he did have a rationale, but the rationale was not rational. You do not gain power by killing. You gain power by keeping people alive and bending them to your will, either by force but even better by deception.

When you go into large-scale killing, you have lost rationality. This can happen only when your mind has been taken over by beings beyond the material realm. You may ask yourself whether these non-material beings have a rationale, and they would say that they do. Some of them believe that it is their task to prove the fallacy of God's design of the universe and especially giving human beings free will. Some of them have gone so far into their downward spiral that this rationale has almost faded away. It is there only in the background, and what really drives them now is just pure hatred.

It can be almost impossible to look at human beings in embodiment and understand pure hatred, but you can find examples, namely the dictators I mentioned, but also individual beings that have been labeled as psychopaths or even mass murderers. As I have explained, everything has a cause in consciousness. You are a conscious being. You can come to a point where you have become so trapped in duality that you have almost lost the ability to reason. There is no reasoning ability left in your mind because it has been taken over by pure hatred. You are not even thinking about why you are killing. You are killing if you have the opportunity to do so. You cannot go into the mind of a being like Hitler or Stalin and find a logical rationale for why they were so obsessed with killing so many people.

How hateful beings are removed from embodiment

In a normal human being, there would come a point where they could no longer do what they were doing, whatever it is they are doing. You will see that even soldiers in war or in concentration camps could come to a breakdown where they could not function any more. They could not even follow orders. Not all experienced this, but some certainly did. There should have come a point where Hitler, Stalin or Mao broke down and could no longer continue doing what they were doing. You could argue that Hitler reached this point, whereas Stalin and Mao never did.

The larger point I am seeking to give you here is that people can be swallowed up by hatred to the point where you cannot reason with them. Why do we of the ascended masters allow such people to remain in physical embodiment? Does there not come a point where we can look at Stalin and see how many people he has killed and see that he is likely to continue to do this for as long as he lives? Does there not come a point where we can activate the Judgment of Christ and take such a being out of embodiment?

My beloved, the stark reality is that there does *not* come such a point—unless a critical mass of people in embodiment transcend the consciousness that precipitated a Hitler, a Stalin or a Mao. As I have said, once groups of people go into a self-reinforcing downward spiral, that spiral must in many cases be taken to some extreme before they begin to wake up. I have said that two groups of people fighting against each other can become substitute teachers. Hitler, Stalin and Mao were substitute teachers for certain groups among humankind.

What is to prevent another dictator equally bad or worse from arising tomorrow? Nothing at all, unless a critical mass of people do two things: They must awaken themselves from the consciousness and transcend that consciousness. They must make the calls for that consciousness to be removed from the earth and for those beings in the physical, emotional, mental and identify realms who embody the consciousness to also be removed from the earth. Until there is an act of conscious free will that says: "Enough is enough," then the law will not allow us to remove such lifestreams. I know this may be a very brutal teaching, but when you look at the brutality of war as it has been happening for thousands of years on this planet, can any teaching given by words be said to be too brutal?

Being aware of but not dwelling on war

My beloved, I have once again given you a big mouthful. You are probably beginning to realize that this book is not a pleasant experience. When you begin to give the calls and invocations we are giving you, I think you will be able to rise above the more unpleasant aspects of reading this book. When you build enough of a momentum, you will not only free yourself from the weight of these matters. You will also begin to give an invaluable service to freeing the planet from the weight of the consciousness behind war.

I am not here encouraging you to dwell on the brutality of war, but I am desiring you to acknowledge that all is not good on this planet. The brutality, the atrocities, that have been precipitated by human beings against other human beings as a result of war are almost unfathomable. Even as an ascended being, I do not often put my attention on the atrocities that have taken place on earth and that are still taking place every day in many parts of the world. I focus on my task of helping people raise their consciousness.

Nevertheless, I am aware of what is happening and has been happening and I wish you to be aware as well. I am not asking you to dwell upon it, but I *am* asking you to realize that there is an incredible hatred behind war. It is time that someone challenges this consciousness and the beings who embody it. If it is not challenged, then what is to stop it from continuing to take over the minds of individuals who will commit the kind of atrocities that you can see in pictures and videos on the Internet of people being beheaded on camera and other atrocities that would have been unthinkable a few decades ago?

Demand an end to the consciousness of war

Can you not see that there is hatred that is being intensified? This is because, as I have explained, at the end of a cycle, things must be allowed to become more extreme so that people can finally see them. I am not asking you to see the brutality of war in the sense that you become overwhelmed or burdened by it. I am asking you to see the brutality of war in the sense that you become determined that you for one will take a stand and demand an end to this consciousness and its manifestations on earth.

I have made that decision, my beloved. I have made it a long time ago. That is one reason I am today and ascended being and that I am still working with earth, instead of moving on to other planets that are at a far higher level of evolution than earth. I could easily have moved on to planets where war is no longer possible. I have chosen not to do this out of love for you and other people who are still stuck on earth. I have a love for this planet itself and the beauty of the matrix that created it in its original form.

Making a positive difference to clean up the planet

I hold that immaculate concept as a result of my spiritual office of the Divine Mother for earth. I hold the immaculate concept for all people on earth that they will transcend the duality consciousness and come up higher. I hold the immaculate concept for *you* that you will awaken and gather the determination to fulfill what you yourself chose that you wanted to fulfill before you took embodiment this time. I am not here asking you to accept something that you are not ready to accept. I am asking you to remember what you already knew and accepted before you came into embodiment. I am asking you to remember the vision you had and the decisions you made on how you wanted to come into embodiment on this planet, in this lifetime, at this particular time in order to make a positive difference.

You make a positive difference by determining that a certain state of consciousness is no longer acceptable to you. Then you make the calls that authorize the ascended masters and the archangels and the angles to step in and consume the energies and remove the beings who, after being confronted with the judgment, will not choose the light. That is how we clean up a planet. This is the only *rational* way to clear up a planet. I know it seems *irrational* to most people in the modern, scientific world, but what can I say, my beloved?

Rationality is reality to the consciousness of the being who is reasoning. I am asking you to raise your consciousness, your vision, so that you can grasp the higher rationality that allows you to play the part that you wanted to play before you took embodiment.

A pure vision for the earth

I see such a grand and beautiful vision for this planet. I see the earth being purified of the dark clouds of war and of the beings who are dark, who are driven by hatred, who are sniveling in their hatred against human beings, in their desire to destroy this planet completely. I see them being bound by the angels and taken to other realms where they actively receive an opportunity to experience an even more intense struggle and, therefore, come closer to their potential awakening. I see those demons and entities who never had self-awareness being bound and consumed by the angels and archangels. I see billions of angels standing ready in the emotional, mental, and identity realms, simply waiting for your call, for your command, for your authorization to step in and purify this earth.

You *below* cannot purify the earth. We *above* cannot purify the earth. What *can* purify the earth is that you here below become all that you already are above so that the earth can be here below as it is above. To this end, I give service. Will you serve also? Mother Mary I AM! What do you think when you say: "I AM"? How do you define yourself? Based on your upbringing, or based on the reality of who you already are above?

8 | SHATTERING THE ILLUSION OF FEAR

In the name of the I AM THAT I AM, Jesus Christ, I call upon Mother Mary, Archangel Michael and Shiva to shatter the fear-based illusions that have caused so many wars on this planet. Awaken people to the reality that we are spiritual beings and that we can co-create a new future by working with the ascended masters. I especially call for …

[Make your own calls here.]

Part 1

1. Archangel Michael, manifest your Presence in the Astral plane and consume the demons that control people through the fear of physically being attacked by others.

Archangel Michael, light so blue,
my heart has room for only you.
My mind is one, no longer two,
your love for me is ever true.

Archangel Michael, you are here,
your light consumes all doubt and fear.
Your Presence is forever near,
you are to me so very dear.

2. Archangel Michael, manifest your Presence in the Astral plane and consume the demons that seek to get one group of people to attack another because they fear being attacked.

Archangel Michael, I will be,
all one with your reality.
No fear can hold me as I see,
this world no power has o'er me.

Archangel Michael, you are here,
your light consumes all doubt and fear.
Your Presence is forever near,
you are to me so very dear.

3. Archangel Michael, manifest your Presence in the Astral plane and consume the demons that cause two groups of people to both build up their armies out of the fear of being attacked by the other.

Archangel Michael, hold me tight,
shatter now the darkest night.
Clear my chakras with your light,
restore to me my inner sight.

> Archangel Michael, you are here,
> your light consumes all doubt and fear.
> Your Presence is forever near,
> you are to me so very dear.

4. Archangel Michael, manifest your Presence in the Astral plane and consume the demons that seek to get one group of people to go to war based on their perception that they would be attacked by others.

> Archangel Michael, now I stand,
> with you the light I do command.
> My heart I ever will expand,
> till highest truth I understand.

> Archangel Michael, you are here,
> your light consumes all doubt and fear.
> Your Presence is forever near,
> you are to me so very dear.

5. Archangel Michael, manifest your Presence in the Astral plane and consume the demons that seek to use dictators to start war or genocide out of the extreme paranoia of fearing another group of people.

> Archangel Michael, in my heart,
> from me you never will depart.
> Of hierarchy I am a part,
> I now accept a fresh new start.

> **Archangel Michael, you are here,**
> **your light consumes all doubt and fear.**
> **Your Presence is forever near,**
> **you are to me so very dear.**

6. Archangel Michael, cut people free so they can see that once you have entered a spiral of fear, you are looking for something outside of yourself that can validate the fear. Your perception actually manifests or magnetizes the external threat.

> Archangel Michael, sword of blue,
> all darkness you are cutting through.
> My Christhood I do now pursue,
> discernment shows me what is true.

> **Archangel Michael, you are here,**
> **your light consumes all doubt and fear.**
> **Your Presence is forever near,**
> **you are to me so very dear.**

7. Archangel Michael, cut people free to see that physical conditions never come before what is happening in the three higher octaves. Fear never springs from a physical condition but exists in the mind.

> Archangel Michael, in your wings,
> I now let go of lesser things.
> God's homing call in my heart rings,
> my heart with yours forever sings.

> **Archangel Michael, you are here,**
> **your light consumes all doubt and fear.**
> **Your Presence is forever near,**
> **you are to me so very dear.**

8. Archangel Michael, cut people free to see that when we are trapped in a downward spiral of fear, we can be free only by experiencing what we fear. Only by experiencing that a physical condition cannot change us, can we escape the paranoia of fearing what is not real.

> Archangel Michael, take me home,
> in higher spheres I want to roam.
> I am reborn from cosmic foam,
> my life is now a sacred poem.

> **Archangel Michael, you are here,**
> **your light consumes all doubt and fear.**
> **Your Presence is forever near,**
> **you are to me so very dear.**

9. Archangel Michael, cut people free so they can see that their fear is an illusion, a product of their perception. Help them see that they are psychological beings and that their life experience depends more on what happens inside their minds than on physical conditions.

> Archangel Michael, light you are,
> shining like the bluest star.
> You are a cosmic avatar,
> with you I will go very far.

Archangel Michael, you are here,
your light consumes all doubt and fear.
Your Presence is forever near,
you are to me so very dear.

Part 2

1. Beloved Shiva, manifest your Presence in the mental realm and consume the demons and fallen beings who seek to control people through the desire for revenge, the desire to punish other people.

O Shiva, God of Sacred Fire,
It's time to let the past expire,
I want to rise above the old,
a golden future to unfold.

O Shiva, clear the energy,
O Shiva, bring the synergy,
O Shiva, make all demons flee,
O Shiva, bring back peace to me.

2. Beloved Shiva, manifest your Presence in the mental realm and consume the demons and fallen beings who seek to use a political ideology or religious teaching to justify revenge and punishment.

O Shiva, come and set me free,
from forces that do limit me,
with fire consume all that is less,
paving way for my success.

**O Shiva, clear the energy,
O Shiva, bring the synergy,
O Shiva, make all demons flee,
O Shiva, bring back peace to me.**

3. Beloved Shiva, manifest your Presence in the mental realm and consume the demons and fallen beings who seek to get people to go to war based on the concept of an epic battle between good and evil. Consume the forces that use this epic mindset to override the command not to kill.

O Shiva, Maya's veil disperse,
clear my private universe,
dispel the consciousness of death,
consume it with your Sacred Breath.

**O Shiva, clear the energy,
O Shiva, bring the synergy,
O Shiva, make all demons flee,
O Shiva, bring back peace to me.**

4. Beloved Shiva, manifest your Presence in the mental realm and consume the demons and fallen beings who use the epic mindset to make a group of people believe their own desire for revenge is justified by God and that God wants them to punish another group of people.

O Shiva, I hereby let go,
of all attachments here below,
addictive entities consume,
the upward path I do resume.

O Shiva, clear the energy,
O Shiva, bring the synergy,
O Shiva, make all demons flee,
O Shiva, bring back peace to me.

5. Beloved Shiva, cut people free to see that an outer enemy is a manifestation of their own state of consciousness, meaning the enemy is a substitute teacher. They only need this teacher because they have not been willing to listen to the ascended masters.

O Shiva, I recite your name,
come banish fear and doubt and shame,
with fire expose within my mind,
what ego seeks to hide behind.

O Shiva, clear the energy,
O Shiva, bring the synergy,
O Shiva, make all demons flee,
O Shiva, bring back peace to me.

6. Beloved Shiva, cut people free so they can use any enemy as a motivation for looking at themselves and transcending the consciousness that precipitated the enemy. If they do not transcend that consciousness, they will attract another enemy.

O Shiva, I am not afraid,
my karmic debt hereby is paid,
the past no longer owns my choice,
in breath of Shiva I rejoice.

O Shiva, clear the energy,
O Shiva, bring the synergy,
O Shiva, make all demons flee,
O Shiva, bring back peace to me.

7. Beloved Shiva, manifest your Presence in the astral plane and consume the demons and fallen beings who seek to control people by using the raw emotions of hatred for another group of people.

O Shiva, show me spirit pairs,
that keep me trapped in their affairs,
I choose to see within my mind,
the spirits that you surely bind.

O Shiva, clear the energy,
O Shiva, bring the synergy,
O Shiva, make all demons flee,
O Shiva, bring back peace to me.

8. Beloved Shiva, manifest your Presence in the astral plane and consume the demons and entities created out of hatred, those that hate human beings, hate life, and are programmed to destroy anything positive.

O Shiva, naked I now stand,
my mind in freedom does expand,
as all my ghosts I do release,
surrender is the key to peace.

> O Shiva, clear the energy,
> O Shiva, bring the synergy,
> O Shiva, make all demons flee,
> O Shiva, bring back peace to me.

9. Beloved Shiva, cut free the people who are driven by hatred towards other people. Help them see that they truly hate something within themselves and that they will only be free by healing their own minds.

> O Shiva, all-consuming fire,
> with Parvati raise me higher,
> when I am raised your light to see,
> all men I will draw onto me.

> O Shiva, clear the energy,
> O Shiva, bring the synergy,
> O Shiva, make all demons flee,
> O Shiva, bring back peace to me.

Part 3

1. Archangel Michael, consume the demons and fallen beings in all four octaves who were behind the Nazi hatred against the Jews and anyone else who was different.

> Archangel Michael, light so blue,
> my heart has room for only you.
> My mind is one, no longer two,
> your love for me is ever true.

**Archangel Michael, you are here,
your light consumes all doubt and fear.
Your Presence is forever near,
you are to me so very dear.**

2. Archangel Michael, consume the demons and fallen beings in all four octaves who were behind the Paranoia of Stalin's Russia and the Soviet Union.

Archangel Michael, I will be,
all one with your reality.
No fear can hold me as I see,
this world no power has o'er me.

**Archangel Michael, you are here,
your light consumes all doubt and fear.
Your Presence is forever near,
you are to me so very dear.**

3. Archangel Michael, consume the demons and fallen beings in all four octaves who were behind the paranoia of Mao's China.

Archangel Michael, hold me tight,
shatter now the darkest night.
Clear my chakras with your light,
restore to me my inner sight.

**Archangel Michael, you are here,
your light consumes all doubt and fear.
Your Presence is forever near,
you are to me so very dear.**

4. Archangel Michael, consume the demons and fallen beings in all four octaves who are behind all paranoid dictatorships in the world today.

> Archangel Michael, now I stand,
> with you the light I do command.
> My heart I ever will expand,
> till highest truth I understand.

> **Archangel Michael, you are here,**
> **your light consumes all doubt and fear.**
> **Your Presence is forever near,**
> **you are to me so very dear.**

5. Archangel Michael, consume the demons and fallen beings in all four octaves who are preventing all nations, but especially Russia and China, from questioning their past.

> Archangel Michael, in my heart,
> from me you never will depart.
> Of hierarchy I am a part,
> I now accept a fresh new start.

> **Archangel Michael, you are here,**
> **your light consumes all doubt and fear.**
> **Your Presence is forever near,**
> **you are to me so very dear.**

6. Archangel Michael, consume the demons and fallen beings in all four octaves who take over the minds of dictators and induce in them an entirely irrational drive to kill all those who could potentially oppose them.

Archangel Michael, sword of blue,
all darkness you are cutting through.
My Christhood I do now pursue,
discernment shows me what is true.

**Archangel Michael, you are here,
your light consumes all doubt and fear.
Your Presence is forever near,
you are to me so very dear.**

7. Archangel Michael, consume the demons and fallen beings in all four octaves who controlled Hitler, Stalin, Mao and all tyrannical dictators, past, present and future.

Archangel Michael, in your wings,
I now let go of lesser things.
God's homing call in my heart rings,
my heart with yours forever sings.

**Archangel Michael, you are here,
your light consumes all doubt and fear.
Your Presence is forever near,
you are to me so very dear.**

8. Archangel Michael, consume the demons and fallen beings in all four octaves who seek to precipitate mass killings because they either want to steal people's light or prove God wrong.

Archangel Michael, take me home,
in higher spheres I want to roam.
I am reborn from cosmic foam,
my life is now a sacred poem.

**Archangel Michael, you are here,
your light consumes all doubt and fear.
Your Presence is forever near,
you are to me so very dear.**

9. Archangel Michael, cut people free to see that there is no material or rational reason for mass killings. The only logical explanation is the demons and fallen beings in the three higher octaves and the fallen beings in embodiment.

Archangel Michael, light you are,
shining like the bluest star.
You are a cosmic avatar,
with you I will go very far.

**Archangel Michael, you are here,
your light consumes all doubt and fear.
Your Presence is forever near,
you are to me so very dear.**

Part 4

1. Beloved Shiva, consume the demons and fallen beings in all four octaves who seek to precipitate the mass killing of millions of people out of their hatred against life itself.

O Shiva, God of Sacred Fire,
It's time to let the past expire,
I want to rise above the old,
a golden future to unfold.

**O Shiva, clear the energy,
O Shiva, bring the synergy,
O Shiva, make all demons flee,
O Shiva, bring back peace to me.**

2. Beloved Shiva, consume the demons and fallen beings in all four octaves who believe it is their task to prove the fallacy of God's design of the universe and especially giving human beings free will.

> O Shiva, come and set me free,
> from forces that do limit me,
> with fire consume all that is less,
> paving way for my success.

**O Shiva, clear the energy,
O Shiva, bring the synergy,
O Shiva, make all demons flee,
O Shiva, bring back peace to me.**

3. Beloved Shiva, I call forth the judgment of Christ upon the dictators, psychopaths or mass murderers who have lost all rationality and kill out of hatred or because they cannot stop. I demand that such people be removed from embodiment.

> O Shiva, Maya's veil disperse,
> clear my private universe,
> dispel the consciousness of death,
> consume it with your Sacred Breath.

**O Shiva, clear the energy,
O Shiva, bring the synergy,
O Shiva, make all demons flee,
O Shiva, bring back peace to me.**

4. Beloved Shiva, cut free the spiritual people to see that we need to transcend the state of consciousness that precipitated these dictators and mass murderers before they can be removed from embodiment.

> O Shiva, I hereby let go,
> of all attachments here below,
> addictive entities consume,
> the upward path I do resume.

**O Shiva, clear the energy,
O Shiva, bring the synergy,
O Shiva, make all demons flee,
O Shiva, bring back peace to me.**

5. Beloved Shiva, I hereby make the call for the consciousness of paranoia and extreme hatred that leads to mass killing to be removed from the earth. I call for those beings in the physical, emotional, mental and identify realms who embody this consciousness to also be removed from the earth.

> O Shiva, I recite your name,
> come banish fear and doubt and shame,
> with fire expose within my mind,
> what ego seeks to hide behind.

**O Shiva, clear the energy,
O Shiva, bring the synergy,
O Shiva, make all demons flee,
O Shiva, bring back peace to me.**

6. Beloved Shiva, I hereby make an act of conscious free will that says: Enough is enough. I demand that the Law of Free Will is activated and that the ascended masters remove such lifestreams and the consciousness they embody.

> O Shiva, I am not afraid,
> my karmic debt hereby is paid,
> the past no longer owns my choice,
> in breath of Shiva I rejoice.

**O Shiva, clear the energy,
O Shiva, bring the synergy,
O Shiva, make all demons flee,
O Shiva, bring back peace to me.**

7. Beloved Shiva, cut free the spiritual people so they can acknowledge the spiritual causes of war without dwelling upon the brutality of war. Help them see that if we do not challenge the consciousness of war, then nothing can stop war.

> O Shiva, show me spirit pairs,
> that keep me trapped in their affairs,
> I choose to see within my mind,
> the spirits that you surely bind.

O Shiva, clear the energy,
O Shiva, bring the synergy,
O Shiva, make all demons flee,
O Shiva, bring back peace to me.

8. Beloved Shiva, I for one hereby determine to take my stand and demand an end to the consciousness of paranoia and its manifestations on earth.

> O Shiva, naked I now stand,
> my mind in freedom does expand,
> as all my ghosts I do release,
> surrender is the key to peace.

O Shiva, clear the energy,
O Shiva, bring the synergy,
O Shiva, make all demons flee,
O Shiva, bring back peace to me.

9. Beloved Shiva, I hereby determine that the consciousness of paranoia and the mindset of hatred of other people is no longer acceptable to me. I hereby use my free will to give the ascended masters the authority to remove the consciousness of war, and all beings who embody it, from the four octaves of earth.

> O Shiva, all-consuming fire,
> with Parvati raise me higher,
> when I am raised your light to see,
> all men I will draw onto me.

O Shiva, clear the energy,
O Shiva, bring the synergy,
O Shiva, make all demons flee,
O Shiva, bring back peace to me.

Sealing

In the name of the I AM THAT I AM, I accept that Archangel Michael, Astrea and Shiva form an impenetrable shield around myself and all constructive people, sealing us from all fear-based energies in all four octaves. I accept that the Light of God is consuming and transforming all fear-based energies that make up the forces behind war!

9 | THE WARRIOR MENTALITY

I am the Ascended Master Mother Mary! I come to discourse with you on another aspect of the hidden causes of war. This one may not be so hidden for those who have paid attention to world history and world events.

The mindset of gaining honor from war

You will know that for a very long time, going back into the mists of history, there has been a culture, a mindset, that has seen war as desirable, as something from which you could gain honor. You can see in many different parts of the world a warrior culture, the Samurai in Japan being but one example. Many other such cultures have existed and are still existing today. There are many people who have seen it as desirable for young men to go to war in order to prove their valor. Some have sought to gain self-worth by going to war and proving your ability to kill other human beings.

How do you gain self-worth from killing other human beings, from being good at killing? You cannot do so when you see yourself as connected to those other human beings, can you, my beloved? You can only see this as desirable when you are trapped in the consciousness of separation and duality. That is when you go into the "us-versus-them" mentality that has played such a dominant part of the mindset you have found on this planet for a very long time.

"Us" versus "them." Consider this mentality, my beloved. This is the essence of duality. Not only do we have a division between "us" and "them," but we also have the value judgment that "us" is better than "them," that we are locked in a struggle against "them" and that we have to prove our superiority by physically defeating "them" in battle or in a war.

Consider how this idea of gaining honor, self-worth or status in your society through war has played a part in the thinking of human beings in different cultures and in different time periods. Where did this warrior culture come from? It did not come from what I would like to call "human beings." I know I have said that all human beings are spiritual beings, but when I talk about human beings, I talk about those who have been created specifically for the earth.

The beginning of the warrior culture

Each planet that has ever been created in the material universe has had a certain group of lifestreams that were the original inhabitants of that planet. They were meant to grow in self-awareness by co-creating their planet, taking it to the point where it could ascend with the rest of the universe when the universe was ready to ascend. Because of free will, there is always the possibility that the inhabitants of a given planet can

9 | The Warrior Mentality

take that planet into a downward spiral instead of the upward, ascending spiral intended.

This is not necessarily wrong or a big sin because it can also become an experience. When people have had enough of going into the downward spiral, they can come back to creating an upward spiral with a different experience. They can do this with an inner knowing that duality truly does not work.

It can be very difficult for a spiritual teacher to explain to lifestreams who have not experienced it, why duality does not work. Innocent lifestreams tend to look at going into duality as just another experience. In a sense, it *is* just another experience. Only, it is not *just* another experience because it so easily becomes a self-reinforcing spiral from which it is very difficult to extricate yourself.

The point I am working towards is that the original inhabitants of the earth did not invent the warrior culture. The warrior culture was invented by the fallen beings. This happened in the fourth sphere [See *Cosmology of Evil*] when that sphere was near the ascension point, and a certain group of fallen beings refused to ascend with the rest of that sphere. They came up with the idea of wanting to prove God wrong, and from this followed the desire to cause other lifestreams to misuse their free will. The simplest way to get people to misuse their free will was to deceive them with the duality consciousness and create the "us-versus-them" mentality. This led to the idea that there had to be a physical struggle to the death between "us" and "them."

The warrior culture and the great struggle

This is the essence of the warrior culture. A warrior spends his entire life – all of his attention, all of his time, all of his physical strength – developing the ability to kill other people in battle, using whatever weapons and methods are there at his time and in his society. The warrior is always adapting to the development of new weapons, always seeking to have the latest, the most lethal and the most effective when it comes to killing other people. The warrior sees this as part of some great struggle. Throughout history, many different philosophies have been used to justify this struggle, but the idea is always that it is *justifiable* for "us" to kill "them."

There may even be ideas that make it seem *desirable* for "us" to kill "them." This warrior culture, this war mentality, has sometimes been justified with the idea that there is some grand struggle between two opposing polarities, such as God and the devil. We are on God's side; those other people over there are on the devil's side. Therefore, it is justifiable and necessary for us kill them. But you have also seen the Omega polarity of this, which is that there is no reason to justify the struggle by some epic mindset. The warrior mentality says that just the fact that we *can* defeat the enemy gives us the right to do so. We are warriors. We go to war. We fight the enemy. We defeat the enemy. Thereby, we gain honor, self-esteem, self-respect.

When you are connected to the reality that all life is one, when you see yourself as connected to a reality outside yourself, then you see yourself as a co-creative being. You know you are co-creating along with this greater reality. When you see yourself as a connected being, you gain honor, self-respect, by co-creating something.

Do you see the essential difference, my beloved? A connected being is directing all of its attention towards co-creating something new, something higher, something that benefits the All. A warrior is directing all of his attention towards destroying other human beings. Do you see that a connected being cannot come up with a warrior mentality? Only those who have gone into separation can do so.

Getting people to accept the warrior mentality

The warrior mentality has its origin with the fallen beings. Not all of the fallen beings were in the warrior mentality. The fallen beings in the identity octave are not trapped in the warrior mentality. They only use the warrior mentality to get human beings in embodiment to fight each other. They do not care about the warrior. They know there is no honor in killing other people. They just see it as a means to an end because, to the fallen beings in the identity octave, there is no concern about what is real, what is unreal, what is true, what is false, what is right, what is wrong. There is only one concern: How can we get human beings in embodiment to fight and destroy each other? What will appeal to them?

The fallen beings discovered very early that the warrior mentality will appeal to those who have gone sufficiently far into the duality consciousness. Once you have created the warrior mentality, you can get people to direct their attention and their physical efforts towards being good at fighting.

Just look at almost any culture in the world and see how this ability to fight, this proficiency in fighting, has been and still is an important part of the culture. Not so long ago it was considered normal in some parts of the world that a man carried a sword and that he was able to use it. The slightest insult could release a duel to the death where people were ready to kill each other over their perceived honor. On an even grander scale, male children were brought up from a very early age to be proficient in using weapons. They were playing war games. They were playing with warlike toys. How many of you, who are adult men today, started out playing with various forms of war toys when you were children?

The closed circle of the warrior mentality

Today, they are not so common in the western world, but there are other parts of the world where they are very common. You may say that, not so long ago, there were many parts of the world where it was necessary to be able to fight in order to survive. You may say that there are parts of the world where this is still necessary, but do you not see that the warrior mentality becomes a closed circle?

A warrior must, by definition, have an enemy or he has no justification for developing his proficiency to fight. Surely, you can go into a training room and get one of these punching bags, and you can pound on it with your boxing gloves for a time. The whole idea of putting on boxing gloves is that you go into a boxing ring, and there is an opponent who is trying to punch you in the nose, as you are trying to punch him. The warrior mentality without an opponent falls apart very quickly.

Is it really necessary in the modern age to bring up young boys to be warriors, to fight, to look at war as something desirable and necessary? I know there are many men in the Western world who themselves have not developed the ability to fight, who have no intention of fighting others physically. They have still taken in an aspect of the warrior mentality because they think it is good that their nation has a large army, has trained soldiers, has superior military hardware. Just look at how many nations in the Western, so-called developed world that still have this large military where all of the people who are professionally involved with the military have the warrior mentality. Look at how many people in the population take pride in

9 | The Warrior Mentality

their countries having this military capability. Take the United States, a country that Saint Germain founded and loves dearly. Look at how the warrior mentality sneaks its way through all aspects, all levels, of that society. From the so-called people on the street to the highest levels of government, you find the idea that the United States is the greatest country in the world. Therefore, it must have the greatest military so that it can fight for freedom and democracy and turn back any threat.

Did the military or the threat come first?

Which came first, my beloved, the chicken or the egg, the threat or the military? Do you not see that when you have millions of people in a nation who direct their attention towards being able to fight any opponent, then they feed their emotional, mental, and identity energies into this matrix? Do you not see that they create an energy impulse that they are sending into the cosmic mirror? What can the mirror do but reflect back at some point what is being sent out? Are you a warrior because there is an opponent or is there an opponent because you are in the warrior mentality and you are projecting out that you want an opponent?

I have talked about the cosmic cycles. I have talked about the transition from Pisces to Aquarius. You can look back at the last hundred years and see the large military conflicts that have taking place. They have taken place only because humankind has not transcended the warrior mentality. If you will not voluntarily transcend the mentality based on the teachings given by the spiritual teacher who is a primary teacher for your age, then you must outlive that mentality to more and more extreme degrees until you begin to see the futility of it. How far does a country like the United States have to go before it discovers that it no longer wants to be in the warrior mentality and, therefore, needs to start behaving as if it is not in the warrior mentality?

Overcoming the addiction to the warrior mentality

There is an aspect of the warrior mentality that is very much tied to the emotional octave, and it becomes an addiction to war, to fighting, to the adrenaline rush, to the excitement, to the sense that you are in a situation where it is a matter of life and death. This can even give some people a certain sense of meaning. You can see soldiers who grew up being bored with their lives. Then, they go to war and now they have a sense of meaning and excitement because there is always a threat. When they come home from war, they no longer know what to do with themselves. They miss the adrenaline rush. They feel that life is empty and has no meaning and they start falling apart psychologically. I would say that they were never really *together* psychologically before they went to war.

How can you grow up in the most free society the world has seen for a long time, a society with so many opportunities and yet you are bored with life? How can you fail to find meaning in life when you have the freedom to do almost whatever you want? You can fail this because you are trapped in the duality consciousness, and there is no real meaning there.

This is not because you are not a developed lifestream. There are millions of people in today's world, especially in the Western world, who have reached a point where, at inner levels, they are ready to step away from duality, to step up to being connected beings. Because they have no outer teaching about this, they do not know how to make the transition consciously, and that is why their lives feel empty. They look at the world and what it has to offer materially, and they cannot find any meaning in seeking material gain or other material goals.

The reason is that they are at the point of their evolution where they need to step up to serving the whole, to serving others. When they cannot do that, their lives are empty. They do not know what to do with themselves, and they deteriorate into various personal downward spirals. This can be drugs, alcohol, materialism, suicide, or the feeling that life is empty because there is no longer the outer situation where you are constantly forced to be alert for the enemy's attack.

There are people who are in physical battle and who are addicted to the adrenaline rush. There are also people who are not in a physical battle situation but who are still addicted to an aspect of the warrior mentality, namely, the feeling that they are the best warriors. These are people for whom war has become a form of contest, almost like a sporting game. When you add to this national pride, you have the idea that your country is better militarily than any other country, that your soldiers are better than any other soldiers.

Look at how, not so long ago, in the British Empire, they thought one British soldier was better than ten or twenty foreigners. How realistic is it that one soldier, no matter how good, could fight off twenty other soldiers? Look at how the German army during Nazism felt that they were superior to any other army. Look at how the Russians, the French, and now the Americans have felt or are feeling the same way.

National pride has nothing on

Where does this idea of national pride based on the ability to kill come from? Again, it comes from the fallen beings. Where else could it come from? Do you not see that nationalism has been used by the fallen beings to create this contest of war between nations? "Our nation is so superior to that other nation. *We* are superior to *them*. We are willing to invest billions of dollars (or whatever the currency may be) into military hardware and training so we can feel sure that we can beat that other army."

How could this be a source of national pride? Does anyone ever question this? Yes, a few people do question it but not enough people question it to have an impact. This needs to change. That is why I need you, who are the spiritually aware people, to make the calls for this mentality to be punctured so that the illusion is shattered, much like the old fairy tale by Hans Christian Anderson about the emperor's new clothes. Everybody is seeing the clothes that do not exist until a young boy suddenly punctures the illusion by saying: "But the emperor has nothing on." Someone needs to say: "But the emperors of war have nothing on. National pride has nothing on."

Shattering the warlike mentality

What is the Olympic Games, what has it deteriorated into? The original idea was to unite the nations and the peoples by bringing them together. This, of course, still works to some degree at the individual level. Look at how it has become a contest for national pride which nation wins the most medals. Is this not simply the war game in a non-lethal version? Is this really necessary? Do we really need to gather the whole world every four years in order to allow a few nations to prove their superiority once again? I am not saying we should not have Olympic Games, but the mentality could change.

Consider what would happen if this warlike mentality was shattered. Consider what would happen, my beloved. What if nations began to realize that your ability to fight a war does

9 | The Warrior Mentality

not prove the superiority of your nation? On the contrary, the more military hardware and capability you have, the more you prove your inferiority when it comes to all of the values that make modern, democratic civilization work. What if the mentality would shift so that those who are able to defeat someone in a physical battle are seen not as the *superior* nations but as the *inferior* ones?

What if the mentality was to shift so that people begin to recognize that separation and duality is the cause of the world's conflicts? What if people were to begin to realize that a new set of values need to be developed, based on the underlying reality of the oneness of all life? In that case, those who are able to fight an enemy would be seen as primitive, as backwards, as behind the times. Those who are able to work together, to negotiate, to come up with solutions that benefit all parties, would be seen as not necessarily the superior ones but certainly the ones who are more developed in terms of the values of oneness. The *values of oneness*—consider that idea.

What is the outcome of the warrior mentality, the warring culture? Is it not what you see in many nations today where the military becomes an end in itself? Look at most of the large nations in the world. If you were to go into the parliament, of say Russia, Great Britain, France or the United States, and suggest that they disband their military, what would be the reaction? The first reaction would likely be: "Oh, but we could not possibly do so, as long as that other nation maintains a large military. If we did not have the ability to defend ourselves against that enemy, they would take over the world." If both sides are saying this, which came first, the chicken or the egg? Was it *our* military that came first, or was it the military of *the enemy*? Do you not see that the military has become an end in itself?

Perpetuating the military indefinitely

The military on both sides are simply using each other to justify their existence. There is a certain military mindset that does not actually want to go to war. Certainly, there is a mindset behind the military that wants to use the military, but there is a mindset in the military itself that does not want to go to war. It just wants to maintain the military indefinitely. It wants to keep nations locked in spending money on the military. It wants to keep millions of soldiers and other personnel locked in training and perpetuating the military capability.

There is a certain fear in many military circles of actually going to war because then that might disprove the sense of superiority that they have developed based on their capability, a capability that has not been tested and proven in war. There is, of course, also a mentality that wants to go to war in order to prove their capability, but what I am pointing out is that there is a deeper, unrecognized mentality that sees the military as an end in itself and simply wants to perpetuate the existence of the military indefinitely.

When will a critical mass of people begin to question the need to maintain and perpetuate the military indefinitely? It has been said that there was a point during the height of the cold war where the West and the Communist Block had created so many nuclear missiles that they could destroy the world and kill all people several times over. The term "overkill" has been used. When does there come a point where one has enough military hardware? According to the mentality I am talking about, that point never arrives. Do you understand why that is so? Do you really understand why that is so?

Imbalanced creation through duality

The very mechanics of the duality consciousness is that there is always an opponent. How do you create a situation where there are two opposing polarities? I have explained in previous books and discourses [See *A Course in Abundance*] how everything in the entire universe is created out of the two forces: the expanding and the contracting, the masculine and feminine. When these two forces are in balance, they are not opposite polarities. They do not oppose each other. They work together. They supplement each other, and then you have a sustainable creation. When you go into duality, you are still using the two basic forces of creation. There is nothing else, but now you are using them as opposites. This means you create an imbalance. Duality is based on a fundamental imbalance that can never be stopped, that can never be balanced. You can only transcend duality and start co-creating again, but you cannot ever, as long as you are in duality, create a state of balance.

What that means in terms of military hardware is that you can develop some kind of weapon, but there will always be a counter measure. You may develop a tank with thicker armor than any tank has had before, but someone will develop a cannon, a rocket or another weapon that can penetrate that armor. What do you, then, have to do? You have to develop a thicker or stronger armor, and then someone else has to develop a stronger cannon or missile. Do you see that there will never come a point in duality where you have developed the ultimate condition? Whether it is weapons or anything else, there can never be an ultimate condition because there will always be an imbalance. This means that for anything you develop, there is an opponent that can destroy it.

The fallacy of the ultimate weapon

Do you understand the dynamics here? When you are connected, when you are using the masculine and feminine forces in balance, they supplement each other. There is no opposition there. They are complementing each other, and you are creating more by combining the two forces. When you go into duality, you make the two forces into opponents, but no force can ever be the ultimate force. No force can ever be decisive. No force can ever be absolute. Do you see this?

Even when you are in balance, no force is absolute. You may say the masculine force, the outgoing force, is the force of the Father, therefore, it should be stronger, but it is not. When you are connected, it does not matter that one force is not the strongest because you are not seeking something ultimate. You are seeking to always transcend the previous state, and it is precisely because no force is ultimate that there will always be the possibility of transcendence. To the Christ mind, this is the essence of growth. To the dualistic mind, this is the ultimate threat.

The fallen beings have from the day they rebelled against God's plan been trying to create some ultimate state in the material world that God cannot override or break down. They believe – in their illusion, in their pride – that one day they will be able to come up with something so ultimate that it cannot be broken down by God or the angels. They do not acknowledge that God and the angels do not need to break down the creation of the fallen beings. As soon as you go into duality, you are creating the opposition that will break down what you have created. It is not God and the angels that need to break down the creation of the fallen beings. They are doing it themselves.

The question is: How much destruction and how much suffering is caused in that process? The question is whether all this suffering actually is necessary for people to grow, or whether there comes a point where they can just look at the suffering and say: "No more! We do not want this anymore. We have had enough of the suffering. We have had enough of having our lives destroyed by the misguided quest of the fallen beings. We have had enough of this arms race that has been so prominent in the world in the last hundred years and even beyond."

Someone can always build a bigger bomb. Whatever you do to increase your military capability, there is a countermeasure. There always has been. There always will be. Yes, you can look at modern technology. You can look back at the cannons and sabers they had a few hundred years ago. You can see how much more sophisticated are the weapons you have created today. You can believe in the illusion that, because you are so much further along technologically today, you will be able to create the ultimate weapon.

Sophistication does not depend on war

My beloved, there have been civilizations before on planet earth that have self-destructed due to war. Those civilizations were far more technologically advanced than what you see today. They also attempted to create the ultimate weapon, but they did not succeed for there was always a countermeasure. When there was a war and both sides used everything they had, the effect was so destructive for the planet that their civilizations were wiped out, to the point where there is still no trace of them.

Surely, you can continue trying to do what no other civilization has done before. You can try to boldly go where no man has gone before. Wherever you go, some man has gone there before and proven that it did not work. There is nothing new under the sun. There is nothing new in the duality consciousness. It has all been done before.

How meaningless that peoples' lives are swallowed up in this impossible quest for the ultimate weapon, the ultimate military capability. How meaningless that the finances of nations are swallowed up in this. Imagine the sums of monies being spent on the military, and then, look at what would happen if they were used for other purposes.

There are children that starve to death every day. There are millions, if not billions, of people who do not have clean drinking water. There are millions of people, by some estimates two-thirds of the world's population, who live beneath the poverty level. Yet, the nations that consider themselves the most sophisticated in the world continue to spend huge amounts of money on developing their ability to kill other human beings.

Is this civilized? Is this sophisticated? I think not. How about you? If you, like I, think this is *not* a sign of sophistication, then I would encourage you to make the calls that will allow the angels to step in and remove the beings in the four levels of the material realm who will not let go of the warrior mentality and the other thoughtforms and ideas that I have talked about in this discourse.

This is a mentality that has been hanging as a cloud for a very long time over this planet. It has been hanging here since the very first fallen beings embodied on earth. It is time and high time that it was punctured by some people going out and saying: "But the warlords have nothing on."

Have you had enough of war

My beloved, I thank you for your attention, not only in hearing or reading this discourse. I trust that you will also be willing to give the invocations and do the work that will allow the angels to step in and remove the energies and the forces, so that one day, not too long into the future, more and more people will begin to wake up and suddenly see what they have never seen before, suddenly dare to question what they have never questioned before.

They will look around and say: "But how can we continue to do this? We no longer want to do this. This is not right. This is not who we are. We want to transcend this entire mentality. We want to look at those warriors and say: 'You have no more place on this planet. Your warrior mentality has no more place on this planet. You must either abandon it or find some other planet for we will no longer allow this one to be destroyed or to live in constant fear because of your war games. Enough of the war games. Enough of the war. Enough of the warriors.'"

My beloved, I thank you for your attention. I am the Ascended Master Mother Mary, and I love all human beings on this planet. I love this planet, and I want to see it be the beautiful jewel in the crown of the galaxy that it has the potential to be. Would you like to see that also?

10 | SHATTERING THE WARRIOR MENTALITY

In the name of the I AM THAT I AM, Jesus Christ, I call upon Mother Mary, Shiva and Archangel Michael to remove the warrior mentality from this planet. Awaken people to the reality that we are spiritual beings and that we can co-create a new future by working with the ascended masters. I especially call for …

[Make your own calls here.]

Part 1

1. Beloved Shiva, manifest your Presence in all four octaves and shatter and consume the warrior mentality in all of its disguises.

O Shiva, God of Sacred Fire,
It's time to let the past expire,
I want to rise above the old,
a golden future to unfold.

O Shiva, clear the energy,
O Shiva, bring the synergy,
O Shiva, make all demons flee,
O Shiva, bring back peace to me.

2. Beloved Shiva, manifest your Presence in all four octaves and shatter the mindset that war is desirable or is something from which one can gain honor.

O Shiva, come and set me free,
from forces that do limit me,
with fire consume all that is less,
paving way for my success.

O Shiva, clear the energy,
O Shiva, bring the synergy,
O Shiva, make all demons flee,
O Shiva, bring back peace to me.

3. Beloved Shiva, manifest your Presence in all four octaves and shatter the mindset that it is desirable for young men to go to war in order to prove their valor or to gain self-worth by proving their ability to kill other human beings.

O Shiva, Maya's veil disperse,
clear my private universe,
dispel the consciousness of death,
consume it with your Sacred Breath.

**O Shiva, clear the energy,
O Shiva, bring the synergy,
O Shiva, make all demons flee,
O Shiva, bring back peace to me.**

4. Beloved Shiva, manifest your Presence in all four octaves and shatter and consume the "us versus them" mentality in all of its disguises.

O Shiva, I hereby let go,
of all attachments here below,
addictive entities consume,
the upward path I do resume.

**O Shiva, clear the energy,
O Shiva, bring the synergy,
O Shiva, make all demons flee,
O Shiva, bring back peace to me.**

5. Beloved Shiva, I call forth the judgment of Christ upon all fallen beings who invented the warrior culture and brought it to earth. Manifest your Presence in all four octaves and remove those fallen beings and all who will not let go of the warrior culture.

O Shiva, I recite your name,
come banish fear and doubt and shame,
with fire expose within my mind,
what ego seeks to hide behind.

**O Shiva, clear the energy,
O Shiva, bring the synergy,
O Shiva, make all demons flee,
O Shiva, bring back peace to me.**

6. Beloved Shiva, manifest your Presence in all four octaves and cut free all people from the warrior culture that causes people to spend an entire lifetime developing the ability to kill other people in battle.

O Shiva, I am not afraid,
my karmic debt hereby is paid,
the past no longer owns my choice,
in breath of Shiva I rejoice.

**O Shiva, clear the energy,
O Shiva, bring the synergy,
O Shiva, make all demons flee,
O Shiva, bring back peace to me.**

7. Beloved Shiva, manifest your Presence in all four octaves and bind and consume the demons and fallen beings who promote any idea that justifies the epic struggle that make it desirable for "us" to kill "them."

O Shiva, show me spirit pairs,
that keep me trapped in their affairs,
I choose to see within my mind,
the spirits that you surely bind.

O Shiva, clear the energy,
O Shiva, bring the synergy,
O Shiva, make all demons flee,
O Shiva, bring back peace to me.

8. Beloved Shiva, manifest your Presence in all four octaves and bind and consume the demons and fallen beings who promote the mindset that warriors have the right to go to war and defeat the enemy in order to get honor and self-respect.

O Shiva, naked I now stand,
my mind in freedom does expand,
as all my ghosts I do release,
surrender is the key to peace.

O Shiva, clear the energy,
O Shiva, bring the synergy,
O Shiva, make all demons flee,
O Shiva, bring back peace to me.

9. Beloved Shiva, manifest your Presence in the identity octave and bind and consume the fallen beings who use the warrior mentality to get human beings in embodiment to fight each other.

O Shiva, all-consuming fire,
with Parvati raise me higher,
when I am raised your light to see,
all men I will draw onto me.

O Shiva, clear the energy,
O Shiva, bring the synergy,
O Shiva, make all demons flee,
O Shiva, bring back peace to me.

Part 2

1. Archangel Michael, manifest your Presence in all four octaves and bind and consume the demons and fallen beings who promote a culture that causes children to play war games or play with war-like toys.

> Archangel Michael, light so blue,
> my heart has room for only you.
> My mind is one, no longer two,
> your love for me is ever true.
>
> **Archangel Michael, you are here,**
> **your light consumes all doubt and fear.**
> **Your Presence is forever near,**
> **you are to me so very dear.**

2. Archangel Michael, manifest your Presence in all four octaves and cut people free to see how the warrior mentality becomes a closed circle because a warrior must justify his or her existence by having an enemy to fight.

> Archangel Michael, I will be,
> all one with your reality.
> No fear can hold me as I see,
> this world no power has o'er me.

**Archangel Michael, you are here,
your light consumes all doubt and fear.
Your Presence is forever near,
you are to me so very dear.**

3. Archangel Michael, manifest your Presence in all four octaves and consume the mentality that their nation needs a large military in which those who are professionally involved have the warrior mentality.

Archangel Michael, hold me tight,
shatter now the darkest night.
Clear my chakras with your light,
restore to me my inner sight.

**Archangel Michael, you are here,
your light consumes all doubt and fear.
Your Presence is forever near,
you are to me so very dear.**

4. Archangel Michael, manifest your Presence in all four octaves and bind and consume the demons and fallen beings who promote the warrior mentality and the need to have an army.

Archangel Michael, now I stand,
with you the light I do command.
My heart I ever will expand,
till highest truth I understand.

**Archangel Michael, you are here,
your light consumes all doubt and fear.
Your Presence is forever near,
you are to me so very dear.**

5. Archangel Michael, cut people free to see that when millions of people direct their attention towards being able to fight any opponent, then they feed their emotional, mental and identity energies into a matrix that attracts an enemy.

Archangel Michael, in my heart,
from me you never will depart.
Of hierarchy I am a part,
I now accept a fresh new start.

**Archangel Michael, you are here,
your light consumes all doubt and fear.
Your Presence is forever near,
you are to me so very dear.**

6. Archangel Michael, manifest your Presence in all four octaves and shatter the warrior mentality that is one cause behind the many large-scale military conflicts seen over the past century.

Archangel Michael, sword of blue,
all darkness you are cutting through.
My Christhood I do now pursue,
discernment shows me what is true.

**Archangel Michael, you are here,
your light consumes all doubt and fear.
Your Presence is forever near,
you are to me so very dear.**

7. Archangel Michael, cut people free to see the futility of the warrior mentality and see that only after they stop behaving like warriors will the outer enemy disappear.

> Archangel Michael, in your wings,
> I now let go of lesser things.
> God's homing call in my heart rings,
> my heart with yours forever sings.

> **Archangel Michael, you are here,**
> **your light consumes all doubt and fear.**
> **Your Presence is forever near,**
> **you are to me so very dear.**

8. Archangel Michael, manifest your Presence in the emotional octave and bind and consume the demons and fallen beings who keep people trapped in the addiction to war, to fighting, to the adrenaline rush.

> Archangel Michael, take me home,
> in higher spheres I want to roam.
> I am reborn from cosmic foam,
> my life is now a sacred poem.

> **Archangel Michael, you are here,**
> **your light consumes all doubt and fear.**
> **Your Presence is forever near,**
> **you are to me so very dear.**

9. Archangel Michael, cut people free from the sense that their lives gain meaning when they go to war. Cut them free from the sense that without war, their lives are empty.

Archangel Michael, light you are,
shining like the bluest star.
You are a cosmic avatar,
with you I will go very far.

Archangel Michael, you are here,
your light consumes all doubt and fear.
Your Presence is forever near,
you are to me so very dear.

Part 3

1. Beloved Shiva, cut free the people who are ready to step out of duality but who feel their lives are empty. Cut them free to find the spiritual path and discover meaning and purpose in serving the whole.

O Shiva, God of Sacred Fire,
It's time to let the past expire,
I want to rise above the old,
a golden future to unfold.

O Shiva, clear the energy,
O Shiva, bring the synergy,
O Shiva, make all demons flee,
O Shiva, bring back peace to me.

2. Beloved Shiva, manifest your Presence in all four octaves and bind and consume the demons and fallen beings who promote the addiction that makes people feel they are the best warriors, that war has become a form of contest or sporting game.

> O Shiva, come and set me free,
> from forces that do limit me,
> with fire consume all that is less,
> paving way for my success.

> **O Shiva, clear the energy,**
> **O Shiva, bring the synergy,**
> **O Shiva, make all demons flee,**
> **O Shiva, bring back peace to me.**

3. Beloved Shiva, manifest your Presence in all four octaves and bind and consume the demons and fallen beings who promote the mentality that a certain country has the best soldiers and could defeat any enemy.

> O Shiva, Maya's veil disperse,
> clear my private universe,
> dispel the consciousness of death,
> consume it with your Sacred Breath.

> **O Shiva, clear the energy,**
> **O Shiva, bring the synergy,**
> **O Shiva, make all demons flee,**
> **O Shiva, bring back peace to me.**

4. Beloved Shiva, manifest your Presence in all four octaves and bind and consume the demons and fallen beings who promote the idea that national pride is based on the ability to kill and that there is a contest of war between nations.

> O Shiva, I hereby let go,
> of all attachments here below,
> addictive entities consume,
> the upward path I do resume.

O Shiva, clear the energy,
O Shiva, bring the synergy,
O Shiva, make all demons flee,
O Shiva, bring back peace to me.

5. Beloved Shiva, manifest your Presence in all four octaves and bind and consume the demons and fallen beings who promote war-like games in a non-lethal version through international sporting competitions.

> O Shiva, I recite your name,
> come banish fear and doubt and shame,
> with fire expose within my mind,
> what ego seeks to hide behind.

O Shiva, clear the energy,
O Shiva, bring the synergy,
O Shiva, make all demons flee,
O Shiva, bring back peace to me.

6. Beloved Shiva, cut people free to see that the ability to fight a war does not prove the superiority of a nation. The more military hardware and capability a nation has, the more it proves its inferiority when it comes to the values behind modern, democratic civilization.

> O Shiva, I am not afraid,
> my karmic debt hereby is paid,
> the past no longer owns my choice,
> in breath of Shiva I rejoice.

> **O Shiva, clear the energy,**
> **O Shiva, bring the synergy,**
> **O Shiva, make all demons flee,**
> **O Shiva, bring back peace to me.**

7. Beloved Shiva, cut people free to see that separation and duality is the cause of the world's conflicts and that a new set of values need to be developed, based on the underlying reality of the oneness of all life.

> O Shiva, show me spirit pairs,
> that keep me trapped in their affairs,
> I choose to see within my mind,
> the spirits that you surely bind.

> **O Shiva, clear the energy,**
> **O Shiva, bring the synergy,**
> **O Shiva, make all demons flee,**
> **O Shiva, bring back peace to me.**

8. Beloved Shiva, cut people free to see that the most sophisticated nations are those who have developed the greatest ability to work together by finding solutions that benefit all parties because they are based on the values of oneness.

> O Shiva, naked I now stand,
> my mind in freedom does expand,
> as all my ghosts I do release,
> surrender is the key to peace.

> **O Shiva, clear the energy,**
> **O Shiva, bring the synergy,**
> **O Shiva, make all demons flee,**
> **O Shiva, bring back peace to me.**

9. Beloved Shiva, manifest your Presence in all four octaves and bind and consume the demons and fallen beings who promote the mentality that the military is an end in itself, based on the illusion that if one side abandoned the military, the other side would take over the world.

> O Shiva, all-consuming fire,
> with Parvati raise me higher,
> when I am raised your light to see,
> all men I will draw onto me.

> **O Shiva, clear the energy,**
> **O Shiva, bring the synergy,**
> **O Shiva, make all demons flee,**
> **O Shiva, bring back peace to me.**

Part 4

1. Archangel Michael, manifest your Presence in all four octaves and bind and consume the demons and fallen beings who promote the mentality that justifies the existence of the military and seeks to perpetuate it indefinitely through an ever-increasing spending on weapons.

> Archangel Michael, light so blue,
> my heart has room for only you.
> My mind is one, no longer two,
> your love for me is ever true.
>
> **Archangel Michael, you are here,**
> **your light consumes all doubt and fear.**
> **Your Presence is forever near,**
> **you are to me so very dear.**

2. Archangel Michael, manifest your Presence in all four octaves and bind and consume the demons and fallen beings who promote the illusion that you can create an ultimate weapon that has no counter-measure.

> Archangel Michael, I will be,
> all one with your reality.
> No fear can hold me as I see,
> this world no power has o'er me.
>
> **Archangel Michael, you are here,**
> **your light consumes all doubt and fear.**
> **Your Presence is forever near,**
> **you are to me so very dear.**

3. Archangel Michael, cut people free to see that when you go into duality, anything you do creates an opposite. Therefore, any weapon that could ever be developed has a counter-measure and this perpetuates military spending indefinitely.

> Archangel Michael, hold me tight,
> shatter now the darkest night.
> Clear my chakras with your light,
> restore to me my inner sight.

> **Archangel Michael, you are here,**
> **your light consumes all doubt and fear.**
> **Your Presence is forever near,**
> **you are to me so very dear.**

4. Archangel Michael, manifest your Presence in all four octaves and bind and consume the demons and fallen beings who are seeking to create some ultimate state in the material world that God cannot override or break down.

> Archangel Michael, now I stand,
> with you the light I do command.
> My heart I ever will expand,
> till highest truth I understand.

> **Archangel Michael, you are here,**
> **your light consumes all doubt and fear.**
> **Your Presence is forever near,**
> **you are to me so very dear.**

5. Archangel Michael, cut free people to see the futility and the fallacy of the quest of the fallen angels so they will awaken to the need to no more allow this to cause conflict and suffering on earth.

> Archangel Michael, in my heart,
> from me you never will depart.
> Of hierarchy I am a part,
> I now accept a fresh new start.

> **Archangel Michael, you are here,**
> **your light consumes all doubt and fear.**
> **Your Presence is forever near,**
> **you are to me so very dear.**

6. Archangel Michael, cut people free to look at suffering and say: "No more! We do not want this anymore. We have had enough of the suffering. We have had enough of having our lives destroyed by the misguided quest of the fallen beings. We have had enough of the arms race that has been so prominent in the world in the last hundred years and even beyond."

> Archangel Michael, sword of blue,
> all darkness you are cutting through.
> My Christhood I do now pursue,
> discernment shows me what is true.

> **Archangel Michael, you are here,**
> **your light consumes all doubt and fear.**
> **Your Presence is forever near,**
> **you are to me so very dear.**

7. Archangel Michael, cut people free to see that it is meaningless that peoples' lives are swallowed up in an impossible quest for the ultimate weapon, the ultimate military capability. It is meaningless that the finances of nations are swallowed up in this.

> Archangel Michael, in your wings,
> I now let go of lesser things.
> God's homing call in my heart rings,
> my heart with yours forever sings.
>
> **Archangel Michael, you are here,**
> **your light consumes all doubt and fear.**
> **Your Presence is forever near,**
> **you are to me so very dear.**

8. Archangel Michael, manifest your Presence in all four octaves and bind and consume the demons and fallen beings who promote the illusion that it is necessary to spend so much money on the military when millions of people are starving and two-thirds of the world's population live beneath the poverty level.

> Archangel Michael, take me home,
> in higher spheres I want to roam.
> I am reborn from cosmic foam,
> my life is now a sacred poem.
>
> **Archangel Michael, you are here,**
> **your light consumes all doubt and fear.**
> **Your Presence is forever near,**
> **you are to me so very dear.**

9. Archangel Michael, I hereby look at those beings in the warrior mentality and by the authority of the Christ within me, I say: "You have no more place on this planet. Your warrior mentality has no more place on this planet. You must either abandon it or find some other planet for I will no longer allow this one to be destroyed or to live in constant fear because of your war games. Enough of the war games. Enough of the war. Enough of the warriors."

> Archangel Michael, light you are,
> shining like the bluest star.
> You are a cosmic avatar,
> with you I will go very far.
>
> **Archangel Michael, you are here,**
> **your light consumes all doubt and fear.**
> **Your Presence is forever near,**
> **you are to me so very dear.**

Sealing

In the name of the I AM THAT I AM, I accept that Archangel Michael, Astrea and Shiva form an impenetrable shield around myself and all constructive people, sealing us from all fear-based energies in all four octaves. I accept that the Light of God is consuming and transforming all fear-based energies that make up the forces behind war!

11 | MATERIAL GAIN THROUGH WAR

I am the Ascended Master Mother Mary. I come to discourse with you on another cause of war, which is war caused by the desire for material gain. This is a complex issue. There is not just one but many undercurrents. Beginning with the most simple one, you have throughout history seen many cases in which wars, or at least aggression on a larger scale, has been caused by the desire for physical plunder. You have seen many groups of people, from the Vikings to the Huns to the pirates, who have waged war or aggressive acts in order to physically plunder those who had greater wealth.

This has to some degree been fed by or spun off from the warrior culture. There has been this culture of educating young men to be good warriors. What did they do with their skills when there were no nations where you could have wars between nations? The warriors would sometimes go out and use their skill for material gain. This is the simplest cause of war over material wealth. There is a direct, visible link between the act of war and the plunder.

In the modern world, things have become much more complex. There is no longer always a direct, physical link – or at least not a *visible* link – between an act of war and the gain of material wealth.

Exposing the industry of war

On a more complicated but still fairly visible level, we can talk about what has been called the military-industrial complex. It is quite obvious that there are large corporations around the world that make money out of making the technology used for war. The so-called defense industry is huge. It has enormous political power in many countries. It has enormous power, either directly or through somewhat indirect means, in that it provides jobs for people. It also has enormous hidden power where it has bought influence through lobbying, bribes or whatever.

This needs to be exposed. It needs to be stopped. When you have a defense industry where the industry itself, the profit of the shareholders, the jobs of the employees, are dependent upon making war materials, then the industry wants to continue making war materials. Not only that, it wants to increase its profits by making more war materials, more sophisticated, more expensive weapons. This ties in with what I have already said, namely that there is no ultimate weapon that could ever be developed because everything has a counter measure.

There are many examples of how the military-industrial complex has presented a new weapons system to the politicians of one country or one side. They have deliberately only presented this weapons system, but from the very beginning that they developed their weapons system, they already knew

11 | Material Gain through War

what the counter measure would be. They had plans for that also, but they are presenting only the one weapons system. They are presenting that this has some ultimate capability compared to existing weapons systems. They get the politicians to buy it because they think that this will give them an edge, perhaps, that it will give them the kind of superiority that might prevent a war.

Sometime later, the industry, perhaps through other companies with which they have no obvious connection, starts developing the counter measure. Now you have an arms race, whereas the promise of the first system was to end the arms race. This takes place over and over again, all in the name of profit. This, I trust, is easy to see. Companies make money on making war materials and other forms of technology used in war, and they sell it to the governments who are responsible for the armed forces.

This is an industry with many branches. There are companies that make money by providing food to the soldiers in the armies or cleaning the toilets on the army bases or doing a number of other things that are not directly related to building and selling war materials such as weapons. You see how big this industry is. You also see, I trust, that when we reach the goal – and my beloved, we *will* reach that goal – of ending war on this planet, then this entire war industry will disappear.

There are many people in today's world, both those who are directly involved with the war industry but also the politicians who see that the jobs of their constituents depend on the war industry, who cannot even conceive of a world without such an industry. They will say: "Where will the jobs come from? How will we even survive without this industry?" I will, therefore, tell you how you will survive.

Prospering through the Law of Multiplied Return

I have talked about the cosmic mirror. You project out something, and the cosmic mirror reflects it back to you multiplied. The very simplest illustration of this principle is that you take one grain of wheat and put it in the ground. It grows to become a plant that provides twenty or more grains of wheat in return for the one you planted. This is the principle described by Jesus in his parable about the servants who were given talents. Two of them multiplied it. One of them buried it in the ground and did nothing with it. This describes the eternal principle of how the spiritual beings who have taken embodiment interact with the matter realm, the Mother realm.

You are the co-creators. When you take an action that is aimed at raising up the whole, then the matter realm will by law multiply your action. When you take an action that is not aimed at benefiting the whole, then the matter realm will also multiply your action. I know this can be difficult to understand, but you simply need to make a switch in your consciousness. Whatever you send out, will be returned multiplied.

If you send out something that is aimed at producing more for everyone, then you will get back a return that gives more to everyone. If you send out an impulse that is aimed at producing more for the few and producing less for the many, then you will receive back an action that actually takes from the whole. When you take a positive action, such as planting wheat in the ground, the matter realm will multiply this by producing many more grains of wheat than you put in the ground. There will be more grains of wheat available on earth. When you take an action that does not multiply, that does not benefit the whole, then the total sum of what is available on earth will be lowered.

11 | Material Gain through War

Decreasing the total amount of wealth through war

If you have an industry that is aimed at producing goods that are not war materials but have a positive purpose, then that industry will create a return from the material universe that will increase the total amount of wealth available on earth. If you have an industry that is aimed at producing war materials, then that industry will not generate a positive return from the matter realm. On the contrary, it will generate a return that will deplete the total amount of resources. You have heard the very old statement that, after having waged war for a time, people realized that it was enough, and they beat their swords into plowshares. When you produce plowshares and use them, you are increasing the total amount of wealth. When you produce swords and use them to kill, you are decreasing the total amount of wealth.

There are entire nations or states in the United States where the politicians believe that their nations or their states are dependent upon the military-industrial complex, the war industry. They will say: "How can our economy survive if we do not have this huge defense industry?" The reality is that the defense industry is not producing something that increases the total amount of wealth on earth. It is producing something that *decreases* that amount of wealth. When the war industry is redirected at spending its resources and ingenuity on producing something that is good for the whole, then the economy of that nation or that state will actually grow. There will be more jobs and more wealth produced when you abandon the military-industrial complex.

I know that this will be difficult to see and accept. I know that there will be a transition period that will seem somewhat chaotic. The fact of the matter is that the military-industrial complex is only producing jobs on a temporary basis. It is not producing an upward trend. If you look at the world today, you can see that there is much more wealth in the world than five hundred years ago. What can account for this increased wealth?

It is the fact that, through the increase of knowledge and understanding, people are now able to produce much more life-supporting activities than they were able to five hundred years ago. It is not the man-made production itself that has increased the wealth; it is the return current from the universe. With men, this is impossible, but not with God, for with God, all things are possible. When you put one grain in the ground, twenty is returned. When you take a simple action aimed at benefiting the whole, the return is much greater than your action. This is simply a natural law. There is no beating it. There is no circumventing it. You can create the *illusion* that you have circumvented it, but this will only be on a temporary basis.

The connection between money and war

This leads me into the topic of one of the more subtle connections between war and material gain or, rather, monetary gain. Many of you will be aware that there is a connection between war and money, but very few people on this planet understand this connection. The reason for this is simple. The people who understand the economy generally do not have a sophisticated spiritual understanding, and the people who have a spiritual understanding generally do not have a sophisticated understanding of money.

You cannot fully understand money without having a spiritual awareness. You cannot understand money and the role of money, and especially the connection between war and money, if you do not incorporate the existence of fallen beings who are not thinking rationally but have other motives, other ways of thinking.

Money has always been linked to profit. Most economists tend to think that people are acting rationally when it comes to money. When they spend money, it is because they want to make a profit. If they do not make a profit, they will not continue to spend money, or so the economist reasons. This is not the case with the fallen beings because they are not necessarily spending money to make a direct profit. They are often spending money for some other goal that cannot easily be understood in terms of rational thinking.

Conspiracy theories and money

Many of you are aware that there are various conspiracy theories that talk about the banking system, the secret bankers, the monetary elite, and how they have manipulated the money systems of the world. What I will give you here is not a conspiracy theory in the traditional term. It goes beyond conspiracy theories.

The reality of the matter is that there is no *conscious* conspiracy that rules the world. There is an *unconscious* conspiracy, but that is not really a conspiracy. It is simply a number of fallen beings in and out of embodiment who are so trapped in their downward spiral that they cannot even see that it is leading to their own destruction.

The issue of money is truly very complicated. Why is it so complicated? Because the fallen beings have, both deliberately and unconsciously, made it very complicated. They have made it complicated so that they can hide what is really going on from the general population. I am not encouraging you to go out and study all of the conspiracy theories out there. The reason for this is that it will simply overwhelm you to the point where you will not know what is up and down, day or night.

This is partly because many of the conspiracy theories are deliberately created by the fallen beings or those they have hired to create conspiracy theories that either muddy the waters or that discredit the conspiracy theories that have some merit. There are some fallen beings who would have preferred that the conspiracy theories never emerged and never found a medium where they could be spread around the world, namely the Internet. When they could not stop this, they took the other measure of creating unreal conspiracy theories in order to confuse people, to overwhelm people, and to discredit the conspiracy theories that do have some bearing on reality.

A Golden-Age perspective on money

I wish to give you a very simple explanation of money. It has been said many times that money is a medium of exchange. This is not what money *is*, but it is what money *should be*. Money should be a medium of exchange.

Today, it is much more, and this is really the central, one might say the *only*, problem with money. In a, shall we say, spiritual, natural or golden age economy, money serves only one function: It is a medium of exchange. This means very simply that there is a direct connection between the money and something of real value, such as goods or services, that needs to be exchanged among people. Money exists for one reason only: to make it easier for people to exchange goods and services. As long as money is seen only as a way to exchange goods and services, then money is not evil and is not the root of all evil. You have heard the saying that money is the root of all evil. This is not correct. The correct understanding is that when money becomes more than a medium of exchange, then *that* is the root of all evil. This is, of course, a figure of speech, for there are certainly other causes of evil than money. There are many evils that follow when you disconnect money from something of real value and make it more than a medium of exchange.

In an ideal economy, money is created and destroyed on a continual basis. Money can be used to store value but only temporarily. Money is used only in direct relation to something that has actual value, inherent, intrinsic value. In an ideal economy, you never allow money to gain intrinsic value. As soon as you allow money to have value in itself, that is disconnected from real goods and services, then money will start to take on a life of its own. Pretty soon, it will own *you*.

Has the world ever had such an ideal economy? Yes, in what you call more primitive societies. In almost all more sophisticated civilizations, money has quickly taken on a value of its own. As soon as this happens, there will be a small elite of the population, namely the fallen beings in embodiment, who will see the potential for making money off of money.

In what I call an *ideal* economy, you are not making money off of money. You are making money off of producing something that benefits the whole, be it goods or services. This is what I earlier said corresponds to you taking a physical grain of wheat and putting it in the ground, thereby producing twenty. When you are doing something that is aimed at creating value, then you are activating the natural law that multiplies what you are creating. Thereby, you are raising up the whole. You are increasing the total amount of wealth in the world. When you are making money off of money, which you can do on a temporary basis, then you are not within the law that raises the whole. Instead, you are decreasing the total amount of wealth in the world.

Becoming rich by taking from the whole

I know this will seem contradictory because a very few people have become so rich that they can go out and spend more money than most people can imagine spending. How can I say that this decreases the total? It does because it not only takes money from other people, but it also takes money out of the economy as a whole.

You can look at the increase in wealth over the last five hundred years. You can see that the world is so much richer today than it was five hundred years ago. Then, you can look at how many billionaires there are in the world and you can say: "How could these people accumulate so much money if they were taking from the whole?" There are more billionaires in the world than ever before, but open your eyes and look at the so-called third world. There are more starving children than ever before. There are more people living beneath the poverty level than ever before. How can you say that the total amount of wealth has been increased to its maximum potential?

The fact of the matter is that the billionaires in today's world have become rich because the fallen beings have created a totally false economy that allows the concentration of wealth in the hands of a small elite. The fact that this elite has become larger than it was five hundred years ago does not mean that the economy is functioning better than it was five hundred years ago. It is the same principle as you saw in the feudal societies where ownership is concentrated in the hands of a small elite, and they have more than they could ever need for personal spending. The price is paid by the many who have less than they need to survive. In an ideal economy where the Law of the Multiplied Return is allowed to function, then all people will have enough. There will be no poverty. There will be no starvation. This planet is designed by the Elohim to sustain ten billion human beings in embodiment. When the Law of the Multiplied Return is functioning unhindered, the planet can easily feed, clothe and give an abundant life to ten billion people.

The fact that there are not ten billion people in embodiment proves an imbalance. The fact that two-thirds of the world population are living beneath the poverty level, while there are more and more billionaires who have more money than they could possible spend on personal consumption, proves this imbalance even more clearly for those who are willing to open their eyes and see.

Questioning the concept of interest

The entire economy of the world today is a false, manipulated economy created by the fallen beings. One of their primary means for creating this false economy is the idea that you can create money and then lend it out with interest.

This idea of interest has become so ingrained in people's minds over the last several hundred years that hardly anyone questions it. You are so used to thinking that if you want to start a business and need to get a loan from the bank, then the bank will only give you that loan if you pay them interest so that they can make money on giving you the loan. What is the purpose for you starting a business? It is to produce goods or services that are aimed at raising the whole. Why, then, should you have to pay interest? In an ideal economy, society would say: "Does this person have the talents, the skills, the attitude, that will allow him or her to run a successful business?" If the answer is "Yes," then society would provide you with the money to start that business. Society would know that you starting the business would activate the Law of Increased Return. Your efforts would be multiplied by the universe, and the entire society would benefit from this. Society would gain a greater return on your investment than the interest you now pay to the bank. Why, then, would society need to have a private bank lend the money to you and gain interest when society would benefit more from lending you the money without interest?

The idea that a private bank needs to create money, lend it out and charge interest is an idea created by the fallen beings. It has one purpose and one purpose only: to concentrate wealth in the hands of a small elite, those who make the interest. There is no other way to look at this. That is why I said that the fallen beings have deliberately made the economy so complicated that hardly anyone can understand it. If you start studying the modern economy, you will be overwhelmed by the knowledge, by the theories, by the different aspects of the economy, but it is really very, very simple.

How the artificial money system was created

Today, you have an economy that is entirely designed to allow a small elite to exploit the general population through money. They have control over the creation of money. All of the monetary instruments you see out there have only one function. It is to camouflage the fact that a small elite controls the money system. In an ideal economy, society will control the

11 | Material Gain through War

money system because society would see that nothing is more important for the prosperity of that society than a naturally functioning money system.

What has allowed the fallen beings to create this artificial money system? It is very simple. The answer is one word: war. What you have today is a wartime economy. This started in the Middle Ages in Europe where you had individual kings. These kings were fallen beings in embodiment. They had what the fallen beings have (and which I will speak about later) a desire for power, raw power. They wanted to expand their territory so that they could say: "I am the greatest king in the world." Doing this costs money, and here is the central dilemma.

Let us use the Middle ages as an example because the economy was more simple back then, but the same principle applies today. You have a king who has an ambition of expanding his territory. Not so far away is another king who is also a fallen being in embodiment and does not want to give up his territory so that the other king can become mightier. The first king knows that he has an opponent. As I have said, when you go into duality, you will always have an opponent. The king is now faced with the question of how he can assemble an army that is large enough to conquer the neighboring territory and defeat the other king.

The concern is very simple here. You have x amount of people in your country. They are right now fully occupied by producing the goods needed for their survival, even for your court and your palaces that are not really part of the naturally functioning economy. How can you create the production capability to produce the weapons and take the soldiers away from producing food and educate them? Where is the money going to come from to do this?

Taking money from the economy to fund war

When you are producing plowshares or growing crops, you are producing something of value. When you are producing cannons, sabers and rifles, you are not producing something that grows the overall economy. You are producing something that has the purpose of destroying something of value, be it human beings or property. Weapons have a destructive capability when they are aimed at war. The simple fact is that, if you create the production capability to produce the weapons and the army, you are taking value away from your country's economy.

How can you do this? It is almost impossible to do. The more sophisticated the economy of a country becomes, the larger the country becomes, the more difficult it becomes to take money out of the economy to produce an army, the more difficult it becomes to take production capability out of the economy to produce an army.

How can you overcome this problem? You can do so through money—when you disconnect money from the exchange of real goods. When you take money to a level where it is no more a medium of exchange but has intrinsic value, then you can create more money than the goods produced in your country. When you have created money that is not needed, that is not a medium of exchange for real goods, then you can use that money to buy something that your normal production capacity cannot produce.

Camouflaging the snowball of debt

When you do this, you will still take some people away from the normal production capability. This means that the young men you take away from the farms are not producing food. There will now be a lack in your economy. There will be a deficit because the real goods are no longer being produced. How can you, then, make this work? Very simple: You cover over the deficit with the money you have created out of nothing. You camouflage the deficit. You make it seem like there is no deficit, but, of course, there *is* a deficit. What you are doing is to push it into the future.

You have now created what we might compare to a snowball. You know that every time you push a snowball one revolution, it gathers more snow and it becomes bigger. You have now created a snowball of debt. The first kings did this to wage war. When the debt had to be paid, they just pushed the snowball further into the future, whereby the snowball became bigger.

Who was it that gave the kings the idea that they could do this? There are different classes of fallen beings. There are the ones who are driven by a more direct primitive quest for power, and they were the kings. Then, there are the ones that are more sophisticated, and they became the bankers. The kings were often controlled by fallen beings in the emotional realm or the mental realm. The bankers were controlled by fallen beings in the identity realm who had a hidden agenda. The more sophisticated fallen beings took advantage of the more primitive fallen beings to create an economy that furthers their ends.

You may say that at a certain level there is a motive that has some rationality to it that human beings can understand. The kings had a motive of expanding their territory, their power. The bankers had a motive of making money or, perhaps, even gaining the power to decide who was going to war. There are bankers who have given loans to two kings. They have also created weapons factories and produced the weapons, sold them to both kings, and then created the spark that made those kings go to war with one another and use up all of the weapons. The bankers were sitting back, making the money and enjoying the power that they were really the ones ruling the world.

I am not saying this is a benevolent rationale, but it is somewhat of a rationale. What neither the kings nor the bankers understood was that they were just pawns in a larger game, and this game was played by the fallen beings in the identity realm. They also have a rationale but not a rationale that most people can understand, and that is why I have attempted to give you the knowledge so that you can understand it. The simple rationale is that they want to prove God wrong by getting self-aware co-creators to misuse their free will to the point where they destroy themselves, rather than grow in self-awareness. They do this by creating war and by creating debt. [For more about the motives of fallen beings, see *Cosmology of Evil*.]

Interest has intrinsic value; debt does not

The debt neutralizes the natural Law of a Multiplied Return by creating an artificial economy. It is a downward spiral because it is constantly pushing a snowball of debt in front of it that becomes bigger and bigger until it can no longer be paid back. The bankers are not concerned about having the debt paid back. Why would they be concerned about having money paid back that they never had because it was created out of nothing? Their concern is only that the nations continue to pay the interest because the interest is what they can use to grow their own wealth and power.

Why is it that there is no value in the money, but there is value in the interest? The money is created out of nothing, but the interest is taken from the people and their labor. The bankers provide something that has no intrinsic value, and they get something back that *has* intrinsic value because it is tied to people's labor. Thereby, the bankers are indirectly reaping the fruits of the peoples' labor, as the feudal lords of the Middle Ages were reaping the fruit of the labor of the peasants that lived on their land. The feudal system of the Middle Ages is still in existence, only it has become hidden, invisible, through the veil of the complexity of the money system. Behind this is the larger rationale of creating a self-destructive economy that decreases the amount of wealth and, thereby, serves the end of causing a self-destructive spiral.

How the fallen beings try to stop economic growth

You will ask yourself why the economy has then grown over the past five hundred years. It is because the fallen beings do not have total control of the earth. There is an upward spiral created by the ascended masters and the many people in embodiment who are activating the Law of Multiplied return. Many of the fallen beings in embodiment would have preferred to keep a closed system, like the feudal system of the Middle Ages, where they were in direct control. They were not able to do this because of the combined efforts of the ascended masters and those in embodiment who had multiplied their talents.

Today, they have realized that they cannot actually stop the growth in the economy, in the total amount of wealth. Many of them are frantically trying to concentrate it in the hands of a few people. Even this is not successful, in the sense that the number of people who have accumulated large amounts of wealth is increasing. It is no longer a small elite that controls most of the wealth; it is a fairly large elite. Not all of the members of this elite are fallen beings. There are, indeed, those who are not fallen beings who have been drawn into this quest for money.

Artificial spending in a false economy

Money is a complex issue, and we need you to make the calls for the exposure of the connection between money and war, the very subtle connection. There are connections I have not even told you about here because I judge that they are too overwhelming at this point. I aim to give you something that is fairly easy to grasp and have you make calls on that. When we have cleared away some of the veil that hides what is going on, we can give you more sophisticated teachings and more sophisticated tools for dealing with these issues. Certainly, if you can make the calls on the issues I have given you here, you will make a great contribution towards ending war on this planet. Truly, people must come to see the connection of how war was used not only to justify a false monetary system but how it has also been used over and over again to create profits, greater and greater profits, for a small elite.

In a false economy, you must create artificial spending. In an ideal or natural economy, there is no need to create anything artificial. The vast majority of the people will quickly fall into seeing that when they make an effort, they get a multiplied return. This will cause them to make a greater effort, and thereby, the amount of wealth will be increased for everyone. What you have in a false economy is that people are making an effort. They are going to work every day, but they do not see the increased return.

They see only a fixed return, namely, what has been artificially defined as the value of their labor. Therefore, they do not make the effort that increases the economy. They only make the effort that keeps them alive and, thereby, sustains the economy at a certain level. In such a false economy, you need to create an artificial need to spend money. You need to create some way to manipulate people into spending more money than they have, more money than can be produced given the state of the production apparatus. What better way to create this artificial spending than war?

In a war, you are in a life-and-death situation. Either you are destroyed by your enemy, or you must buy weapons enough to defeat the enemy. Who supplies the money to pay for the weapons and who supplies the weapons? They are the ones who will make the profit. Naturally, in the quest for making a greater and greater profit, more and more weapons have to be produced. Every once in a while, those weapons also have to be used. Surely, there is money in having weapons sitting there being maintained, but there is much more money in having two sides who are both blowing up their weapons and, therefore, having to buy more. This is simply the greatest money-making machine on earth. War is the greatest money-making machine on earth.

The removal of money manipulation

This you need to make the calls on so that the angels can step in and remove those people from embodiment who will not give up the manipulation of the money system and the use of war to manipulate that money system. You need to make the calls for the removing of the beings in the astral plane, in the emotional realm, who want to escalate war so they can steal the energy and who want to escalate the debt economy so they can enslave more and more people under this burden of debt and, thereby, also extract their energy.

Whenever people are burdened by something, whenever they are limited, there are beings in the emotional realm who can steal people's energy. A person who is imprisoned and knows it is giving more energy to the beings in the astral realm than a person who is happy and free.

You also need to make the calls for the removal of those beings in the mental realm who are fueling war by providing the justification. Many of these beings in the mental realm are justifying the current economy. They are using their intellectual capability to explain why the economy is the way it is, why it has to be the way it is and how it can be made to function even though it is becoming increasingly clear that it cannot function. You need to make the calls for the removal of those beings in the identity realm who have a deeper agenda of using money to enslave people, using war to cause them to destroy themselves in order to prove God wrong.

Taking the opportunity without feeling overwhelmed

Surely, I have once again given you more than you can handle in one sitting so I shall end this release. I will return to give you more. I realize that this book is a challenge for all spiritual people. It will be difficult for many to read this book without feeling overwhelmed, but I ask you to deliberately look at yourself and ask yourself why you are feeling overwhelmed.

I am not asking you to solve the problem of war in an afternoon, my beloved. This has been going on for thousands of years. I am asking you to realize that, in the current cycle, there is a great opportunity to end war by the spiritual people making the calls and raising their awareness. I am not asking you to become burdened, whereby you release or produce negative energy and lower your awareness. I am asking you to become determined to make the calls, to increase your awareness and to enter a positive spiral.

Do you understand, my beloved, that there are many people who study the conspiracy theories and end up being completely overwhelmed and feeling completely pacified? They feel like: "If there *is* such a conspiracy, if things are so complex and serious, what could I possibly do?" This is not what I am asking you to do in this book. I am asking you to be awakened to the realization that there is *something* you can do. There is nothing you can do personally to change these things, but what you can do is make the call and thereby give the ascended masters and the angels the authority to change things on earth. We *will* respond to your call!

When you realize that you are not the doer, that you do not have to solve these problems, then you can enter an upward spiral because you are not alone. You are not alone having to fight the fallen beings and solve the serious problems on earth. You are in a partnership with the ascended masters. Every time you give a decree or an invocation, you are activating the Law of the Multiplication of the Return. Whatever energy you put into giving that invocation, we will multiply the energy and use it to remove the forces of war from this planet. You are in a positive, upward spiral with us. You may say: "But I do not have time to give more than one invocation a day." Anything you give is better than doing nothing. Anything you give will have an impact, a positive impact, on this planet. Anything you do will be multiplied by us and have a far greater impact.

There is no reason to feel burdened by the knowledge I give you. You should feel joyful, you should feel relieved by knowing these things. By knowing it, you can make the calls. When you make the calls, we *will* do the work. When we do the work, more people will begin to wake up. The entire collective consciousness will be shifted upwards until we reach that point where a certain consciousness of war, and the beings who will not let go of it, can be taken from the earth. This will be a momentous change.

Building the upward movement to change earth

You might look at the economy and see how complex it is and say: "How could this possibly be changed?" It could be changed so quickly that most people would fail to accept it if I told them. Things can shift almost in the blinking of an eye when enough people wake up and demand change.

I am not giving you a utopian pipe dream. I am giving you the absolute reality. The tools I am giving you in this book *will* activate the Law of the Multiplied Return, and this law is sufficient to produce change on earth. Surely, the change that can be produced is in direct proportion to the number of people who give the invocations, but nevertheless, when you personally make an effort, it will make a difference, a positive difference. You will, therefore, put yourself in the upward spiral that has been built over a long time on this planet. If you make that shift in awareness (away from focusing on the problems), you will feel that you are part of the positive, upward movement that is changing the earth.

Lock in to my enthusiasm. It is not based on belief. It is based on knowledge. It is based on experience. It is based on being proven time and time again on this and many other planets. What we are presenting you, as the ascended masters in this age, is not something that is a pipe dream or that has just been invented. The program that we are putting forth on this planet (through this and other messengers) has been proven over and over again on thousands upon thousands of other planets who have been in a similar downward spiral as earth.

They have turned things around and are now in an upward spiral. It is by no means an impossibility. It is by no means beyond the capability of the people in embodiment.

There are many people who have embodied at this time specifically to help this transition along. You have embodied because you have the capability, you have the growth in awareness, you have the momentum from past lives. I am simply asking you to tune in to what you already know in your heart and to make that leap forward and be positive about the difference that you can make when you activate the Law of the Multiplication of the Return. We of the ascended masters are the multiplication. We will multiply what you give us to multiply. Therefore, rest assured that our combined efforts *are* making a decisive difference in removing war from the earth. Mother Mary I AM!

12 | JUDGING WAR FOR PROFIT

In the name of the I AM THAT I AM, Jesus Christ, I call upon Mother Mary, Archangel Michael, the Divine Director and the seven Archangels to judge and remove all beings, in and out of embodiment, who promote war as a means to gain profit. Awaken people to the reality that we are spiritual beings and that we can co-create a new future by working with the ascended masters. I especially call for …

[Make your own calls here.]

Part 1

1. Archangel Michael, I call forth the judgment of Christ upon the people who are committing or planning war or aggression for material gain.

Archangel Michael, light so blue,
my heart has room for only you.
My mind is one, no longer two,
your love for me is ever true.

**Archangel Michael, you are here,
your light consumes all doubt and fear.
Your Presence is forever near,
you are to me so very dear.**

2. Archangel Michael, I call forth the judgment of Christ upon the demons and fallen beings in the astral plane who are behind warfare for physical plunder. I command you to remove these beings from earth.

Archangel Michael, I will be,
all one with your reality.
No fear can hold me as I see,
this world no power has o'er me.

**Archangel Michael, you are here,
your light consumes all doubt and fear.
Your Presence is forever near,
you are to me so very dear.**

3. Archangel Michael, I call forth the judgment of Christ upon the military-industrial complex and the corporations who make money on war.

Archangel Michael, hold me tight,
shatter now the darkest night.
Clear my chakras with your light,
restore to me my inner sight.

> Archangel Michael, you are here,
> your light consumes all doubt and fear.
> Your Presence is forever near,
> you are to me so very dear.

4. Archangel Michael, I call forth the judgment of Christ upon the defense industry. I call for the exposure of its political power through job creation, corruption or lobbying.

> Archangel Michael, now I stand,
> with you the light I do command.
> My heart I ever will expand,
> till highest truth I understand.

> **Archangel Michael, you are here,
> your light consumes all doubt and fear.
> Your Presence is forever near,
> you are to me so very dear.**

5. Archangel Michael, I call forth the judgment of Christ upon upon the fallen beings and demons in the three higher octaves who are behind the defense industry. I command you to remove these beings from earth.

> Archangel Michael, in my heart,
> from me you never will depart.
> Of hierarchy I am a part,
> I now accept a fresh new start.

> **Archangel Michael, you are here,
> your light consumes all doubt and fear.
> Your Presence is forever near,
> you are to me so very dear.**

6. Archangel Michael, I call forth the judgment of Christ upon the war industry and its desire to increase its profits by making more war materials plus more sophisticated and expensive weapons.

> Archangel Michael, sword of blue,
> all darkness you are cutting through.
> My Christhood I do now pursue,
> discernment shows me what is true.
>
> **Archangel Michael, you are here,**
> **your light consumes all doubt and fear.**
> **Your Presence is forever near,**
> **you are to me so very dear.**

7. Archangel Michael, I call forth the judgment of Christ upon the fallen beings and demons in the three higher octaves who are behind the war industry and who induce the never-ending desire for greater profits. I command you to remove these beings from earth.

> Archangel Michael, in your wings,
> I now let go of lesser things.
> God's homing call in my heart rings,
> my heart with yours forever sings.
>
> **Archangel Michael, you are here,**
> **your light consumes all doubt and fear.**
> **Your Presence is forever near,**
> **you are to me so very dear.**

8. Archangel Michael, I call forth the judgment of Christ upon the military-industrial complex and the strategy of developing a seemingly ultimate weapon while hiding its counter measure.

> Archangel Michael, take me home,
> in higher spheres I want to roam.
> I am reborn from cosmic foam,
> my life is now a sacred poem.
>
> **Archangel Michael, you are here,**
> **your light consumes all doubt and fear.**
> **Your Presence is forever near,**
> **you are to me so very dear.**

9. Archangel Michael, I call forth the judgment of Christ upon the war industry and its willingness to sell weapons to the highest bidder, even to sell the counter measure to one weapon to the opposing side in order to create or maintain an arms race.

> Archangel Michael, light you are,
> shining like the bluest star.
> You are a cosmic avatar,
> with you I will go very far.
>
> **Archangel Michael, you are here,**
> **your light consumes all doubt and fear.**
> **Your Presence is forever near,**
> **you are to me so very dear.**

Part 2

1. Divine Director, I call forth the judgment of Christ upon the fallen beings and demons in the three higher octaves who are behind the arms race and who seek to turn it into a never-ending quest for the ultimate weapon. I command you to remove these beings from earth.

> Divine Director, I now see,
> the world is unreality,
> in my heart I now truly feel,
> the Spirit is all that is real.
>
> **Divine Director, send the light,**
> **from blindness clear my inner sight,**
> **my vision free, my vision clear,**
> **your guidance is forever here.**

2. Divine Director, I call forth the judgment of Christ upon all people who believe the economy depends on the war industry and that sufficient jobs cannot be created without it. Awaken people to the lie behind this belief.

> Divine Director, vision give,
> in clarity I want to live,
> I now behold my plan Divine,
> the plan that is uniquely mine.
>
> **Divine Director, send the light,**
> **from blindness clear my inner sight,**
> **my vision free, my vision clear,**
> **your guidance is forever here.**

3. Divine Director, I call forth the judgment of Christ upon the fallen beings and demons in the three higher octaves who are hiding the fact that the cosmic mirror returns whatever we send out multiplied. I command you to remove these beings from earth.

> Divine Director, show in me,
> the ego games, and set me free,
> help me escape the ego's cage,
> to help bring in the golden age.
>
> **Divine Director, send the light,**
> **from blindness clear my inner sight,**
> **my vision free, my vision clear,**
> **your guidance is forever here.**

4. Divine Director, I call forth the judgment of Christ upon the fallen beings and demons in the three higher octaves who are hiding the fact that an industry that has a positive purpose will increase the amount of wealth available. I command you to remove these beings from earth.

> Divine Director, I'm with you,
> my vision one, no longer two,
> as karma's veil you do disperse,
> I see a whole new universe.
>
> **Divine Director, send the light,**
> **from blindness clear my inner sight,**
> **my vision free, my vision clear,**
> **your guidance is forever here.**

5. Divine Director, I call forth the judgment of Christ upon the fallen beings and demons in the three higher octaves who are hiding the fact that the war industry is decreasing the total amount of wealth by generating a profit for a small elite. I command you to remove these beings from earth.

Divine Director, I go up,
electric light now fills my cup,
consume in me all shadows old,
bestow on me a vision bold.

**Divine Director, send the light,
from blindness clear my inner sight,
my vision free, my vision clear,
your guidance is forever here.**

6. Divine Director, I call forth the judgment of Christ upon the politicians who believe that their nations or their states are dependent upon the military-industrial complex, the war industry. Awaken people to the lie behind this belief.

Divine Director, heart of gold,
my sacred labor I unfold,
o blessed Guru, I now see,
where my own plan is taking me.

**Divine Director, send the light,
from blindness clear my inner sight,
my vision free, my vision clear,
your guidance is forever here.**

7. Divine Director, I call forth the judgment of Christ upon the fallen beings and demons in the three higher octaves who will do anything in their power to prevent people from seeing the true cost of the war industry. I command you to remove these beings from earth.

> Divine Director, by your grace,
> in grander scheme I find my place,
> my individual flame I see,
> uniqueness God has given me.
>
> **Divine Director, send the light,**
> **from blindness clear my inner sight,**
> **my vision free, my vision clear,**
> **your guidance is forever here.**

8. Divine Director, awaken people to the fact that when industry is redirected at spending resources and ingenuity on producing something that is good for the whole, then the economy will create more jobs and more wealth than the military-industrial complex.

> Divine Director, vision one,
> I see that I AM God's own Sun,
> with your direction so Divine,
> I am now letting my light shine.
>
> **Divine Director, send the light,**
> **from blindness clear my inner sight,**
> **my vision free, my vision clear,**
> **your guidance is forever here.**

9. Divine Director, I call for the exposure of the most subtle connections between money and war. I call for the judgment of Christ upon the fallen beings and demons in the three higher octaves and the human beings in embodiment who seek to hide these connections.

> Divine Director, what a gift,
> to be a part of Spirit's lift,
> to raise mankind out of the night,
> to bask in Spirit's loving sight.
>
> **Divine Director, send the light,**
> **from blindness clear my inner sight,**
> **my vision free, my vision clear,**
> **your guidance is forever here.**

Part 3

1. Mother Mary, awaken people to see the connection of how war has been used to justify a false monetary system and create greater and greater profits for a small elite.

> O blessed Mary, Mother mine,
> there is no greater love than thine,
> as we are one in heart and mind,
> my place in hierarchy I find.
>
> **O Mother Mary, generate,**
> **the song that does accelerate,**
> **the earth into a higher state,**
> **all matter does now scintillate.**

2. Mother Mary, awaken people to the fact that in a false economy, one must create artificial spending, and war or the threat of war is the primary means for doing this.

> I came to earth from heaven sent,
> as I am in embodiment,
> I use Divine authority,
> commanding you to set earth free.

> **O Mother Mary, generate,**
> **the song that does accelerate,**
> **the earth into a higher state,**
> **all matter does now scintillate.**

3. Mother Mary, I call forth the judgment of Christ upon the fallen beings and demons in the three higher octaves and the human beings in embodiment who are maintaining the false economy and its artificial spending justified by war. I command you to remove these beings from earth.

> I call now in God's sacred name,
> for you to use your Mother Flame,
> to burn all fear-based energy,
> restoring sacred harmony.

> **O Mother Mary, generate,**
> **the song that does accelerate,**
> **the earth into a higher state,**
> **all matter does now scintillate.**

4. Mother Mary, I call forth the judgment of Christ upon the fallen beings and demons in the three higher octaves and the human beings in embodiment who are deliberately using war in order to force nations to spend more money than they have. I command you to remove these beings from earth.

> Your sacred name I hereby praise,
> collective consciousness you raise,
> no more of fear and doubt and shame,
> consume it with your Mother Flame.

O Mother Mary, generate,
the song that does accelerate,
the earth into a higher state,
all matter does now scintillate.

5. Mother Mary, I call forth the judgment of Christ upon the fallen beings in embodiment who are supplying the money and the weapons to one or both sides in order to make a profit on war. I command you to remove these beings from earth.

> All darkness from the earth you purge,
> your light moves as a mighty surge,
> no force of darkness can now stop,
> the spiral that goes only up.

O Mother Mary, generate,
the song that does accelerate,
the earth into a higher state,
all matter does now scintillate.

6. Mother Mary, I call forth the judgment of Christ upon the fallen beings and demons in the three higher octaves and the human beings in embodiment who are deliberately creating war in order to force nations to use their weapons and buy more. I command you to remove these beings from earth.

> All elemental life you bless,
> removing from them man-made stress,
> the nature spirits are now free,
> outpicturing Divine decree.
>
> **O Mother Mary, generate,**
> **the song that does accelerate,**
> **the earth into a higher state,**
> **all matter does now scintillate.**

7. Mother Mary, I call forth the judgment of Christ upon the fallen beings and demons in the three higher octaves and the human beings in embodiment who have turned war into the greatest money-making machine. I command you to remove these beings from earth.

> I raise my voice and take my stand,
> a stop to war I do command,
> no more shall warring scar the earth,
> a golden age is given birth.
>
> **O Mother Mary, generate,**
> **the song that does accelerate,**
> **the earth into a higher state,**
> **all matter does now scintillate.**

8. Mother Mary, I call forth the judgment of Christ upon the fallen beings and demons in the three higher octaves and the human beings in embodiment who are behind the creation of the false money system. I command you to remove these beings from earth.

> As Mother Earth is free at last,
> disasters belong to the past,
> your Mother Light is so intense,
> that matter is now far less dense.

> **O Mother Mary, generate,**
> **the song that does accelerate,**
> **the earth into a higher state,**
> **all matter does now scintillate.**

9. Mother Mary, I call forth the judgment of Christ upon the fallen beings and demons in the three higher octaves and the human beings in embodiment who are behind the use of war as a way to manipulate the money system. I command you to remove these beings from earth.

> In Mother Light the earth is pure,
> the upward spiral will endure,
> prosperity is now the norm,
> God's vision manifest as form.

> **O Mother Mary, generate,**
> **the song that does accelerate,**
> **the earth into a higher state,**
> **all matter does now scintillate.**

Part 4

1. I call to the seven Archangels to remove the people from embodiment who will not give up the manipulation of the money system.

> Archangel Michael, light so blue,
> my heart has room for only you.
> My mind is one, no longer two,
> your love for me is ever true.
>
> **Archangel Michael, you are here,**
> **your light consumes all doubt and fear.**
> **Your Presence is forever near,**
> **you are to me so very dear.**

2. I call to the seven Archangels to remove the people from embodiment who are using war to manipulate the money system.

> Archangel Michael, I will be,
> all one with your reality.
> No fear can hold me as I see,
> this world no power has o'er me.
>
> **Archangel Michael, you are here,**
> **your light consumes all doubt and fear.**
> **Your Presence is forever near,**
> **you are to me so very dear.**

3. I call to the seven Archangels to remove the beings in the astral plane who want to escalate war so they can steal people's energy.

> Archangel Michael, hold me tight,
> shatter now the darkest night.
> Clear my chakras with your light,
> restore to me my inner sight.
>
> **Archangel Michael, you are here,**
> **your light consumes all doubt and fear.**
> **Your Presence is forever near,**
> **you are to me so very dear.**

4. I call to the seven Archangels to remove the beings in the astral plane who want to escalate the debt economy so they can enslave more and more people under this burden of debt and thereby steal their energy.

> Archangel Michael, now I stand,
> with you the light I do command.
> My heart I ever will expand,
> till highest truth I understand.
>
> **Archangel Michael, you are here,**
> **your light consumes all doubt and fear.**
> **Your Presence is forever near,**
> **you are to me so very dear.**

5. I call to the seven Archangels to remove the beings in the mental realm who are fueling war by providing the justification for war and for the current economy.

Archangel Michael, in my heart,
from me you never will depart.
Of hierarchy I am a part,
I now accept a fresh new start.

**Archangel Michael, you are here,
your light consumes all doubt and fear.
Your Presence is forever near,
you are to me so very dear.**

6. I call to the seven Archangels to remove the beings in the mental realm who are using their intellectual capability to explain why the economy is the way it is, why it has to be the way it is and how it can be made to function even though it cannot function.

Archangel Michael, sword of blue,
all darkness you are cutting through.
My Christhood I do now pursue,
discernment shows me what is true.

**Archangel Michael, you are here,
your light consumes all doubt and fear.
Your Presence is forever near,
you are to me so very dear.**

7. I call to the seven Archangels to remove the beings in the identity realm who have a deeper agenda of using money to enslave people and using war to cause them to destroy themselves in order to prove God wrong.

Archangel Michael, in your wings,
I now let go of lesser things.
God's homing call in my heart rings,
my heart with yours forever sings.

**Archangel Michael, you are here,
your light consumes all doubt and fear.
Your Presence is forever near,
you are to me so very dear.**

8. I call to the seven Archangels to awaken all people from hopelessness and the sense of being powerless. Awaken people to the reality that when we work with the ascended masters, there is indeed something we can do.

Archangel Michael, take me home,
in higher spheres I want to roam.
I am reborn from cosmic foam,
my life is now a sacred poem.

**Archangel Michael, you are here,
your light consumes all doubt and fear.
Your Presence is forever near,
you are to me so very dear.**

9. I call to the seven Archangels to awaken the people who have embodied at this time in order to be part of the upward movement that will take earth away from the control of the fallen beings. Awaken people to their potential to activate the Law of the Multiplied Return by working with the ascended masters.

Archangel Michael, light you are,
shining like the bluest star.
You are a cosmic avatar,
with you I will go very far.

**Archangel Michael, you are here,
your light consumes all doubt and fear.
Your Presence is forever near,
you are to me so very dear.**

Sealing

In the name of the I AM THAT I AM, I accept that Archangel Michael, Astrea and Shiva form an impenetrable shield around myself and all constructive people, sealing us from all fear-based energies in all four octaves. I accept that the Light of God is consuming and transforming all fear-based energies that make up the forces behind war!

13 | EXPOSING THE FALSE MONEY SYSTEM

In the name of the I AM THAT I AM, Jesus Christ, I call upon Mother Mary, Saint Germain and the Divine Director to awaken people from the illusions behind the false money system. Awaken people to the reality that we are spiritual beings and that we can co-create a new future by working with the ascended masters. I especially call for …

[Make your own calls here.]

Part 1

1. Saint Germain, awaken people to the reality that one cannot fully understand money without having a spiritual awareness.

> O Saint Germain, you do inspire,
> my vision raised forever higher,
> with you I form a figure-eight,
> your Golden Age I co-create.
>
> **O Saint Germain, what love you bring,**
> **it truly makes all matter sing,**
> **your violet flame does all restore,**
> **with you we are becoming more.**

2. Saint Germain, awaken people to the reality that one cannot understand the connection between war and money if one does not incorporate the existence of fallen beings who are not thinking rationally but have other motives, other ways of thinking.

> O Saint Germain, what Freedom Flame,
> released when we recite your name,
> acceleration is your gift,
> our planet it will surely lift.
>
> **O Saint Germain, what love you bring,**
> **it truly makes all matter sing,**
> **your violet flame does all restore,**
> **with you we are becoming more.**

3. Saint Germain, awaken people to the reality that the fallen beings are not necessarily spending money to make a direct profit. They have some other goal that cannot easily be understood through rational thinking.

> O Saint Germain, in love we claim,
> our right to bring your violet flame,
> from you Above, to us below,
> it is an all-transforming flow.
>
> **O Saint Germain, what love you bring,**
> **it truly makes all matter sing,**
> **your violet flame does all restore,**
> **with you we are becoming more.**

4. Saint Germain, awaken people to the reality that there is no conscious conspiracy that rules the world. There is an unconscious conspiracy, namely a number of fallen beings in and out of embodiment who are so trapped in their downward spiral that they cannot see that it is leading to their own destruction.

> O Saint Germain, I love you so,
> my aura filled with violet glow,
> my chakras filled with violet fire,
> I am your cosmic amplifier.
>
> **O Saint Germain, what love you bring,**
> **it truly makes all matter sing,**
> **your violet flame does all restore,**
> **with you we are becoming more.**

5. Saint Germain, awaken people to the reality that the issue of money is complicated because the fallen beings have made it so in order to hide what is really going on.

O Saint Germain, I am now free,
your violet flame is therapy,
transform all hang-ups in my mind,
as inner peace I surely find.

**O Saint Germain, what love you bring,
it truly makes all matter sing,
your violet flame does all restore,
with you we are becoming more.**

6. Saint Germain, awaken people to the reality that the fallen beings have created many conspiracy theories in order to discredit the theories that expose their existence and methods.

O Saint Germain, my body pure,
your violet flame for all is cure,
consume the cause of all disease,
and therefore I am all at ease.

**O Saint Germain, what love you bring,
it truly makes all matter sing,
your violet flame does all restore,
with you we are becoming more.**

7. Saint Germain, awaken people to the reality that money should be nothing more than a medium of exchange. In a golden age economy there is a direct connection between money and something of real value, such as goods or services.

O Saint Germain, I'm karma-free,
the past no longer burdens me,
a brand new opportunity,
I am in Christic unity.

**O Saint Germain, what love you bring,
it truly makes all matter sing,
your violet flame does all restore,
with you we are becoming more.**

8. Saint Germain, awaken people to the reality that money is not the root of all evil. It is when money becomes more than a medium of exchange that it becomes a tool for evil.

O Saint Germain, we are now one,
I am for you a violet sun,
as we transform this planet earth,
your Golden Age is given birth.

**O Saint Germain, what love you bring,
it truly makes all matter sing,
your violet flame does all restore,
with you we are becoming more.**

9. Saint Germain, awaken people to the fact that in an ideal economy money must never gain intrinsic value. If you allow money to take on a life of its own, it will own you.

O Saint Germain, the earth is free,
from burden of duality,
in oneness we bring what is best,
your Golden Age is manifest.

**O Saint Germain, what love you bring,
it truly makes all matter sing,
your violet flame does all restore,
with you we are becoming more.**

Part 2

1. Divine Director, awaken people to the reality that when money takes on inherent value, a small elite, namely the fallen beings in embodiment, will use the potential for making money off of money.

> Divine Director, I now see,
> the world is unreality,
> in my heart I now truly feel,
> the Spirit is all that is real.
>
> **Divine Director, send the light,**
> **from blindness clear my inner sight,**
> **my vision free, my vision clear,**
> **your guidance is forever here.**

2. Divine Director, awaken people to the reality that when you are making money off of money, then you are not within the law that raises the whole. You are decreasing the total amount of wealth in the world.

> Divine Director, vision give,
> in clarity I want to live,
> I now behold my plan Divine,
> the plan that is uniquely mine.
>
> **Divine Director, send the light,**
> **from blindness clear my inner sight,**
> **my vision free, my vision clear,**
> **your guidance is forever here.**

3. Divine Director, awaken people to the reality that the billionaires in today's world have become rich because the fallen beings have created a false economy that allows the concentration of wealth in the hands of a small elite.

> Divine Director, show in me,
> the ego games, and set me free,
> help me escape the ego's cage,
> to help bring in the golden age.

> **Divine Director, send the light,**
> **from blindness clear my inner sight,**
> **my vision free, my vision clear,**
> **your guidance is forever here.**

4. Divine Director, awaken people to the reality that the entire economy of the world is a false, manipulated economy created by the fallen beings. One of their primary means for creating this false economy is the idea that you can create money and then lend it out with interest.

> Divine Director, I'm with you,
> my vision one, no longer two,
> as karma's veil you do disperse,
> I see a whole new universe.

> **Divine Director, send the light,**
> **from blindness clear my inner sight,**
> **my vision free, my vision clear,**
> **your guidance is forever here.**

5. Divine Director, awaken people to the reality that in a golden age economy, a business producing goods or services that are aimed at raising the whole will not have to pay interest.

> Divine Director, I go up,
> electric light now fills my cup,
> consume in me all shadows old,
> bestow on me a vision bold.

> **Divine Director, send the light,**
> **from blindness clear my inner sight,**
> **my vision free, my vision clear,**
> **your guidance is forever here.**

6. Divine Director, awaken people to the reality that in an ideal economy, society will provide the money to start a business because this will activate the Law of Increasing Return.

> Divine Director, heart of gold,
> my sacred labor I unfold,
> o blessed Guru, I now see,
> where my own plan is taking me.

> **Divine Director, send the light,**
> **from blindness clear my inner sight,**
> **my vision free, my vision clear,**
> **your guidance is forever here.**

7. Divine Director, awaken people to the reality that there is no need to have private banks lend money and gain interest when society would benefit more from lending the money without interest.

> Divine Director, by your grace,
> in grander scheme I find my place,
> my individual flame I see,
> uniqueness God has given me.
>
> **Divine Director, send the light,**
> **from blindness clear my inner sight,**
> **my vision free, my vision clear,**
> **your guidance is forever here.**

8. Divine Director, awaken people to the reality that the idea that private banks needs to create money, lend it out and charge interest is created by the fallen beings. It has one purpose, namely to concentrate wealth in the hands of a small elite.

> Divine Director, vision one,
> I see that I AM God's own Sun,
> with your direction so Divine,
> I am now letting my light shine.
>
> **Divine Director, send the light,**
> **from blindness clear my inner sight,**
> **my vision free, my vision clear,**
> **your guidance is forever here.**

9. Divine Director, awaken people to the reality that the fallen beings have deliberately made the economy so complicated that hardly anyone can understand it. Yet the economy is very simple.

Divine Director, what a gift,
to be a part of Spirit's lift,
to raise mankind out of the night,
to bask in Spirit's loving sight.

Divine Director, send the light,
from blindness clear my inner sight,
my vision free, my vision clear,
your guidance is forever here.

Part 3

1. Saint Germain, awaken people to the reality that we have an economy that is designed to allow a small elite to exploit the general population through money. All monetary instruments camouflage the fact that a small elite controls the money system.

O Saint Germain, you do inspire,
my vision raised forever higher,
with you I form a figure-eight,
your Golden Age I co-create.

O Saint Germain, what love you bring,
it truly makes all matter sing,
your violet flame does all restore,
with you we are becoming more.

2. Saint Germain, awaken people to the reality that in an ideal economy, society will control the money system because people will see that nothing is more important for the prosperity of a society than a naturally functioning money system.

> O Saint Germain, what Freedom Flame,
> released when we recite your name,
> acceleration is your gift,
> our planet it will surely lift.

> **O Saint Germain, what love you bring,**
> **it truly makes all matter sing,**
> **your violet flame does all restore,**
> **with you we are becoming more.**

3. Saint Germain, awaken people to the reality that what has allowed the fallen beings to create the artificial money system is war. What we have today is a wartime economy.

> O Saint Germain, in love we claim,
> our right to bring your violet flame,
> from you Above, to us below,
> it is an all-transforming flow.

> **O Saint Germain, what love you bring,**
> **it truly makes all matter sing,**
> **your violet flame does all restore,**
> **with you we are becoming more.**

4. Saint Germain, awaken people to the reality that the wartime economy began with medieval kings who wanted to expand their territory. They needed to raise money for war beyond what could be produced by their citizens.

O Saint Germain, I love you so,
my aura filled with violet glow,
my chakras filled with violet fire,
I am your cosmic amplifier.

**O Saint Germain, what love you bring,
it truly makes all matter sing,
your violet flame does all restore,
with you we are becoming more.**

5. Saint Germain, awaken people to the reality that producing weapons for war will not grow the overall economy. If you create the production capability to produce weapons and an army, you are taking value away from your country's economy.

O Saint Germain, I am now free,
your violet flame is therapy,
transform all hang-ups in my mind,
as inner peace I surely find.

**O Saint Germain, what love you bring,
it truly makes all matter sing,
your violet flame does all restore,
with you we are becoming more.**

6. Saint Germain, awaken people to the reality that the only way to produce weapons is to disconnect money from the exchange of real goods, giving money intrinsic value.

O Saint Germain, my body pure,
your violet flame for all is cure,
consume the cause of all disease,
and therefore I am all at ease.

**O Saint Germain, what love you bring,
it truly makes all matter sing,
your violet flame does all restore,
with you we are becoming more.**

7. Saint Germain, awaken people to the reality that a leader can now create more money than the goods produced in his country. He can use that money to buy something that the normal production capacity cannot produce.

> O Saint Germain, I'm karma-free,
> the past no longer burdens me,
> a brand new opportunity,
> I am in Christic unity.

**O Saint Germain, what love you bring,
it truly makes all matter sing,
your violet flame does all restore,
with you we are becoming more.**

8. Saint Germain, awaken people to the reality that war always produces a deficit in the economy. The fallen beings then cover over the deficit with the money they have created out of nothing, but this pushes the debt into the future.

> O Saint Germain, we are now one,
> I am for you a violet sun,
> as we transform this planet earth,
> your Golden Age is given birth.

> O Saint Germain, what love you bring,
> it truly makes all matter sing,
> your violet flame does all restore,
> with you we are becoming more.

9. Saint Germain, awaken people to the reality that there are different classes of fallen beings. Some have a primitive quest for power, and they were the kings. The more sophisticated fallen beings became the bankers.

> O Saint Germain, the earth is free,
> from burden of duality,
> in oneness we bring what is best,
> your Golden Age is manifest.

> O Saint Germain, what love you bring,
> it truly makes all matter sing,
> your violet flame does all restore,
> with you we are becoming more.

Part 4

1. Divine Director, awaken people to the reality that the kings were often controlled by fallen beings in the emotional realm or the mental realm. The bankers were controlled by fallen beings in the identity realm who had a hidden agenda.

> Divine Director, I now see,
> the world is unreality,
> in my heart I now truly feel,
> the Spirit is all that is real.

**Divine Director, send the light,
from blindness clear my inner sight,
my vision free, my vision clear,
your guidance is forever here.**

2. Divine Director, awaken people to the reality that the more sophisticated fallen beings took advantage of the more primitive fallen beings to create an economy that furthers their ends.

Divine Director, vision give,
in clarity I want to live,
I now behold my plan Divine,
the plan that is uniquely mine.

**Divine Director, send the light,
from blindness clear my inner sight,
my vision free, my vision clear,
your guidance is forever here.**

3. Divine Director, awaken people to the reality that the kings waging war and the bankers making money were just pawns in a larger game, and this game was played by the fallen beings in the identity realm.

Divine Director, show in me,
the ego games, and set me free,
help me escape the ego's cage,
to help bring in the golden age.

**Divine Director, send the light,
from blindness clear my inner sight,
my vision free, my vision clear,
your guidance is forever here.**

4. Divine Director, awaken people to the reality that the fallen beings in the identity realm want to prove God wrong by getting self-aware co-creators to misuse their free will to the point where they destroy themselves, rather than grow in self-awareness. They do this by creating war and by creating debt.

> Divine Director, I'm with you,
> my vision one, no longer two,
> as karma's veil you do disperse,
> I see a whole new universe.
>
> **Divine Director, send the light,**
> **from blindness clear my inner sight,**
> **my vision free, my vision clear,**
> **your guidance is forever here.**

5. Divine Director, awaken people to the reality that debt neutralizes the natural Law of a Multiplied Return by creating an artificial economy. It is a downward spiral because it is constantly pushing a snowball of debt in front of it that becomes bigger and bigger until it can no longer be paid back.

> Divine Director, I go up,
> electric light now fills my cup,
> consume in me all shadows old,
> bestow on me a vision bold.
>
> **Divine Director, send the light,**
> **from blindness clear my inner sight,**
> **my vision free, my vision clear,**
> **your guidance is forever here.**

6. Divine Director, awaken people to the reality that the fallen beings are not concerned about having the debt paid back. They want the nations to continue to pay the interest because the interest is what they can use to grow their own wealth and power.

> Divine Director, heart of gold,
> my sacred labor I unfold,
> o blessed Guru, I now see,
> where my own plan is taking me.
>
> **Divine Director, send the light,**
> **from blindness clear my inner sight,**
> **my vision free, my vision clear,**
> **your guidance is forever here.**

7. Divine Director, awaken people to the reality that money is created out of nothing, but the interest is taken from the people and their labor. The bankers provide something that has no intrinsic value, and they get something back that has intrinsic value because it is tied to people's labor.

> Divine Director, by your grace,
> in grander scheme I find my place,
> my individual flame I see,
> uniqueness God has given me.
>
> **Divine Director, send the light,**
> **from blindness clear my inner sight,**
> **my vision free, my vision clear,**
> **your guidance is forever here.**

8. Divine Director, awaken people to the reality that the fallen beings are indirectly reaping the fruits of peoples' labor. The feudal system of the Middle Ages is still in existence, only it has become hidden through the veil of the complexity of the money system.

> Divine Director, vision one,
> I see that I AM God's own Sun,
> with your direction so Divine,
> I am now letting my light shine.
>
> **Divine Director, send the light,**
> **from blindness clear my inner sight,**
> **my vision free, my vision clear,**
> **your guidance is forever here.**

9. Divine Director, awaken people to the reality that behind this is the larger rationale of creating a self-destructive economy that decreases the amount of wealth and, thereby, serves the end of causing a self-destructive spiral.

> Divine Director, what a gift,
> to be a part of Spirit's lift,
> to raise mankind out of the night,
> to bask in Spirit's loving sight.
>
> **Divine Director, send the light,**
> **from blindness clear my inner sight,**
> **my vision free, my vision clear,**
> **your guidance is forever here.**

Sealing

In the name of the I AM THAT I AM, I accept that Archangel Michael, Astrea and Shiva form an impenetrable shield around myself and all constructive people, sealing us from all fear-based energies in all four octaves. I accept that the Light of God is consuming and transforming all fear-based energies that make up the forces behind war!

14 | WAR AND THE QUEST FOR POWER

I am the Ascended Master Mother Mary. In this discourse I will talk about another of the spiritual causes of war. This time I will talk about the quest for raw power. Although I have mentioned some of the aspects of the quest for power in my previous discourses, I want to give you more depth and detail.

When you look at history, you will see that there have been empires, there have been certain leaders, that have been driven by this quest to extend their power. Sometimes, it has been mixed with a quest for material gain. Other times, it has been mixed with the desire to gain territory, to conquer territory. In some cases, it has been mixed with the clever use of ideas, such as the desire to spread a certain religion or a certain political ideology. It has even been clothed in the seemingly benign quest for extending civilization.

Look at some of the leaders who have been driven by this desire for raw power, this quest to extend their power. You quickly see that even though they may seem to have great power over men or power to build empires, they are actually not free in themselves.

The spiritual realm and the material world

There is something you need to understand about what it means to be a human being in embodiment on earth. Earth is a quite dense planet. With this, I mean that the energies on earth are quite dense compared to the energies in the spiritual realm.

If you are a being who has some inner memory, some inner sense of the reality of the spiritual realm, then you will know that the energies on earth are quite dense. You will know and feel that everything you do in the material world is limited, that there is an opposition, that there is a resistance. It is difficult on a planet as dense as earth to have a free flow of creative energies because the collective consciousness opposes transcendence, which is the essence of creativity.

Where this is important is in understanding how the contrast between the freedom of the spiritual realm and the restrictions of the material realm can give rise to various desires. You may be mature enough to realize that your inner longing for something more is really a longing for the spiritual realm. You then direct your attention towards raising your consciousness and attuning it to the spiritual realm and also winning your ascension so you do not have to re-embody in the dense material world. When you do this, you will have a desire that cannot be fulfilled in the material realm because it will not be fulfilled until you exit the material realm permanently through the ascension. Nevertheless, it is not a longing that will be obsessive-compulsive. It will not swallow up your life. It will not prevent you from engaging in active life on earth or seeking the fulfillment of the desires you have concerning life on earth.

How longing for freedom can cause rebellion

There is an old tendency to say that your physical body and its desires are an enemy of your spiritual growth. This we of the ascended masters do not teach. What we do teach is the healthy balance where you do not allow the desires related to the material realm to run your life, to take over your life, to become insatiable desires. When you do have the inner memory that the goal of life is to ascend, then you can accomplish this fairly easily.

If you do not quite have the maturity to know that there is a spiritual quest, then it is possible that your inner knowing that there is something more than the earth can give you a desire for freedom, a desire to rebel against the restrictions you feel on earth. This is what you see in some revolutionaries, even in many of the young people who were part of what they call the sixties, the youth movement, the youth rebellion against authority.

These people had such a quest for freedom, but because they did not quite understand how to direct it towards raising their consciousness, they became ensnared by the desire to rebel against authority. They thought it was the outer authority, such as the institutions of society, that were restricting them. They did not understand that it was actually the denseness of the energies in the material realm that were the greatest restriction.

How extreme desires give rise to addictions

If you are at an even lower level of consciousness, you may still have some inner memory of the spiritual realm. This gives you a quest for infinity, for something beyond the finite world.

Because you do not understand that this is a spiritual quest (a spiritual path, a raising of your consciousness) you direct it towards finding some ultimate fulfillment of the desires that relate to the material realm.

You will see many people in today's world who are pursuing such an extreme fulfillment of desires. Look at how many people are allowing their lives to be swallowed up by the quest for material goods, material possessions. Look how many people are completely focused on making money, even to the point of making more money than they could personally spend for the rest of their lifetime. Look at how many people are pursuing the quest for sex, for sexual conquest. So many other of these desires can be taken to the extreme, and any time you take any desire related to the finite world and pursue it with the desire to gain something infinite through the fulfillment of a finite desire, then you will have an addiction.

An addiction is when you are seeking a goal that cannot be attained through the means you are using. A drug addict may be seeking some inner experience. During the 1960s, many of the people who could have been forerunners for raising the collective consciousness allowed themselves to be caught up in the drug culture. Their quest for freedom, their quest for spiritual experiences, was replaced by this misguided quest of seeking them through chemical experiences. Even though a chemical reaction in the brain can lead to a state of consciousness that is beyond your normal state of consciousness, this is not spiritual freedom. Spiritual freedom is when you attain a higher state of consciousness without any material means. You attain it through your inner growth in consciousness.

When you are seeking an infinite experience through finite means, you cannot ever reach the goal. You may have an experience that is beyond your normal level of consciousness, but your brain will quickly adapt to the introduction of this chemical substance. Now, it takes more chemical substance to have the same experience again, and this can go on, not indefinitely, but until your entire life is swallowed up in either being affected by these chemicals or longing to have the experience.

You may also pursue an infinite experience through sex, but again it becomes an addiction because you can never quite reach that ultimate experience. You are always chasing the pot of gold at the end of the rainbow. It is never quite enough, no matter how much sex you have or how intense it is. What I am seeking to point out here is that many people have this desire for something ultimate, something infinite, but when you seek to fulfill it through finite means, you end up in an addiction, whereby I mean your life becomes a self-reinforcing downward spiral that swallows up your attention and energy.

Civilizations and the quest for power

There are a few people in the history of the world who have not been fallen beings but who have been sucked into the desire for power. They have been misled into thinking that, by pursuing conquests in some form, they could establish a higher civilization or even God's kingdom on earth. This quest for the Utopia, the ideal society, has caused some people to be drawn into this quest for power. The vast majority of the people who have been caught up in this quest for power have, indeed, been the fallen beings. There is an entire class of fallen beings who are completely trapped in this quest for power. You need to understand that this quest can never be fulfilled. It will never be enough power.

You may say: "But what if they managed to take over and control the entire earth?" You have seen in the past some empires that thought they had conquered the whole world. In the Roman civilization, they thought there was nothing more to the world than what they had conquered. Of course, their knowledge of the world was limited, but they had conquered vast territories. As you will see from the Roman emperors, it was not enough.

You will also see the mechanical aspect that the Roman Empire was financially dependent on new conquest. When it became difficult to find new conquest, at least new conquest that paid a healthy dividend, so to speak, then the Roman Empire could not sustain itself financially.

You have in the modern world seen at least two empires, the Nazi Empire and the Communist Empire, that were also aimed at world conquest. You may say that they achieved some dominion over vast territories. What if, with the further development of technology and weapons, there one day was a single power that would attain world dominion? Would it be enough for those who were the leaders of that world power if they could sit there in their seat of government and know that one person or a few persons had total power over the entire planet? Would that be enough for them?

In duality, nothing is ever enough

You need to understand that it would not be enough. When you go into the duality consciousness, nothing will ever be enough.

Even fallen beings started out as self-aware co-creators or self-aware angels. When you are a spiritual being, you can have a sense of touching the hem of God's garment, touching the hem of the garment of Christ, as the woman who touched Jesus when he was walking through the crowd. By touching the infinite, you can have a sense that it is enough. You are filled. You are satisfied. You are whole. You are at peace. Once you go into duality, you cannot touch the infinite, you must now seek to fulfill desires through the finite world, and this can never give you that sense that you are full. Once you go into duality, you are engaged in the impossible quest.

Going into duality is one thing, and it may take you into an impossible quest of seeking to fulfill your personal desires, but when you go into the fallen consciousness, another psychological mechanism comes into play. There is a difference between having personal desires for what you want to experience, own, have or do and then being in the fallen consciousness where you want to achieve a goal that is outside yourself.

Imagine that you are walking through the marketplace, and you feel hungry. You find a suitable looking eating place. You go in and order a meal and you eat until you are full. This is a goal that is relatively easy to fulfill. Of course, in a few hours you will be hungry again, but you can be full because it is only yourself that needs to be filled. Now imagine that you go into the marketplace, and you desire for all people in the entire world to be full. This would be a much more difficult desire to fulfill, would it not? It might very well go beyond your powers.

This is essentially what the fallen beings are seeking to do. They are always seeking to attain a goal that is outside themselves and their own personal powers. This goal always involves some kind of force, and as I have explained in my previous discourses, any impulse you create will have an opposite. Every action has a reaction. This makes it impossible that the fallen ones could ever attain their goals.

They do not see this, and therefore, they become addicted to the fulfillment of their goals and seeking that fulfillment by forcing other human beings to comply with whatever vision the fallen beings have of how their goals can be fulfilled. If they have locked themselves on the idea that the spreading of the ideology of communism will fulfill their quest for power, then they cannot rest until that goal has been fulfilled.

Why the fallen beings have embodied on earth

I know there are those who say that, with the advent of modern technology, the world has become smaller. It is easier to travel; it is easier to communicate. Some believe that it will be easier today to achieve an empire, a one-world government, that can control the entire world.

You might ask yourself why the ascended masters allowed fallen beings to embody on earth. As I have attempted to explain, once the collective consciousness on a planet goes below a certain level, the inhabitants of that planet are no longer open to the direct teachings from the ascended masters. They, therefore, need substitute teachers who can take their tendencies to such an extreme that people can see the futility of it. The fallen beings are, so to speak, the perfect teachers for teaching people how the dualistic games do not work. The fallen beings will immediately upon arriving on a planet start taking everything towards extremes, and therefore it becomes easier for the original inhabitants of the planet to see that this is simply too much.

Does that mean we would allow the fallen beings to embody on any planet where the inhabitants had gone into a downward spiral? It does not. There are certain conditions that need to be fulfilled, and one of them relates to the size of the planet. You could come up with a mathematical equation that would show the relationship between the size of the earth and the capabilities of the human body. You could even make an equation that compared the size of the earth to the capabilities of the human brain: its ability to see, to understand, to

14 | War and the Quest for Power

organize information. If you did this, you would see that there is a precise correlation that would make it impossible for any power controlled by one or a few human beings to physically dominate and control this planet. The world may have become smaller because of technology, but it will never become small enough that human beings from a centralized vantage point on this planet can control the entire planet and all of the people upon it.

The fallen beings may have a dream that they are doing something benign by establishing this utopian, advanced civilization that will finally bring peace and prosperity to this planet, but it can never be achieved as the fallen ones envision it. It can never be achieved through human, physical, material means. It could be achieved by spiritual means, by all people being connected to the Holy Spirit within, being directed by that Holy Spirit to work on a greater vision. You cannot create a vision with the human mind, the mind trapped in duality, of an ideal society and then manifest that vision as a physical reality on the planet. You cannot extend your control of this planet to the entire planet through material means. It would be impossible, due to the ratio between the size of the earth and the capabilities of the human brain and body.

This planet was chosen carefully in order to allow the incarnation of fallen beings. We knew that there was a limit to how far they could go in their quest for conquest and raw power. As spiritual people, you need to be aware of this. You need to see that there are certain fallen beings who are completely trapped in their quest for power. You need to see that it is an impossible quest that can never be fulfilled. You need to give up your own desire for some benign power to control the entire planet. There are many spiritual people who have been drawn in by the religious or political ideologies and thought systems created by the fallen beings in order to justify their quest for power, their search for this utopian society. I will talk more about these in a coming discourse, but what I want you to realize here is that it is all camouflage.

Ruling through raw power or false ideas

There are two main classes of fallen beings. One class is completely caught up in this quest for power. They want to have power for their own sake. They want to prove that they are the most powerful, the most superior beings. There is another class of fallen beings who are not primarily seeking personal power. They are seeking to prove God wrong. Both of these classes of fallen beings have created and used these epic philosophies that portray the world as being in an epic battle between good and evil.

In many cases, the more sophisticated fallen beings who are seeking to prove God wrong are using the fallen beings who are driven by a quest for power. The more sophisticated fallen beings are saying that the power-hungry fallen beings are evil, are bad, are negative. You, the spiritual people, should join themselves in working against the power-hungry fallen beings in various ways. This may be anything from fighting them directly to fighting them with ideas. Both classes of fallen beings are pursuing an impossible quest, and they are driven by an illusion.

What I am addressing in this discourse is those who are driven by the illusion that, if they had some ultimate state of power, then that would be enough for them. Even if the fallen beings or one fallen being managed to conquer the entire earth and have control over the entire earth, it would not be enough for that person. He or she would then instantly begin to say: "But earth is not the only planet. I need to conquer the entire universe." Of course, you know very well that the universe is so big that you could not even physically travel to the farthest reaches of the universe in a lifetime. Even if time slows down during space travel, you still could not travel very far in a lifetime. The desire to conquer the entire universe is obviously an impossible quest, but as I have attempted to explain to you, even the desire to conquer the earth is physically impossible.

You need to see this so that you are not sucked in by the fallen beings and their quest for the impossible. You also need to make the calls that the fallen beings who are driven by this impossible quest for raw power are judged by the mind of Christ and that those who will not abandon the quest for power are removed from the earth. Right now, you see many conflicts going on in, for example, Africa and the Middle East. There is an element here of the desire for material gain, but there is a deeper element of the desire for raw power and the willingness to do anything in order to attain that power.

The Muslim religion is in subtle ways perverted by the fallen beings and their mindset. Under the guise of the seemingly benign goal of extending Islam to the entire world, there is a quest for raw power. This was inserted in this religion at a very early stage because the mindset was there in the Arabic culture where Islam emerged. The reason why the mindset was there is that the Arabic culture and the Jewish culture have for thousands of years had a collective consciousness that allowed many fallen beings to embody there.

Calling for the removal of a state of consciousness

There are other planets that have actually self-destructed due to the warring of the people on those planets. Some of the beings from those planets have been allowed to embody on earth and many have embodied in the Middle East. These are what we have sometimes called "laggard" beings because they are lagging behind the evolution of the entire universe. They are not willing to give up their quest for raw power, and they can only embody on planets that are not part of the upward spiral of the material universe.

These planets are either in a downward spiral, or they are moving far slower than the rest of the universe. Earth is a planet where there is currently an upward spiral, but the upward spiral of earth is still behind the upward spiral created by the universe as a whole. This is why such beings can continue to embody here. You, as the spiritual people, have a right to make the calls that these laggard beings will be faced with the choice to either transcend their consciousness or be removed from this planet. They can then embody in other places or go into the astral plane for some time.

It is your right to look at the earth and say: "There are obviously people who will not abandon war and conflict. They are creating conflict where none exists. They are seeking to draw as many people as possible into this meaningless conflict, and there is no realistic hope that they will end this in the foreseeable future. Therefore, we who are the spiritual people choose to transcend that consciousness, to abandon it. From our higher state of consciousness, we choose to demand that those who will not abandon this consciousness will be removed from the earth so that this planet can move higher in its evolution." This is your right, my beloved, as spiritual people on earth. You are not doing this in anger. You are not doing this with hatred of these laggard evolutions and their quest for power. You are simply seeing that what is going on, for example, in the Middle East, is not an expression of who you are as a spiritual being.

14 | War and the Quest for Power

Why you are in embodiment right now

I wish to address a very subtle state of consciousness. I have said that those who are more mature lifestreams will know that their desire for infinity is really a desire for the spiritual realm. There are many spiritual people who have been led into believing that the main focus of their life should be to qualify for their ascension so that they can get out of this planet with all of its problems.

I am in no way discouraging you from striving towards your ascension, but there is a balance to be found. There are many spiritual people in embodiment today who have the potential to qualify for their ascension in this lifetime, but you see, you had that potential before you came into embodiment. Why did you choose to come into embodiment at this particular time? You did so because you knew, first of all, that, by qualifying for your ascension, you would raise the earth. You also knew that, while you are in embodiment, you have the potential to do something that will make a difference.

I am not here talking about going out fighting some battle but I am talking about raising your awareness and claiming your right to be a spiritual person in embodiment. I am talking about claiming your right to look at what is happening on this planet and say: "This activity is not acceptable to me. It is not an expression of my state of consciousness. Because I have transcended it, I have a right to demand that it be removed from the earth."

You are not here working against specific people or specific groups of people. As I have explained, everything is an expression of consciousness. There are certain people who are on this impossible quest for power, whose lives are completely swallowed up by it. I am not here talking about singling out such people and going into some kind of anger or hatred against these people. I am talking about looking beyond the people and seeing that their minds are taken over by a non-personal state of consciousness, even by non-personal beings in the emotional, mental or identity octaves.

When you see this, you realize that you are not opposing other people. You are not even opposing the lower state of consciousness. You are separating yourself from it. In doing so, you are claiming your right to demand that this state of consciousness be removed from the earth. This means that you give the authority to the ascended masters and the angels to confront the people who are blinded by this state of consciousness.

What happens when you call forth the judgment

Right now, these people are blinded by that state of consciousness. This means they cannot see that there is an alternative. They cannot even see that there is something outside of that state of consciousness. They think this is the *only* way to look at life. When you call for this consciousness to be removed and when you call for the Judgment of Christ upon those who are trapped in this consciousness, you are giving us the authority to confront these people.

This does not mean that we go in and angrily judge them. It means we go in, and we show them that there is an alternative to their state of consciousness. We are actually giving them a choice they do not have right now.

You may say that when you call forth the judgment and when we confront a lifestream, are we not violating their free will? Nay, because on a planet you do have individual free will, but you are also living on a unit with many other beings who have individual free will. Your individual free will is individual and free when it comes to fulfilling your own desires. As soon as you begin doing something that is aimed at forcing the will of other people, you are making yourself subject to the will of the whole.

When the fallen beings started embodying here, it was because the majority of the people on earth were not able or willing to listen to the ascended masters. This meant the fallen beings were free to do whatever they wanted, if they could deceive people into supporting their quest for power. If no one protests, then the fallen beings are literally given free reign on a planet, and they can wreak havoc as they have done many, many times. When no one is objecting, people are silently accepting what the fallen beings are doing. Silence means consent. When a critical mass of people awaken themselves and look at a certain state of consciousness and say: "This is not acceptable to us," then their choice now has an impact on the will of the collective.

We are not *forcing* the fallen beings because the fallen beings are seeking to force others. When you go into the mindset of deliberately seeking to force the will of other people, then the law makes it legal for us to go in and confront these people with the fact that there is an alternative to their state of consciousness. Again, we are not forcing the fallen beings. We are actually giving them a choice they do not have right now where they see no alternative to the fallen consciousness. We confront them with a choice.

This does not, in most cases, happen at the level of people's conscious minds. It happens at inner levels, below the level of conscious awareness. We confront the lifestream with a choice between its present state of consciousness and a higher state of consciousness, and then we allow that lifestream to choose between the two. Of course, if it chooses to remain in its present state of consciousness and refuses the higher state of consciousness, then the consequence can in many cases be that the being is taken out of embodiment either immediately or fairly quickly.

There are also some cases where, due to complicated factors that I do not want to go into here, a fallen lifestream has received the judgment but is allowed to stay in embodiment for some time. This is mainly because there are some people who are following that fallen being and they need to see certain things outplayed. In that case, the fallen being after it dies physically will not be allowed to reincarnate on earth. This was the case, for example, with Hitler, Stalin and Mao.

How the angels confront and neutralize demons

There is a very complex equation that is determining which lifestreams can be allowed to embody on earth. It is very much tied to the choices made by the people in embodiment. You who are the more mature spiritual people can have a major impact on this planet by raising your own consciousness and then by making the choice that you have a right to demand that a certain lower state of consciousness be removed from the earth. Once we have confronted the fallen lifestreams with the need to abandon a certain state of consciousness, we also have the authority to go into, for example, the astral plane and bind the demons and entities who never had self-awareness.

Archangel Michael and the other Archangels have legions of angels who are specially trained for this task. You may have seen or read the old stories from the Bible about the angels fighting a war in heaven against the devil and his seed. This was not a physical war as you envision it on earth. These were illustrations given based on the consciousness of the people, but there was certainly a confrontation between the angels of light and the fallen angels, the fallen beings. This did not take place in Heaven because, as we have explained in other books [See *Cosmology of Evil*], there can be no conflict in the spiritual realm. The real conflict took place in a previous sphere that was not ascended.

There is also a confrontation that takes place in the three higher octaves of the material world. This confrontation is ongoing. When a sufficient number of human beings in embodiment have made the calls for a certain state of consciousness to be bound, then the Archangels can send their angels into, for example, the astral plane. They will come across a certain demon, and with the spiritual tools that they have, they will be able to bind that demon and thereby neutralize it. They will then, through a complicated process that they have been specially trained to perform, liberate the energies that are trapped.

A demon that has never had self-awareness is essentially a vortex of fear-based energy, like a maelstrom or a tornado. As long as that energy is swirling, it has a momentum that would be beyond human power to stop, just as you cannot stop a tornado by going into it with your physical body. The angels have been trained to go into such a spiral and gradually stop its rotation. Once the rotation has been stopped, then the energies can be separated out so that they no longer have that collective magnetic effect that actually creates the swirling movement. Then, the energies can be separated. In many cases, a demon may be a combination of the perversions of several of the spiritual rays, perhaps even all seven spiritual rays. The angels for a given ray will go in and take the energies that are a perversion of their ray, and then they will raise the vibration of these energies.

The angels and archangels have the power to right now go in and instantly dissolve all of the fear-based energies associated with planet earth in all four octaves. As I have explained, we do not have the authority. There has to be a certain amount of energy invoked by people in embodiment before we can dissolve a certain amount of demons in the astral plane or other forces in the mental and identity octaves.

The victories achieved through invoking light

There is a proportional relationship between the energies you invoke while you are in physical embodiment and what the angels are allowed to use in terms of purifying energies in the other octaves. It is not so that there is a one-to-one relationship. The energies that you invoke are multiplied. There are various multiplication factors that we can apply, and this is, again, a very complex scenario that I do not wish to explain in detail, for it is not really significant for your work.

What *is* significant is that you understand that every invocation you give is multiplied many, many times, and it has a tremendous effect. The trick is, of course, that the effect is in the three higher octaves, which most people do not see. Therefore, you do not see a direct, physical result of your efforts. I know very well that we are asking you to give invocations based on a certain amount of faith that this will work. In many cases, you may give invocations for a long time without seeing a direct physical result; yet, I can assure you that there have been physical results.

The students of the ascended masters over the past century have attained many victories by invoking spiritual light through decrees and invocations. Of course, you can look at the earth, and you do not know what difference it made. There were many students of Saint Germain who gave violet flame decrees during the Second World War. Had it not been for them, the war would have lasted several years longer and millions of more people would have died. Nazism would ultimately have been defeated anyway, but it was possible that communism, the Soviet Union, would have gained even more power after the war.

Likewise, many students of the ascended masters gave decrees for the fall of communism. Without this, communism would not have collapsed when it did. It would have lasted longer. There was even the potential that the Cold War would become a hot war, even with nuclear exchanges. The fact that the Soviet Union collapsed without a third world war was a direct effect of the many decrees given by ascended master students during the 60s, 70s, 80s, and early 90s. Many, many other physical conditions would have been far worse had it not been for the calls made.

"The prayer of a just man availeth much," as it says in the Bible. The same, of course, goes for a just woman. A just man and a just woman means one who has begun to raise his or her consciousness above duality. Only when you have transcended a certain state of consciousness, do you gain the full authority to make the calls for its removal from the earth. That is why Jesus told you to first remove the beam from your own eye. Then you will see how to remove the splinter from the eyes of your brother because you will not start fighting your brother.

You will start seeing beyond the person and see that the person is trapped in a state of consciousness. You know that it is the state of consciousness that needs to be removed. You also know that it is not you who can fight or remove it. It is only the angels and the ascended masters. You see your correct relationship to us, namely that you are a partner with us. You do not think that you are the doer, that you have to go out and fight other people or fight a state of consciousness.

The difference between oneness and sameness

This is a subtle outcome of the quest for power. There is a certain desire, even among some spiritual students, to be the prince on the white horse, to be the knight in shining armor, who singlehandedly comes in and saves the damsel in distress or the entire community, the entire country or the entire world. There are people, who are not fallen beings, who have been trapped by this consciousness of wanting to be the hero who singlehandedly made a difference. Even Jesus and the Buddha did not singlehandedly make a difference. What good would it have done for Jesus to go around and give his teachings and perform miracles, if people had forgotten them as soon as he left physical embodiment? It was only the efforts of his disciples that spread the Christian movement and made it a movement with any significant impact.

No human being can singlehandedly change the world or save the world, but many individuals who see themselves as part of the Body of God on earth can make a decisive difference. Being part of the Body of God means that you know that there is a vertical oneness and a horizontal oneness. You see yourself as one with your I AM Presence and with the ascended masters above. You see yourself as one with your spiritual brothers and sisters below and ultimately with all people below. You stop seeing yourself in conflict or in opposition to other people. You stop seeing yourself as being different from other people. You stop seeking sameness.

I have talked about the fact that there are various philosophies that are created by the fallen beings in order to camouflage their quest for power and make it seem benign. What is it that the fallen beings are attempting to do? They are always attempting to establish one centralized control point, be it a government or an emperor or whatever it may be, even a religion. The fallen beings are driven to establish power through force. This means they have to control, and how do you attain control? By destroying or suppressing differences so that you create either a forced or even a voluntary sameness.

The whole idea that one religion needs to eradicate other religions and become the only religion on earth springs from the fallen mindset. God has no desire to see one religion dominate the earth. Jesus has no desire to see Christianity dominate the earth. We of the ascended masters are not seeking sameness. Why not? Because we have become ascended masters by daring to acknowledge and express our divine individuality. We know that our divine individuality is unique. I know that I am a unique individual being. So is Jesus, so is Saint Germain and so is every human being in embodiment.

God created diversity, not sameness

We are seeking to raise every human being up to where that person can express his or her divine individuality. We are not seeking to establish sameness, my beloved. We are not even seeking to create an ascended master religion that will dominate the earth. We celebrate differences. The fallen beings want sameness because it allows them to control. It allows them to suppress the individual creativity that is the greatest threat to their power over the earth. Sameness is a sign of the fallen consciousness; diversity is an expression of the God consciousness.

God has no desire to see a planet with seven billion people who all believe the same and act the same way. God has created those people as individual expressions of its own being, and it wants to see them express their individuality, rather than suppress it. The fallen beings want you to suppress your individuality or express the human individuality, which puts you in conflict with others. When you are expressing your divine individuality, there is no conflict between yourself and others. You are not threatened by others and they are not threatened by you. You are complementing each other, as the different flowers on a spring meadow complement each other. Surely, it can be beautiful to have a spring meadow filled with yellow dandelions, but does there not quickly come a point where the human mind tires of the conformity and looks for something different? Is it not more interesting to look at a meadow with many different colors of flowers?

What you have seen in history is how the fallen beings have been driven by this quest to establish one dominant religion, one dominant political ideology, one dominant nation, one dominant civilization, one dominant corporation or one dominant army. Have they ever been successful? Nay, because when one group of fallen beings attempts to create one dominant religion, it is inevitable that another group of fallen beings will create another religion to rival the first one.

What you see on earth is a quest for power perpetrated by the fallen beings. Even though the aim of this quest for power is to establish one dominant force, you should not be fooled into thinking that the fallen beings are united in this quest. The fallen beings will, by the very nature of the dualistic consciousness, always be divided into at least two rivaling factions. The power struggle that has been going on is nothing more than the rivalry between at least two groups of fallen beings.

They may each claim that they are benign and that they are working for some ultimate cause. Each of them is completely wrong. They are driven by an illusion. They may believe that they are working for God's cause by seeking to establish their religion as the dominant one, but it is a complete illusion. God's cause is not sameness. God's cause is not control. God's cause is individual creativity leading to individual beings attaining God consciousness.

You need to recognize that neither capitalism nor communism was a force established by God. Neither Islam nor Christianity, as they fought in the Crusades, was a cause established by God or Christ. This is nothing more than the rivalry of fallen beings. None of them could ever win. Even if they could, it would not be God's cause or God's kingdom that was established on earth. It would only be the kingdom of the fallen beings.

Free yourself from the ideas of the fallen beings

Is this what you want as a spiritual being? If it is not, then make an effort to free yourself from the very subtle ideas and beliefs that have been inserted by the fallen beings into the collective consciousness on this earth. If you have grown up on this planet, you will have been affected. You will have been programmed with some of these ideas, which is precisely why I will talk about them in my next discourse.

I have, once again, given you a lot to handle. I trust that as you work your way through this book, your experience will become an upward spiral where you will be able to handle more and more. Therefore, I can give you more and more advanced teachings. I look forward to returning with my next installment in this course on how to truly make love, not war.

15 | JUDGING THE INSATIABLE QUEST FOR POWER

In the name of the I AM THAT I AM, Jesus Christ, I call upon Mother Mary, Archangel Michael and Sanat Kumara for the judgment of the beings in all four octaves who have an insatiable desire for power. Awaken people to the reality that we are spiritual beings and that we can co-create a new future by working with the ascended masters. I especially call for ...

[Make your own calls here.]

Part 1

1. Archangel Michael, I call forth the judgment of Christ upon the fallen beings who are trapped in the insatiable desire for power, expressed as the quest for a higher civilization, a Utopia, based on centralized control. I demand that these beings be removed from the earth.

Archangel Michael, light so blue,
my heart has room for only you.
My mind is one, no longer two,
your love for me is ever true.

**Archangel Michael, you are here,
your light consumes all doubt and fear.
Your Presence is forever near,
you are to me so very dear.**

2. Archangel Michael, I call forth the judgment of Christ upon the consciousness and the fallen beings who will not see that it will never be enough power because in the duality consciousness, nothing can be enough. I demand that this consciousness and these beings be removed from the earth.

Archangel Michael, I will be,
all one with your reality.
No fear can hold me as I see,
this world no power has o'er me.

**Archangel Michael, you are here,
your light consumes all doubt and fear.
Your Presence is forever near,
you are to me so very dear.**

3. Archangel Michael, I call forth the judgment of Christ upon the consciousness and the fallen beings behind the Roman civilization and its attempt to conquer the world. I demand that this consciousness and these beings be removed from the earth.

> Archangel Michael, hold me tight,
> shatter now the darkest night.
> Clear my chakras with your light,
> restore to me my inner sight.
>
> **Archangel Michael, you are here,**
> **your light consumes all doubt and fear.**
> **Your Presence is forever near,**
> **you are to me so very dear.**

4. Archangel Michael, I call forth the judgment of Christ upon the consciousness and the fallen beings behind the Nazi empire. I demand that this consciousness and these beings be removed from the earth.

> Archangel Michael, now I stand,
> with you the light I do command.
> My heart I ever will expand,
> till highest truth I understand.
>
> **Archangel Michael, you are here,**
> **your light consumes all doubt and fear.**
> **Your Presence is forever near,**
> **you are to me so very dear.**

5. Archangel Michael, I call forth the judgment of Christ upon the consciousness and the fallen beings behind the Communist empire. I demand that this consciousness and these beings be removed from the earth.

> Archangel Michael, in my heart,
> from me you never will depart.
> Of hierarchy I am a part,
> I now accept a fresh new start.
>
> **Archangel Michael, you are here,
> your light consumes all doubt and fear.
> Your Presence is forever near,
> you are to me so very dear.**

6. Archangel Michael, I call forth the judgment of Christ upon the consciousness and the fallen beings who think that with the development of technology, they can conquer and control the world. I demand that this consciousness and these beings be removed from the earth.

> Archangel Michael, sword of blue,
> all darkness you are cutting through.
> My Christhood I do now pursue,
> discernment shows me what is true.
>
> **Archangel Michael, you are here,
> your light consumes all doubt and fear.
> Your Presence is forever near,
> you are to me so very dear.**

7. Archangel Michael, I call forth the judgment of Christ upon the consciousness and the fallen beings behind the quest to conquer something outside yourself through force. I demand that this consciousness and these beings be removed from the earth.

> Archangel Michael, in your wings,
> I now let go of lesser things.
> God's homing call in my heart rings,
> my heart with yours forever sings.
>
> **Archangel Michael, you are here,**
> **your light consumes all doubt and fear.**
> **Your Presence is forever near,**
> **you are to me so very dear.**

8. Archangel Michael, I call forth the judgment of Christ upon the consciousness and the fallen beings who are addicted to forcing other people to comply with a dualistic vision. I demand that this consciousness and these beings be removed from the earth.

> Archangel Michael, take me home,
> in higher spheres I want to roam.
> I am reborn from cosmic foam,
> my life is now a sacred poem.
>
> **Archangel Michael, you are here,**
> **your light consumes all doubt and fear.**
> **Your Presence is forever near,**
> **you are to me so very dear.**

9. Archangel Michael, I call forth the judgment of Christ upon the consciousness and the fallen beings who take everything towards an extreme in an unbalanced quest for power and control. I demand that this consciousness and these beings be removed from the earth.

Archangel Michael, light you are,
shining like the bluest star.
You are a cosmic avatar,
with you I will go very far.

**Archangel Michael, you are here,
your light consumes all doubt and fear.
Your Presence is forever near,
you are to me so very dear.**

Part 2

1. Sanat Kumara, I call forth the judgment of Christ upon the consciousness and the fallen beings and their dream that they are doing something benign, even doing something for God, by establishing a centralized civilization based on force and control. I demand that this consciousness and these beings be removed from the earth.

Sanat Kumara, Ruby Fire,
I seek my place in love's own choir,
with open hearts we sing your praise,
together we the earth do raise.

**Sanat Kumara, Ruby Ray,
bring to earth a higher way,
light this planet with your fire,
clothe her in a new attire.**

2. Sanat Kumara, I call forth the judgment of Christ upon the consciousness and the fallen beings who refuse to see that the earth is too big for human beings to control the entire planet. I demand that this consciousness and these beings be removed from the earth.

> Sanat Kumara, Ruby Fire,
> initiations I desire,
> I am for you an electrode,
> Shamballa is my true abode.

> **Sanat Kumara, Ruby Ray,**
> **bring to earth a higher way,**
> **light this planet with your fire,**
> **clothe her in a new attire.**

3. Sanat Kumara, I call forth the judgment of Christ upon the consciousness and the fallen beings who are completely trapped in their quest for power for the sake of their own sense of superiority. I demand that this consciousness and these beings be removed from the earth.

> Sanat Kumara, Ruby Fire,
> I follow path that you require,
> initiate me with your love,
> the open door for Holy Dove.

> **Sanat Kumara, Ruby Ray,**
> **bring to earth a higher way,**
> **light this planet with your fire,**
> **clothe her in a new attire.**

4. Sanat Kumara, I call forth the judgment of Christ upon the consciousness and the fallen beings who are seeking to prove God wrong by using an epic philosophy. I demand that this consciousness and these beings be removed from the earth.

> Sanat Kumara, Ruby Fire,
> your great example all inspire,
> with non-attachment and great mirth,
> we give the earth a true rebirth.

> **Sanat Kumara, Ruby Ray,**
> **bring to earth a higher way,**
> **light this planet with your fire,**
> **clothe her in a new attire.**

5. Sanat Kumara, I call forth the judgment of Christ upon the consciousness and the sophisticated fallen beings who portray the power-hungry fallen beings as evil in order to justify getting people to fight them. I demand that this consciousness and these beings be removed from the earth.

> Sanat Kumara, Ruby Fire,
> you are this planet's purifier,
> consume on earth all spirits dark,
> reveal the inner Spirit Spark.

> **Sanat Kumara, Ruby Ray,**
> **bring to earth a higher way,**
> **light this planet with your fire,**
> **clothe her in a new attire.**

6. Sanat Kumara, I call forth the judgment of Christ upon the consciousness and the fallen beings that seek to prevent people from seeing the illusion of the duality consciousness. I demand that this consciousness and these beings be removed from the earth.

> Sanat Kumara, Ruby Fire,
> you are a cosmic amplifier,
> the lower forces can't withstand,
> vibrations from Venusian band.
>
> **Sanat Kumara, Ruby Ray,**
> **bring to earth a higher way,**
> **light this planet with your fire,**
> **clothe her in a new attire.**

7. Sanat Kumara, I call forth the judgment of Christ upon the consciousness and the fallen beings who in their quest for power have started wars and conflicts. I demand that this consciousness and these beings be removed from the earth.

> Sanat Kumara, Ruby Fire,
> I am on earth your magnifier,
> the flow of love I do restore,
> my chakras are your open door.
>
> **Sanat Kumara, Ruby Ray,**
> **bring to earth a higher way,**
> **light this planet with your fire,**
> **clothe her in a new attire.**

8. Sanat Kumara, I call forth the judgment of Christ upon the consciousness and the fallen beings who use religion, especially Islam and Christianity, to justify war and conflict. I demand that this consciousness and these beings be removed from the earth.

Sanat Kumara, Ruby Fire,
Venusian song the multiplier,
as we your love reverberate,
the densest minds we penetrate.

**Sanat Kumara, Ruby Ray,
bring to earth a higher way,
light this planet with your fire,
clothe her in a new attire.**

9. Sanat Kumara, I call forth the judgment of Christ upon the consciousness and the laggard beings who embody in the Middle East and will not stop warring. I demand that this consciousness and these beings be removed from the earth.

Sanat Kumara, Ruby Fire,
you are for all the sanctifier,
the earth is now a holy place,
purified by cosmic grace.

**Sanat Kumara, Ruby Ray,
bring to earth a higher way,
light this planet with your fire,
clothe her in a new attire.**

Part 3

1. Archangel Michael, I call forth the judgment of Christ upon the laggard beings so they are faced with the choice to stop warring or be removed from this planet. I demand that this consciousness and these beings be removed from the earth.

> Archangel Michael, light so blue,
> my heart has room for only you.
> My mind is one, no longer two,
> your love for me is ever true.
>
> **Archangel Michael, you are here,**
> **your light consumes all doubt and fear.**
> **Your Presence is forever near,**
> **you are to me so very dear.**

2. Archangel Michael, I call forth the judgment of Christ upon the consciousness and the fallen beings who will not abandon war and conflict as a tool for gaining power and control. I demand that this consciousness and these beings be removed from the earth.

> Archangel Michael, I will be,
> all one with your reality.
> No fear can hold me as I see,
> this world no power has o'er me.
>
> **Archangel Michael, you are here,**
> **your light consumes all doubt and fear.**
> **Your Presence is forever near,**
> **you are to me so very dear.**

3. Archangel Michael, I call forth the judgment of Christ upon the consciousness and the fallen beings who create conflict in order to gain power and control. I demand that this consciousness and these beings be removed from the earth.

> Archangel Michael, hold me tight,
> shatter now the darkest night.
> Clear my chakras with your light,
> restore to me my inner sight.

> **Archangel Michael, you are here,**
> **your light consumes all doubt and fear.**
> **Your Presence is forever near,**
> **you are to me so very dear.**

4. Archangel Michael, cut free the spiritual people so they can see and transcend the fallen consciousness and demand that those who will not abandon this consciousness will be removed from the earth so that this planet can move higher in its evolution.

> Archangel Michael, now I stand,
> with you the light I do command.
> My heart I ever will expand,
> till highest truth I understand.

> **Archangel Michael, you are here,**
> **your light consumes all doubt and fear.**
> **Your Presence is forever near,**
> **you are to me so very dear.**

5. Archangel Michael, cut free the spiritual people to claim their right to look at what is happening on this planet and say: "This activity is not acceptable to me. It is not an expression of my state of consciousness. Because I have transcended it, I have a right to demand that it be removed from the earth."

> Archangel Michael, in my heart,
> from me you never will depart.
> Of hierarchy I am a part,
> I now accept a fresh new start.

> **Archangel Michael, you are here,**
> **your light consumes all doubt and fear.**
> **Your Presence is forever near,**
> **you are to me so very dear.**

6. Archangel Michael, cut free the spiritual people to see that we are not opposing other people or the lower state of consciousness. We are separating ourselves and claiming our right to demand that this state of consciousness be removed from the earth.

> Archangel Michael, sword of blue,
> all darkness you are cutting through.
> My Christhood I do now pursue,
> discernment shows me what is true.

> **Archangel Michael, you are here,**
> **your light consumes all doubt and fear.**
> **Your Presence is forever near,**
> **you are to me so very dear.**

7. Archangel Michael, by the authority of the Christ within me, I hereby give the authority to the ascended masters and the seven Archangels to confront the people who are blinded by the fallen state of consciousness.

> Archangel Michael, in your wings,
> I now let go of lesser things.
> God's homing call in my heart rings,
> my heart with yours forever sings.

> **Archangel Michael, you are here,**
> **your light consumes all doubt and fear.**
> **Your Presence is forever near,**
> **you are to me so very dear.**

8. Archangel Michael, cut free the spiritual people to see that if no one is objecting, people are silently accepting what the fallen beings are doing. Awaken them to their right to say: "This is not acceptable to us," whereby we give the ascended masters authority to step in.

> Archangel Michael, take me home,
> in higher spheres I want to roam.
> I am reborn from cosmic foam,
> my life is now a sacred poem.

> **Archangel Michael, you are here,**
> **your light consumes all doubt and fear.**
> **Your Presence is forever near,**
> **you are to me so very dear.**

9. Archangel Michael, awaken the spiritual people to see that because the fallen beings are deliberately seeking to force the will of other people, the law makes it legal for the ascended masters to confront these people with the fact that there is an alternative to their state of consciousness.

> Archangel Michael, light you are,
> shining like the bluest star.
> You are a cosmic avatar,
> with you I will go very far.
>
> **Archangel Michael, you are here,**
> **your light consumes all doubt and fear.**
> **Your Presence is forever near,**
> **you are to me so very dear.**

Part 4

1. Sanat Kumara, I call forth the judgment of Christ upon the consciousness and the fallen beings in the three higher octaves of earth. I demand that this consciousness and these beings be removed from the earth.

> Sanat Kumara, Ruby Fire,
> I seek my place in love's own choir,
> with open hearts we sing your praise,
> together we the earth do raise.

**Sanat Kumara, Ruby Ray,
bring to earth a higher way,
light this planet with your fire,
clothe her in a new attire.**

2. Sanat Kumara, I demand that the seven archangels send your legions to clear out all perverted energies of the seven rays that form vortexes in the four octaves of earth.

Sanat Kumara, Ruby Fire,
initiations I desire,
I am for you an electrode,
Shamballa is my true abode.

**Sanat Kumara, Ruby Ray,
bring to earth a higher way,
light this planet with your fire,
clothe her in a new attire.**

3. Sanat Kumara, awaken the spiritual people to see our correct relationship with the ascended masters, so that we can collectively invoke enough energy for the Archangels to remove all fallen beings and demons of war and power from the earth.

Sanat Kumara, Ruby Fire,
I follow path that you require,
initiate me with your love,
the open door for Holy Dove.

**Sanat Kumara, Ruby Ray,
bring to earth a higher way,
light this planet with your fire,
clothe her in a new attire.**

15 | Judging the Insatiable Quest for Power

4. Sanat Kumara, cut free the spiritual people from the desire to be the prince on the white horse, to be the knight in shining armor, who saves the world.

> Sanat Kumara, Ruby Fire,
> your great example all inspire,
> with non-attachment and great mirth,
> we give the earth a true rebirth.
>
> **Sanat Kumara, Ruby Ray,**
> **bring to earth a higher way,**
> **light this planet with your fire,**
> **clothe her in a new attire.**

5. Sanat Kumara, awaken the spiritual people to see that we are all part of the Body of God on earth when we achieve vertical oneness and horizontal oneness. We are one with the ascended masters above and one with all people below.

> Sanat Kumara, Ruby Fire,
> you are this planet's purifier,
> consume on earth all spirits dark,
> reveal the inner Spirit Spark.
>
> **Sanat Kumara, Ruby Ray,**
> **bring to earth a higher way,**
> **light this planet with your fire,**
> **clothe her in a new attire.**

6. Sanat Kumara, I call forth the judgment of Christ upon the consciousness and the fallen beings and their quest to establish control through sameness. I demand that this consciousness and these beings be removed from the earth.

> Sanat Kumara, Ruby Fire,
> you are a cosmic amplifier,
> the lower forces can't withstand,
> vibrations from Venusian band.

> **Sanat Kumara, Ruby Ray,**
> **bring to earth a higher way,**
> **light this planet with your fire,**
> **clothe her in a new attire.**

7. Sanat Kumara, I call forth the judgment of Christ upon the consciousness and the fallen beings promoting the idea that one religion or ideology needs to eradicate all competitors. I demand that this consciousness and these beings be removed from the earth.

> Sanat Kumara, Ruby Fire,
> I am on earth your magnifier,
> the flow of love I do restore,
> my chakras are your open door.

> **Sanat Kumara, Ruby Ray,**
> **bring to earth a higher way,**
> **light this planet with your fire,**
> **clothe her in a new attire.**

8. Sanat Kumara, I call forth the judgment of Christ upon the consciousness and the fallen beings who are on a quest to establish a dominant religion, ideology or nation. I demand that this consciousness and these beings be removed from the earth.

Sanat Kumara, Ruby Fire,
Venusian song the multiplier,
as we your love reverberate,
the densest minds we penetrate.

**Sanat Kumara, Ruby Ray,
bring to earth a higher way,
light this planet with your fire,
clothe her in a new attire.**

9. Sanat Kumara, awaken the spiritual people from the tendency to be pulled into the rivalry between competing groups of fallen beings, all of them blinded by the illusion of ultimate power and control.

Sanat Kumara, Ruby Fire,
you are for all the sanctifier,
the earth is now a holy place,
purified by cosmic grace.

**Sanat Kumara, Ruby Ray,
bring to earth a higher way,
light this planet with your fire,
clothe her in a new attire.**

Sealing

In the name of the I AM THAT I AM, I accept that Archangel Michael, Astrea and Shiva form an impenetrable shield around myself and all constructive people, sealing us from all fear-based energies in all four octaves. I accept that the Light of God is consuming and transforming all fear-based energies that make up the forces behind war!

16 | HOW IDEAS ARE USED TO JUSTIFY WAR

I am the Ascended Master Mother Mary. I wish to speak to you about another cause of war, we might say another justification for war. What I am seeking to help you see through the discourses in this book is that one can make a distinction between the causes of war and then the justification for war.

Much of what human beings would see as the causes of war, based on a superficial or materialistic view, are simply camouflage. They are the conditions that are used to justify going to war, but the real causes of war are at a much deeper level, namely in the minds and mindset of the fallen beings. This mindset I will address in a coming discourse, but for now, I wish to speak about one of the elements that are used to justify war, one of the elements that are used to get people to go to war. This element is the use of ideas. Ideas, of course, take many forms, but why is it necessary to use ideas to get people to go to war?

The complexity of the physical body

The worldview that we of the ascended masters seek to give you is that you are not human, material beings. You are spiritual beings who are inhabiting, on a temporary basis, a human, material body. This means that you do have the potential to take command over the body, to master the body. It also means that if you do not exercise this potential, the body may take command over you.

The human body is a very, very complex creation. You may have heard various figures of how there are more neurons in the brain than stars in the universe. There are many other such facts that can be used to describe how complex the human brain is. You may have heard how many cells there are in the body and how complex the different systems of the body really are.

It should be obvious that with such a complex machinery, there are certain rules or laws that are working in the body. The human body is an organism that can in some ways be compared to a machine controlled by a computer. When I talk about your four lower bodies or the four levels of your mind, I am talking about an identity body, a mental body and an emotional body. I am even talking about a level of the physical mind that is very much tied to how you, as a spiritual being, interact with a material body on earth.

There are elements of this soul vehicle that you take with you from lifetime to lifetime. Therefore, one can say that this soul vehicle is not produced by or part of the material body. There is also an aspect of the physical body you are wearing right now that is unique to this lifetime, to this body. This aspect is still a mind, although not a self-aware mind. It is so complex that one can compare it to one of these supercomputers that has taken on an almost human-like intelligence. I am not thereby saying that researchers or scientists will be able to create artificial intelligence, as many dream of doing. They will be able to create something that mimics it, but they will never be able to create life that has self-awareness, for self-awareness comes only from above.

The complex programming in the physical body

There is an aspect of the body that contains a very complex programming. This is programmed into the physical body. You can override this consciously, but for the vast majority of the people on this planet, they are not able to do this. What they *can* do is override the programming in an unconscious, unaware manner. They are overriding the programming, but they are not consciously aware of what they are doing. They have, so to speak, been tricked into overriding the programming. Where this plays into the understanding of war is that one of the deepest programmings in the human mind-body is that of survival.

You do, of course, have a programming aimed at preserving your specific physical body. If this program perceives a threat to the life of your body, it will do whatever necessary to preserve your body, including killing the body of another human being. This is self-preservation. For most people in the modern world this program rarely comes into action. It is not a program that controls your normal day-to-day behavior when you are not in a stressful or life-threatening situation. It simply lies dormant, as the program you have created for riding a bicycle only gets activated when you get on a bicycle.

There is another program that is aimed at preserving your species as a whole. This program is aimed at preserving the whole of the species rather than individuals. It is more important to preserve the species than a given individual because the species can survive without a particular individual, but if the species itself becomes extinct, then, of course, no more individuals can exist.

When the body's programs clash

The human mind-body has two programs that can very easily clash with each other. There can be a conflict in the psyche of an individual when it comes to the entire concept of killing other human beings. You can be in a situation where there seems to be such a threat to the life of your body that you will kill another human being. There is a deeper more powerful program that prompts you *not* to kill other human beings in order to preserve the species.

Do you understand what I am saying? The human mind-body is programmed in such a way as to strongly discourage killing other human beings. This is a very deep and very powerful program in the body. When you add to this the fact that you are a spiritual being inhabiting a physical body, you see that, as long as you have some intuitive sense of being connected to a greater whole than yourself, then you have some sense of the oneness of all life. You may not use this expression consciously, but you do have a sense that life is a whole. If you see yourself as a spiritual being, you would not want to kill another human being because you realize that you are part of the Body of God and so is that other person.

There is a disconnect between the reality that I am explaining to you and a very popular idea that is floating around in the collective consciousness. This idea is in part based on the observation of history and in part based on the theory of

16 | How Ideas Are Used to Justify War

evolution and its idea of the survival of the fittest, or as the popular saying is: "nature red in tooth and claw." The idea is that, for the human species, killing is almost normal, almost natural. You must kill in order to survive. You may even have to kill those of your own species in order to survive. This idea is an idea—not a reality.

It is an idea created by the fallen beings and projected into the collective consciousness. Both your spiritual identity and the programming of the physical body make it extremely difficult for a human being to kill another human being. This is simply part of the self-preservation of the species that in many cases overrides the self-preservation of the individual.

War is not an individual conflict. If you are in a situation where your physical life is threatened, then the program aimed at preserving your physical body will kick in and may cause you to kill another human being. If you are a soldier and you are on a battlefield, then you may have your life threatened and the program may kick in and cause you to kill an enemy soldier who otherwise would kill you. The question is: "How do you ever get yourself from a normal human life to the rather extreme condition of being on a battlefield? What motivates you to go there? What prevents you from objecting to going there?"

The deeper, more powerful program that programs you *not* to kill other human beings works directly against the entire concept of war. In order to get human beings to engage in war, the fallen beings have had to find a way to neutralize the program that is aimed at preserving the species and to inflate the importance of the program that makes you kill in order to preserve yourself. The program aimed at preserving the species would say it is wrong to assemble an army and to attack another country because this works against the preservation of the human species. The fallen beings must find a way to neutralize this program and then over-inflate the individual preservation program so that you think that this other group of people, this other nation or this other race is a direct threat to your survival. Now it becomes acceptable or necessary to kill them.

Humans are not designed to kill their own species

One of the many ideas that are aimed at accomplishing this goal is the idea that it is natural or normal for human beings to kill each other. You can look at human history and see that it *has* been normal for human beings to kill each other. It has been "normal" in the sense that it has been common. It has not been normal in the sense that this is what human beings are designed to do, because human beings are designed *not* to kill each other in order to preserve the species.

When you look at animals, you will see, as the idea of "nature red in tooth and claw" shows, that animals are constantly killing each other. There is a so-called balance in nature, where carnivores must kill herbivores in order to prevent the herbivores from becoming too numerous so that they destroy the food supply, or at least this is the interpretation of nature that has been floated by the fallen beings. The deeper reality is that what you see in nature right now is not a natural condition. It is an unnatural condition that only came into existence after fallen beings started embodying on earth.

This statement will contradict everything you have been brought up to believe by both religion and science. Religion says that the world is not very old and was created instantly by an almighty God. Science says the world is older, but it still says that, even though the planet is billions of years old, there has only been human life on this planet for a few thousand or tens of thousands of years. Certainly, there has only been civilized life for a handful of millennia.

This is completely out of touch with reality. Human life, intelligent life, has, as we have explained before, existed for a very, very long time on this planet. This means that human beings have had an influence on what evolutionary theory sees as completely natural processes. The fact that you need carnivores to prevent the population of herbivores from getting too big is a reflection of the imbalance introduced by human beings. There can be balance in nature without animals killing each other because nature can be completely controlled by the flow of the Holy Spirit. The need to maintain a "balance" in nature by killing is a reflection of an imbalance, and such an imbalance is introduced only by the human beings who incarnate on earth.

They are the co-creators, and they are the only beings who are capable of creating imbalance. The Elohim who created the earth in its original design could not create imbalance. They created a completely balanced planet, and it is only the descent of human beings into the duality consciousness, and especially the incarnation of fallen beings, that has led to the current state of imbalance. You have grown up to see the current state of imbalance as normal, and you do not realize how extreme of an imbalance it is, compared to the original state of this planet.

War is neither natural nor normal

It is neither natural nor normal for human beings to kill each other. It is especially not natural and normal for human beings to engage in large-scale killings of other human beings, such as what you see in war. As I have hinted at before, war is not an invention of the original inhabitants of the earth. They had descended into a downward spiral, where the planet was not following the ascending movement of the rest of the universe, but they still had not invented war amongst themselves.

This was not introduced to the planet until the fallen beings were allowed to incarnate here. This did not mean that human beings were not killing each other on a smaller scale. There was a certain competition among various groups, but war as you see it today was not invented by the original inhabitants of the earth. It was introduced here by the fallen beings who taught the original inhabitants to wage war. It was also the fallen beings who introduced the ideas that justified war and made it seem necessary, even natural, even honorable.

I have said before that you truly cannot gain through war because, even though you may reap a temporary, material gain, the consequence is that you lower the overall wealth and abundance found on the planet, and this will in the future hit you as well. It has sometimes been said about the debt that has been accrued by many Western nations that you are mortgaging your children's future, but when you know the reality of reincarnation, who are your children? Your children's children might be you in a future lifetime. By going to war, by destroying resources and life and lowering the level of abundance on the planet, you create an imbalance for yourself that you will have to experience in a coming lifetime. There is no way around this.

It is neither natural nor normal in a higher way for human beings to wage war. What does this mean? It means something very interesting that you need to be aware of. Warfare was not normal human behavior before the fallen beings came to this planet. One can argue that right now it *is* almost normal human behavior. Certainly, this is what the fallen beings are arguing, but do you see what they are doing? They are using a condition, a state of imbalance, that *they* have created in order to define a new norm, and then they use the new norm to justify perpetuating the condition. This is how the fallen beings work. This is the essence of the duality consciousness. As the serpent said to Eve: "When you eat of the forbidden fruit of the duality consciousness, you become as a god, knowing good and evil." The meaning is that you are now *defining* what is good and what is evil.

This is what has sometimes been called the "privilege of formulating the problem," and the fallen beings are very skilled at capturing this privilege. They define what is the problem or define what is the "normal" way to solve such a problem. Thereby, they can define that this other group of people is "the problem" and the normal, inevitable, honorable, desirable or God-ordained way to solve the problem is to kill those human beings, preferably exterminating them completely from the surface of the earth. You, as the spiritual people, need to look beyond this programming and see that this is not normal. "The Emperor has nothing on." Killing, especially large-scale killing, is not normal, is not natural, is not God-ordained, is not honorable, is not justifiable, is not beneficial to anyone—including yourself.

The effect of the duality consciousness

What makes it possible for human beings to override the very deep programming in the mind-body that programs them not to kill? Most people cannot do this consciously, but they can be manipulated into doing it without being aware of what they are doing. This is done primarily through ideas but ideas of a special kind. These ideas are all based on an underlying idea, namely, that there are two opposites that are mutually exclusive. One of these opposites is desirable and the other is undesirable. The option that your group represents is the desirable one, but it is being threatened by the opposite, which will destroy it unless you destroy the opposition first. Destroying the opposition means destroying the people who are promoting the idea that is opposing your idea. You may even be aware that *they* claim to be the rightful ones, that you are the bad ones and that you are a threat to them.

This is the effect of the duality consciousness. You can have two groups of people who both believe that they are being threatened by the other, and they have to take aggressive action against the other. If two groups of people go to war, and both of them claim that they are not the aggressors but that they had to go to war in order to avoid the aggression from the other group, then is it not obvious that they are both blinded by what I would like to call the serpentine logic. The serpentine logic is *dualistic* logic. It is not logical in a higher sense. It is not logical when seen from the Christ mind.

Creating opponents through serpentine logic

When you step away from a situation and you look at it from the outside, it is not difficult to see that Group A and Group B are both reasoning that they are threatened by the other. If they both claim to be peaceful and non-aggressive, then, in reality, none of them can be threatened by the other if this claim is true. It cannot be logical and rational that they would have to go to war against each other, if both of them are as peaceful and non-aggressive as they claim to be.

You can see this very clearly from the outside, but once you step into the perception filter, the thought bubble, created by the serpentine logic, you will not be able to see this. You are not seeing your own actions from a neutral or objective perspective. You are not seeing that they are illogical. Neither are you, of course, seeing the other side's actions from a neutral perspective. You can only see the opposing side as a threat. You can only see your own reasoning and behavior as logical, rational and justifiable because you have to defend yourself against the opponent and its aggression.

So many times in history the fallen beings have managed to get two groups of people to engage in a war based on this particular deception. They both believe they are threatened by the other. None of them can step outside the veil of illusion that has been created by the fallen beings and see that this cannot be true, rational or logical.

There is even the larger logic that, if you truly are peaceful, you cannot be threatened by an opponent. If you are sending only peace into the cosmic mirror, the cosmic mirror cannot reflect back the opposite of what you are sending out. It can only reflect back what you are sending out multiplied.

Imagine you were willing to look at this simple fact and say: "We perceive that we are threatened by an opponent. What is it in our collective consciousness that has sent a signal into the cosmic mirror that has been reflected back in the form of this opponent?" If you were willing to look at yourself and pull the beam from your own eye, then I can assure you that you would not have to fight that opponent. There would be other ways to resolve the situation without going to war.

So many times in history, even in recent history, you have seen nations go to war, claiming they had no other choice. There was no other option than going to war because of what the enemy did, said or thought. There is *always* an alternative to going to war. It is simply that you cannot see it, and the reason you cannot see it is that you will not look at the beam in your own eye. The reason you will not look at this is that you will not realize that war is caused by the idea that there is an epic struggle and that you represent good and the other side represents evil. You will not see that this is an illusion and that you do not represent good in an unqualified sense and your opponent does not represent evil in an unqualified sense.

Your side, your nation, your group, is made up of individual human beings. They have flaws. They have opinions. They have limitations. The enemy is also made up of individual human beings with flaws and limitations. How can you claim that you are fundamentally different from and superior to the enemy and therefore it is justifiable that you kill the enemy? If you are willing to look at the beam in your own eye, you cannot make this claim. You cannot believe this. When you see a nation, such as Nazi Germany, the Soviet Union or China, that claims to be fundamentally different because of its ideology and fundamentally superior to another group of people, then you know this nation is trapped in the serpentine logic and the dualistic mindset. This nation has been sucked into the epic struggle between two opponents.

The epic struggle between "God" and the devil

As we have explained in several other books, the epic struggle was not created by God. The epic struggle has no necessity. It has no reality. It is an entirely artificial creation that is completely created by the fallen beings. You may say: "But so many of the religions in the world say that there is a God and there is a devil. And the devil is opposing God, threatening God's plan and God's kingdom." The reality is that the devil is the fallen beings. In their arrogance, in their spiritual blindness, in their pride, they have made themselves believe that they are powerful enough to be the opponent of God and to threaten God's plan. This would be comparable to a flea thinking it could control an elephant, only God is infinitely greater than an elephant. The fallen beings have no power to threaten God.

You know, because you have been brought up to believe, that the earth is a very, very small speck of dust in an infinitely large universe. There was a time only a few hundred years ago when people believed that the universe was much smaller than it is. They believed the earth was the center of the universe and was extremely important to God's plan. This was, again, an idea created by the fallen ones in order to make themselves, the fallen beings on earth, appear to be so important.

You know very well that the earth is very, very small compared to the rest of the universe. You also know that, even though the earth exerts a gravitational force on the moon, there is absolutely no chance that the gravitational force of the earth could affect faraway galaxies. It is ridiculous to believe that the earth is the center of the universe and that the earth has some cosmic significance for the entire universe.

I can tell you that as large as the physical universe is, it is infinitely small compared to the totality of the spiritual realm and of previous spheres created. The fallen beings exist only in the material realm, in this latest unascended sphere. An unascended sphere has no permanence. It can be said to have no reality, compared to the spiritual realm that has attained permanence. The idea that anything that happens in an unascended sphere could be a threat to God or God's plan is simply so out of touch with reality that one is almost at a loss for words to describe how ridiculous it is. There *is* no devil, there *is* no force of evil that has *any* chance whatsoever of threatening God or God's plan for the unfoldment of the universe.

This is another idea floating around in the collective consciousness on earth. There is, however, a certain reality in the sense that there *is* a devil that opposes a god, but the deeper reality is that both the devil and the god that is being opposed is created by the fallen beings. It is not the real God that is being threatened by a devil. It is a false god, created by the fallen beings. It has gained some power because it exists as a demon in both the emotional, mental and identity realms. This god, this finite god, can be threatened by a finite devil because this god is created out of the duality consciousness and it must have an opponent. Again, the fallen beings have created a false god and its opposite, the devil, and they are using the existence of these two opposing demons to create the idea of an epic struggle that justifies an ultimate war.

The epic struggle throughout history

You have seen this epic struggle take on many different disguises. A few hundred years ago, you saw it in the form of the Crusades where there was this epic struggle between two religions, Christianity and Islam. Both of these religions claimed to be based on the Old Testament. They claimed to be worshiping the same God, the God who gave the Ten Commandments, one of which is: "Thou shalt not kill." They both believed that the same God who gave this command was so threatened by the other religion that he had set aside his unqualified, unconditional command not to kill and would not only validate but reward you for killing the other side. Your opponent was supposedly such a threat to this almighty God that he needed you to step in and do his dirty work for him by killing these people.

In more modern times, you have seen another version of the epic struggle, namely the tension between communism and the so-called free world. You may have grown up in the West and been conditioned to believe that communism was a threat to the West. You may have believed it was justified that the West opposed the communist expansion by building a big army and by engaging in the Cold War, building nuclear weapons that could kill the human population several times over in order to prevent a takeover of communist forces.

You may even have read that it was capitalists in the West who financed Lenin's takeover of Russia and the creation of the Soviet Union and that it was continued financing that upheld the Soviet Union until it finally became impossible to sustain it. Why would capitalists in the West create a system that completely opposed the capitalism that they had used to enrich themselves? It was because those capitalists in the West were fallen beings, and they wanted to create an opponent in order to justify spending on war. They would not only build the weapons but would also provide the financing that fueled the military-industrial complex and the incredible spending that took place during the Cold War.

Do you, again, see the fallen beings creating conflict, creating an epic struggle between two opponents that now can justify something that should be seen as completely insane? Both the programming of your physical mind-body and your spiritual awareness should have made most people on earth see the lie behind the epic struggle between capitalism and communism, the struggle between Islam and Christianity and so many other struggles. They should have said: "But the emperor has nothing on. We will not support this. We will not give up our sons as cannon fodder for this ridiculous quest of the fallen beings."

Why didn't people do this? Because they had become so blinded by the illusions promoted by the fallen beings. I need you, as a spiritual person, to unblind yourself from these illusions and to make the calls so that other people can be set free. I need you to make the calls so that the Archangels and the angels can step in and bind the demons and the entities in the astral, mental and identity realms that are continuing to create a magnetic force that makes it difficult for people to see through the illusion and to free their minds from it.

Fanaticism overrides the mind-body programming

I also need you to increase your awareness of a very simple fact. You have in the Western world been conditioned to believe that some of the greatest evils perpetrated in history were caused by fanaticism. You have, for example, been conditioned to believe that Adolph Hitler and many of the Nazi leaders (and even many among the German people at the time) had become fanatical because of the ideology of Nazism. You have come to believe that this was an extreme condition that blinded people temporarily and that somehow was punctured when Germany was defeated at the end of the war. You have also been conditioned to believe that the communists in the Soviet Union or China were also fanatical and had a hatred of the West and wanted to spread their system to the entire world. You have in recent years been conditioned to believe that Al Qaeda and I.S. or ISIS are Muslim fanatics who hate the West and who want to destroy the great Satan of America.

You have been conditioned to believe that fanaticism is a major cause of war. This is correct in the sense that fanaticism is not really a cause of war but is the most common way to justify war. It is a mindset that justifies war. We can say that any time human beings are able to override the mind-body programming not to kill, they can do so only by going into a fanatical state of mind.

My beloved, did you take note of what I just said? I said that *any time* human beings believe it is necessary and justifiable to kill at a large scale, they have been blinded by fanaticism. What did the American president. Many among the American leaders and many among the American people believe when they went to war in Iraq? They believed it was necessary and justified to go to war and kill tens of thousands of people. How was this *not* fanaticism, my beloved?

Do you see what fanaticism does? It makes you project that the problem is "out there" in those other people. Therefore, it is necessary and justified to kill them. The *common* definition of fanaticism is that it is any idea or belief taken to an extreme, to an excess. The *real* definition of fanaticism that I want to give you here is that fanaticism is the mindset that overrides the mind-body programming not to kill. Fanaticism, of course, also overrides your spiritual awareness of the Oneness of all life, but this is not so important because if you have a spiritual awareness, you will not go into fanaticism. You will not be susceptible to fanaticism, if you have a true spiritual awareness of the Oneness of all life.

I know very well that you can claim to be a religious person or even a spiritual person, even an ascended master student, and still become susceptible to fanaticism. You will not think you are fanatical, you will think it is those other people who are fanatical and you simply have to oppose them. Many spiritual and religious people (who claim to be spiritual and religious in an outer sense) have been deceived by the fanatical mindset. If you are a true spiritual person, who has an intuitive knowing of the oneness of all life, you are not likely to be drawn into fanaticism. You will know that you cannot kill another human being any more than you can chop off a part of your own body.

Fanaticism is a state of mind. It is produced by the ideas promoted by the fallen beings, first of all, the epic struggle that takes on a specific disguise. It then defines that, in order to win this epic struggle, it is justifiable and necessary to kill this other group of people. It also defines that winning the epic struggle is absolutely necessary for some reason or other.

Anytime there is a conflict between two groups of people and anytime that conflict is justified by ideas, those ideas produce the fanatical mindset on both sides. It is never so that one side represents right, good, God, truth or reality and the other represents the opposite. Both sides are in a fanatical state of mind, and this means that both sides are controlled by the fallen beings in the emotional, mental and identity realms. There is *no* other explanation.

There is no justification for fanaticism

The willingness to kill on a large scale is the very definition of fanaticism. Fanaticism is a state of mind that is neither normal nor natural for a human being or a spiritual being. It is an artificial state of mind, deliberately and maliciously created by the fallen beings in order to get human beings to kill each other. My beloved, there is no other explanation. You can come up with all kinds of subtle reasonings. Perhaps your mind is already churning, coming up with what you have been programmed to believe. I am telling you: There *is* no other explanation. There is no justification or necessity for fanaticism, and there is no way to kill on a large scale unless you have been blinded and taken over by fanaticism.

You may say: "But Nazism was clearly evil and therefore the free world was not fanatical in fighting the war against Nazism." I am telling you: This is a complete lie and a smokescreen created by the fallen beings. It is a product of your unwillingness to look at the beam in your own eye. What you should be thinking is: "What was it in the collective consciousness in the 1920s and 30s that produced the emergence of Nazism? What was the rest of the world and even the German people sending into the cosmic mirror that came back in the form of Nazism? What was the beam in our own eye that we did not see, that we still have not seen and that we still have not pulled?"

There are those who have said that the dilemma of war is that in order to defeat the enemy, you have to become as ruthless as the enemy. The risk is that you can become worse than the enemy. You may look at the Nazi leaders, and you may clearly see that they were in a fanatical state of mind. If you were to look objectively at the leaders in England and America who fought the war against Nazism, then you would see that they were also in a fanatical state of mind. It was not as obvious as the German one, but let me tell you that one of the reasons for this was that Germany lost the war. Therefore, to the victor goes the spoils and the right to write history. You have heard the saying that history is written for the winners because the winners write it to make themselves look good.

You will know that towards the end of the war, the Americans and the British conducted large-scale bombings of German cities. In some of those cities there were no military targets. It was a punishment of the German civil population that killed tens of thousands of women and children. What was the obvious way to cover up this and other war crimes committed by the allies? It was to demonize the Germans and make them seem even worse than they were.

Fanaticism is always the mindset behind war

This is not to excuse the holocaust. I am not here seeking to go into a discussion about who was bad and who was not bad. I am not trying to excuse the war crimes and atrocities committed by the Nazis. I am simply trying to point out that whenever two sides are opposing each other in a conflict, especially if that conflict is seen as an epic struggle between good and evil, then both sides will have become affected by the mindset of fanaticism. Fanaticism can take many forms. It can even appear benign. The Christian Crusaders were fanatical, but they thought they were fighting for God's cause. So did the Muslims who opposed them.

I need you, as the spiritual people, to see that fanaticism is always the mindset that leads to war. I need you to make the calls for this to be exposed for people to see. I need you to give the authority to the angels to remove those demons and entities in the emotional, mental and identity realms who are feeding off fanaticism and encouraging it so that people will commit further atrocities as a result of the fanatical mindset.

You cannot push men, women and children into a gas chamber unless you are blinded by fanaticism. Neither can you send hundreds of bombers to bomb an undefended city, killing tens of thousands of civilians, unless you are in the fanatical mindset. It makes you do things that are not necessary in order to achieve the end that you claim to be working towards. You do not see that what you are doing is not necessary, rational, logical or humane.

I am not here trying to say that war is in any way rational. You can step back and say if there is an end that needs to be achieved, such as defeating the enemy, then from a rational, logical standpoint, we would do only what is absolutely necessary in order to defeat the enemy and nothing more. Why would we spend money on things that are not necessary to achieve our end? This is what you could do from a rational evaluation of war. What I am pointing out here is that so many times in war, you see that both sides go far beyond what is absolutely necessary, and the explanation for this is that they are blinded by fanaticism.

16 | *How Ideas Are Used to Justify War*

The Alpha and Omega of transcending fanaticism

There are two ways out of fanaticism, the Alpha and the Omega, the masculine and the feminine. The Alpha way is to recognize and to reconnect with your own vertical oneness to something higher, meaning your spiritual self, your spiritual teachers, the ascended masters and God. When you see the oneness of all life in yourself, you see the oneness of all life in other people. You are freed from fanaticism, for you realize that all people are part of the same Body of God of which you are a part.

The Omega way is to look at it rationally and say: "Is what we are doing necessary? Does it produce any end? What are the consequences of what we are doing for ourselves?" The Omega way is to look at the mechanics of how the material universe works, and the mechanics are simple: action and reaction. Any action you take creates a consequence. When you evaluate the consequences, you start thinking: "Well, is it worth it? Is this what we want to achieve?" Either way, you can free yourself from fanaticism, and I am asking you to make the calls so that people will be freed in both ways.

There is still much fanaticism in the world, and it is not always "out there." There is still much fanaticism in the West. It should be possible for you to see that after the World Trade Center attacks in 2001, fanaticism in the West has increased and been directed towards defeating this new enemy. This fanaticism goes far back. Certainly, it was there before the second world war and even further back in history. It is a mindset that has been created by the fallen beings, and it has been sustained for a very, very long time on this planet.

Calling forth the Judgment of Christ

We are now in a spiritual cycle where the spiritual people on earth have an unprecedented opportunity to make the calls and authorize the ascended masters and the angels to not only consume the energies of fanaticism but to bind the demons and entities and take them from the earth and dissolve them. You also have an unprecedented opportunity to call for the Judgment of Christ upon the fallen beings who are promoting fanaticism, and who will not let it go, so that they can be removed from the earth, both from physical incarnation and from the emotional, mental and identity realms.

There is a whole class, a whole rung, of fallen beings who are ready for the Judgment of Christ. When Jesus appeared in physical embodiment and attained Christhood 2,000 years ago, he said: "For judgment, I am come." There was an entire group of fallen beings who were judged by their killing of the Christ incarnate. The plan behind Jesus' coming into physical embodiment was to set an example that others could follow so that at the end of this 2,000-year cycle there would be 10,000 people who had attained full Christhood. They could call forth the Judgment of Christ upon the fallen beings without them having to be physically killed by the fallen beings.

As Jesus has said in his book [*The Mystical Teachings of Jesus*], there are ten thousand people in embodiment who have the potential to awaken and accept or quickly develop their Christhood. Thereby, you can make the calls for the judgment of the fallen beings who are ready to be taken from the earth in this age. You will not have to be physically killed; you will not have to have the bloodshed.

When there was only one Christ in embodiment, he had to allow himself to be physically killed in order to bring about the judgment of the fallen beings. When there are ten thousand

Christed beings in embodiment, you can make the calls and give the invocations and transcend the fallen consciousness. Thereby, you can authorize the removal of the fallen beings from the earth, and with them will go their fanaticism and their warring. This, my beloved, is an unprecedented opportunity.

The purpose for which you came into embodiment

You have taken embodiment because, before you took embodiment, you saw how unique this opportunity was and you felt an inner longing to be part of this movement. That is why you took embodiment on this dense planet in this very difficult time. You did not look at the difficulties you are facing now. You looked at the opportunity.

I am here to reconnect you to that sense of opportunity. It was not fanaticism you felt. It was enthusiasm. It was joy. It was the joy of seeing what an incredible opportunity there is to take a planet as dark as earth and to lighten it so much that it can quickly accelerate into the golden age that Saint Germain envisions for this planet for the next 2,000 years. You saw this. You felt such a deep love, a deep joy, well up from the core of your being that you volunteered to take embodiment.

Many of you did not have to take embodiment for karmic reasons. You could have balanced the remainder of your karma from the etheric realm and, thereby, ascended without taking embodiment. You volunteered to take embodiment because you saw that by you awakening to your potential and making the call, then these fallen beings could be judged and taken from the earth. Thereby, their warring and their warring ways would be lifted from this planet, as a dark cloud that has been hanging for far too long. You saw how this earth could be lifted from being the dark star it is today to being freedom's star that could radiate a new light and bring hope to other planets that are as dark or darker than the earth.

I am not here in any way seeking to convince you of something. I am not asking you to believe anything. I am asking you to tune in to your heart, to the core of your being, to your higher self. I am asking you to acknowledge consciously what you already know in your identity body, what you already understand in your mental body and what you already feel in your emotional body—when you look beyond your normal state of consciousness.

I am not asking you to follow me or believe me. I am asking you to tune in to who you really are and accept who you really are. I am asking you to accept your role, your potential, your right and the very purpose for which you came into embodiment at this time. Will you acknowledge who you are, as I have acknowledged who I AM? For I am the Ascended Master Mother Mary!

17 | JUDGING FANATICISM

In the name of the I AM THAT I AM, Jesus Christ, I call upon Mother Mary, Jesus, Lord Maitreya, Gautama Buddha and Sanat Kumara for the judgment of the consciousness of fanaticism and the beings who embody it in all four octaves. Awaken people to the reality that we are spiritual beings and that we can co-create a new future by working with the ascended masters. I especially call for …

[Make your own calls here.]

Part 1

1. Beloved Jesus, I call forth the judgment of Christ upon the fallen beings and demons who use ideas to justify getting people to go to war. Archangel Michael, remove these beings from the earth.

O Jesus, blessed brother mine,
I walk the path that you outline,
a great example to us all,
I follow now your inner call.

**O Jesus, let the Fire of Joy,
consume the devil's subtle ploy,
transfigured is our planet earth,
the golden age is given birth.**

2. Beloved Jesus, I call forth the judgment of Christ upon the fallen beings and demons who know that in order to get people to kill each other on a large scale, they have to override the programming that prompts people not to kill in order to preserve the species. Archangel Michael, remove these beings from the earth.

O Jesus, open inner sight,
the ego wants to prove it's right,
but this I will no longer do,
I want to be all one with you.

**O Jesus, let the Fire of Joy,
consume the devil's subtle ploy,
transfigured is our planet earth,
the golden age is given birth.**

3. Beloved Jesus, I call forth the judgment of Christ upon the fallen beings and demons who promote the idea of "nature red in tooth and claw" and that it is normal or natural to kill. Archangel Michael, remove these beings from the earth.

17 | Judging Fanaticism

> O Jesus, I now clearly see,
> the Key of Knowledge given me,
> my Christ self I hereby embrace,
> as you fill up my inner space.
>
> **O Jesus, let the Fire of Joy,**
> **consume the devil's subtle ploy,**
> **transfigured is our planet earth,**
> **the golden age is given birth.**

4. Beloved Jesus, I call forth the judgment of Christ upon the fallen beings and demons who promote the idea that we must kill others in order to survive, thereby neutralizing the programming not to kill. Archangel Michael, remove these beings from the earth.

> O Jesus, show me serpent's lie,
> expose the beam in my own eye,
> as Christ discernment you me give,
> in oneness I forever live.
>
> **O Jesus, let the Fire of Joy,**
> **consume the devil's subtle ploy,**
> **transfigured is our planet earth,**
> **the golden age is given birth.**

5. Beloved Jesus, I call forth the judgment of Christ upon the fallen beings and demons who use science to promote killing as normal, natural or justifiable. Archangel Michael, remove these beings from the earth.

> O Jesus, I am truly meek,
> and thus I turn the other cheek,
> when the accuser attacks me,
> I go within and merge with thee.

> **O Jesus, let the Fire of Joy,**
> **consume the devil's subtle ploy,**
> **transfigured is our planet earth,**
> **the golden age is given birth.**

6. Beloved Jesus, I call forth the judgment of Christ upon the fallen beings and demons who use religion to promote killing as normal, natural or justifiable. Archangel Michael, remove these beings from the earth.

> O Jesus, ego I let die,
> surrender ev'ry earthly tie,
> the dead can bury what is dead,
> I choose to walk with you instead.

> **O Jesus, let the Fire of Joy,**
> **consume the devil's subtle ploy,**
> **transfigured is our planet earth,**
> **the golden age is given birth.**

7. Beloved Jesus, I call forth the judgment of Christ upon the fallen beings and demons who seek to hide the reality that they themselves have created the imbalance in nature that makes killing seem natural. Archangel Michael, remove these beings from the earth.

> O Jesus, help me rise above,
> the devil's test through higher love,
> show me separate self unreal,
> my formless self you do reveal.
>
> **O Jesus, let the Fire of Joy,**
> **consume the devil's subtle ploy,**
> **transfigured is our planet earth,**
> **the golden age is given birth.**

8. Beloved Jesus, I call forth the judgment of Christ upon the fallen beings and demons who seek to hide the reality that it was the descent of human beings into the duality consciousness, and the incarnation of fallen beings, that led to the current imbalance. Archangel Michael, remove these beings from the earth.

> O Jesus, what is that to me,
> I just let go and follow thee,
> with this I do pass ev'ry test,
> to find with you eternal rest.
>
> **O Jesus, let the Fire of Joy,**
> **consume the devil's subtle ploy,**
> **transfigured is our planet earth,**
> **the golden age is given birth.**

9. Beloved Jesus, I call forth the judgment of Christ upon the fallen beings and demons who seek to hide the idea that war, and the ideas that justify it, were introduced to this planet by the fallen beings who incarnated here. Archangel Michael, remove these beings from the earth.

O Jesus, fiery master mine,
my heart now melting into thine,
I love with heart and mind and soul,
the God who is my highest goal.

**O Jesus, let the Fire of Joy,
consume the devil's subtle ploy,
transfigured is our planet earth,
the golden age is given birth.**

Part 2

1. Lord Maitreya, I call forth the judgment of Christ upon the fallen beings and demons who seek to hide the reality that war creates imbalances and karma that people themselves will experience in a future lifetime. Archangel Michael, remove these beings from the earth.

Maitreya, I am truly meek,
your counsel wise I humbly seek,
your vision I so want to see,
with you in Eden I will be.

**Maitreya, kindness is the cure,
in fires of kindness I am pure.
Maitreya, now release the fire,
that raises me forever higher.**

2. Lord Maitreya, I call forth the judgment of Christ upon the fallen beings and demons who are using a state of imbalance they have created in order to define a new norm, and then they use the new norm to justify perpetuating the condition. Archangel Michael, remove these beings from the earth.

> Maitreya, help me to return,
> to learn from you, I truly yearn,
> as oneness is all I desire
> I feel initiation's fire.

> **Maitreya, kindness is the cure,**
> **in fires of kindness I am pure.**
> **Maitreya, now release the fire,**
> **that raises me forever higher.**

3. Lord Maitreya, I call forth the judgment of Christ upon the fallen beings and demons who have captured the "privilege of formulating the problem" and are using it to justify getting people to kill each other through war. Archangel Michael, remove these beings from the earth.

> Maitreya, I hereby decide,
> from you I will no longer hide,
> expose to me the very lie
> that caused edenic self to die.

> **Maitreya, kindness is the cure,**
> **in fires of kindness I am pure.**
> **Maitreya, now release the fire,**
> **that raises me forever higher.**

4. Lord Maitreya, I call forth the judgment of Christ upon the fallen beings and demons who use the serpentine logic to define two opposites and say they are in a fatal conflict. Archangel Michael, remove these beings from the earth.

> Maitreya, blessed Guru mine,
> my heart of hearts forever thine,
> I vow that I will listen well,
> so we can break the serpent's spell.
>
> **Maitreya, kindness is the cure,**
> **in fires of kindness I am pure.**
> **Maitreya, now release the fire,**
> **that raises me forever higher.**

5. Lord Maitreya, I call forth the judgment of Christ upon the fallen beings and demons who use serpentine logic to get two groups of people to go to war while both believe they are peaceful and the other is the aggressor. Archangel Michael, remove these beings from the earth.

> Maitreya, help me see the lie
> whereby the serpent broke the tie,
> the serpent now has naught in me,
> in oneness I am truly free.
>
> **Maitreya, kindness is the cure,**
> **in fires of kindness I am pure.**
> **Maitreya, now release the fire,**
> **that raises me forever higher.**

6. Lord Maitreya, I call forth the judgment of Christ upon the fallen beings and demons who use serpentine logic to hide that there is always an alternative to going to war. Archangel Michael, remove these beings from the earth.

> Maitreya, truth does set me free
> from falsehoods of duality,
> the fruit of knowledge I let go,
> so your true spirit I do know.

> **Maitreya, kindness is the cure,**
> **in fires of kindness I am pure.**
> **Maitreya, now release the fire,**
> **that raises me forever higher.**

7. Lord Maitreya, I call forth the judgment of Christ upon the fallen beings and demons who use serpentine logic to dehumanize both groups so they will not see each other as individual human beings. Archangel Michael, remove these beings from the earth.

> Maitreya, I submit to you,
> intentions pure, my heart is true,
> from ego I am truly free,
> as I am now all one with thee.

> **Maitreya, kindness is the cure,**
> **in fires of kindness I am pure.**
> **Maitreya, now release the fire,**
> **that raises me forever higher.**

8. Lord Maitreya, I call forth the judgment of Christ upon the fallen beings and demons who promote the idea of the epic struggle and use it to create the fanaticism that can override the programming not to kill. Archangel Michael, remove these beings from the earth.

> Maitreya, kindness is the key,
> all shades of kindness teach to me,
> for I am now the open door,
> the Art of Kindness to restore.
>
> **Maitreya, kindness is the cure,**
> **in fires of kindness I am pure.**
> **Maitreya, now release the fire,**
> **that raises me forever higher.**

9. Lord Maitreya, I call forth the judgment of Christ upon the fallen beings and demons who hide the reality that the epic struggle was not created by God and that it is a complete illusion. Archangel Michael, remove these beings from the earth.

> Maitreya, oh sweet mystery,
> immersed in your reality,
> the myst'ry school will now return,
> for this, my heart does truly burn.
>
> **Maitreya, kindness is the cure,**
> **in fires of kindness I am pure.**
> **Maitreya, now release the fire,**
> **that raises me forever higher.**

Part 3

1. Gautama Buddha, I call forth the judgment of Christ upon the fallen beings and demons who in their pride have made themselves believe that they are powerful enough to be the opponent of God and to threaten God's plan. Archangel Michael, remove these beings from the earth.

> Gautama, show my mental state
> that does give rise to love and hate,
> your exposé I do endure,
> so my perception will be pure.

> **Gautama, Flame of Cosmic Peace,**
> **unruly thoughts do hereby cease,**
> **we radiate from you and me**
> **the peace to still Samsara's Sea.**

2. Gautama Buddha, I call forth the judgment of Christ upon the fallen beings and demons who promote the idea that the devil is powerful enough to oppose God. Archangel Michael, remove these beings from the earth.

> Gautama, in your Flame of Peace,
> the struggling self I now release,
> the Buddha Nature I now see,
> it is the core of you and me.

> **Gautama, Flame of Cosmic Peace,**
> **unruly thoughts do hereby cease,**
> **we radiate from you and me**
> **the peace to still Samsara's Sea.**

3. Gautama Buddha, I call forth the judgment of Christ upon the fallen beings and demons who hide the reality that they have created both the devil and the false god being opposed. Archangel Michael, remove these beings from the earth.

> Gautama, I am one with thee,
> Mara's demons do now flee,
> your Presence like a soothing balm,
> my mind and senses ever calm.
>
> **Gautama, Flame of Cosmic Peace,**
> **unruly thoughts do hereby cease,**
> **we radiate from you and me**
> **the peace to still Samsara's Sea.**

4. Gautama Buddha, I call forth the judgment of Christ upon the fallen beings and demons who have used the epic struggle in many disguises in order to justify war. Archangel Michael, remove these beings from the earth.

> Gautama, I now take the vow,
> to live in the eternal now,
> with you I do transcend all time,
> to live in present so sublime.
>
> **Gautama, Flame of Cosmic Peace,**
> **unruly thoughts do hereby cease,**
> **we radiate from you and me**
> **the peace to still Samsara's Sea.**

5. Gautama Buddha, I call for the seven Archangels to cut all people free from the illusions of the epic struggle and the fanaticism that is its psychological consequence.

> Gautama, I have no desire,
> to nothing earthly I aspire,
> in non-attachment I now rest,
> passing Mara's subtle test.
>
> **Gautama, Flame of Cosmic Peace,
> unruly thoughts do hereby cease,
> we radiate from you and me
> the peace to still Samsara's Sea.**

6. Gautama Buddha, I call forth the judgment of Christ upon the fallen beings and demons who seek to hide the reality that any time human beings are able to override the mind-body programming not to kill, they can do so only by going into a fanatical state of mind. Archangel Michael, remove these beings from the earth.

> Gautama, I melt into you,
> my mind is one, no longer two,
> immersed in your resplendent glow,
> Nirvana is all that I know.
>
> **Gautama, Flame of Cosmic Peace,
> unruly thoughts do hereby cease,
> we radiate from you and me
> the peace to still Samsara's Sea.**

7. Gautama Buddha, I call forth the judgment of Christ upon the fallen beings and demons who seek to hide the reality that anyone who engages in war or believes it is justified is in a fanatical state of mind. Archangel Michael, remove these beings from the earth.

Gautama, in your timeless space,
I am immersed in Cosmic Grace,
I know the God beyond all form,
to world I will no more conform.

**Gautama, Flame of Cosmic Peace,
unruly thoughts do hereby cease,
we radiate from you and me
the peace to still Samsara's Sea.**

8. Gautama Buddha, I call forth the judgment of Christ upon the fallen beings and demons who seek to hide the reality that fanaticism is the mindset that overrides the mind-body programming not to kill. Archangel Michael, remove these beings from the earth.

Gautama, I am now awake,
I clearly see what is at stake,
and thus I claim my sacred right
to be on earth the Buddhic Light.

**Gautama, Flame of Cosmic Peace,
unruly thoughts do hereby cease,
we radiate from you and me
the peace to still Samsara's Sea.**

9. Gautama Buddha, I call for the seven Archangels to cut free all spiritual and religious people who have been deceived by the fanatical mindset and project that the problem is "out there."

17 | Judging Fanaticism

Gautama, with your thunderbolt,
we give the earth a mighty jolt,
I know that some will understand,
and join the Buddha's timeless band.

Gautama, Flame of Cosmic Peace,
unruly thoughts do hereby cease,
we radiate from you and me
the peace to still Samsara's Sea.

Part 4

1. Sanat Kumara, I call forth the judgment of Christ upon the fallen beings and demons who seek to hide the reality that anytime there is a conflict between two groups of people, and anytime that conflict is justified by ideas, those ideas produce the fanatical mindset on both sides. Archangel Michael, remove these beings from the earth.

Sanat Kumara, Ruby Fire,
I seek my place in love's own choir,
with open hearts we sing your praise,
together we the earth do raise.

Sanat Kumara, Ruby Ray,
bring to earth a higher way,
light this planet with your fire,
clothe her in a new attire.

2. Sanat Kumara, I call forth the judgment of Christ upon the fallen beings and demons who seek to hide the reality that in any war, both sides are controlled by the fallen beings in the emotional, mental and identity realms. Archangel Michael, remove these beings from the earth.

> Sanat Kumara, Ruby Fire,
> initiations I desire,
> I am for you an electrode,
> Shamballa is my true abode.
>
> **Sanat Kumara, Ruby Ray,**
> **bring to earth a higher way,**
> **light this planet with your fire,**
> **clothe her in a new attire.**

3. Sanat Kumara, I call forth the judgment of Christ upon the fallen beings and demons who seek to hide the reality that fanaticism is an artificial state of mind, deliberately and maliciously created by the fallen beings in order to get human beings to kill each other. Archangel Michael, remove these beings from the earth.

> Sanat Kumara, Ruby Fire,
> I follow path that you require,
> initiate me with your love,
> the open door for Holy Dove.
>
> **Sanat Kumara, Ruby Ray,**
> **bring to earth a higher way,**
> **light this planet with your fire,**
> **clothe her in a new attire.**

4. Sanat Kumara, I call for the seven Archangels to cut all people free to see that fanaticism can take many forms and that it is always the mindset that leads to war.

> Sanat Kumara, Ruby Fire,
> your great example all inspire,
> with non-attachment and great mirth,
> we give the earth a true rebirth.

> **Sanat Kumara, Ruby Ray,**
> **bring to earth a higher way,**
> **light this planet with your fire,**
> **clothe her in a new attire.**

5. Sanat Kumara, by the Christ within me, I hereby give the seven Archangels the authority to remove the demons and entities in the emotional, mental and identity realms who are feeding off fanaticism and encouraging it so that people will commit further atrocities as a result of the fanatical mindset.

> Sanat Kumara, Ruby Fire,
> you are this planet's purifier,
> consume on earth all spirits dark,
> reveal the inner Spirit Spark.

> **Sanat Kumara, Ruby Ray,**
> **bring to earth a higher way,**
> **light this planet with your fire,**
> **clothe her in a new attire.**

6. Sanat Kumara, I call for the seven Archangels to cut free all spiritual people to see that at this time we have an unprecedented opportunity to make the calls and authorize the ascended masters and the Archangels to consume the energies of fanaticism and to bind the demons and entities and take them from the earth.

> Sanat Kumara, Ruby Fire,
> you are a cosmic amplifier,
> the lower forces can't withstand,
> vibrations from Venusian band.

> **Sanat Kumara, Ruby Ray,**
> **bring to earth a higher way,**
> **light this planet with your fire,**
> **clothe her in a new attire.**

7. Sanat Kumara, I call forth the judgment of Christ upon the fallen beings who are promoting fanaticism. I demand that they are removed from the earth, both from physical incarnation and from the emotional, mental and identity realms. Archangel Michael, remove these beings from the earth.

> Sanat Kumara, Ruby Fire,
> I am on earth your magnifier,
> the flow of love I do restore,
> my chakras are your open door.

> **Sanat Kumara, Ruby Ray,**
> **bring to earth a higher way,**
> **light this planet with your fire,**
> **clothe her in a new attire.**

8. Sanat Kumara, I call forth the judgment of Christ upon the rung of fallen beings who are ready to be removed from the earth in this age. Archangel Michael, remove these beings from the earth.

> Sanat Kumara, Ruby Fire,
> Venusian song the multiplier,
> as we your love reverberate,
> the densest minds we penetrate.
>
> **Sanat Kumara, Ruby Ray,**
> **bring to earth a higher way,**
> **light this planet with your fire,**
> **clothe her in a new attire.**

9. Sanat Kumara, I call for the seven Archangels to awaken the 10,000 Christed beings in embodiment, so they can accept their potential to remove war from the earth. Awaken them to the reason they chose to be in embodiment at this time.

> Sanat Kumara, Ruby Fire,
> you are for all the sanctifier,
> the earth is now a holy place,
> purified by cosmic grace.
>
> **Sanat Kumara, Ruby Ray,**
> **bring to earth a higher way,**
> **light this planet with your fire,**
> **clothe her in a new attire.**

Sealing

In the name of the I AM THAT I AM, I accept that Archangel Michael, Astrea and Shiva form an impenetrable shield around myself and all constructive people, sealing us from all fear-based energies in all four octaves. I accept that the Light of God is consuming and transforming all fear-based energies that make up the forces behind war!

18 | THE NEED TO CLEAN UP THE ASTRAL PLANE

I am the Ascended Master Mother Mary! I wish to discourse with you on the hidden agendas of the fallen beings. These agendas are the true cause of war. All of the outer reasons for war given on this planet are simply camouflage that are designed to hide the true cause.

It is important for you, as a spiritual person, to understand the incredible difference between the worldview you have been given as you were growing up, and then the reality of how the world actually works. The official worldview of how life works on earth and how history has progressed and what has been the cause of the progression of history is woefully inadequate. This lack of knowledge of what is really happening on this planet is not due to *innocent* ignorance; it is a *produced* ignorance, a state that has been produced by the fallen beings deliberately.

Artificially produced ignorance

The equation is very simple. If you are feeling pain in your foot and you know the cause is that you have stepped on a nail that has gone through the sole of your shoe, then what would you do? Well, you would take the shoe off and pull the nail out. If you are feeling pain in your foot and you either do not know what is causing it or you believe there is nothing you could do to avoid it, then you cannot take this simple measure, can you?

Human beings are not stupid. If they are feeling pain or discomfort and they discover the cause of it, then they will do something about it. Many human beings on this planet are feeling the pain of the existence of war and conflict. Many people would like to do something about it. If these people could be helped to understand that the real cause of war and conflict is the presence of the fallen beings, then they would instantly stop following the fallen beings. This is the simple equation: The fallen beings cannot keep their power if people see them and see them for what they are. They can keep their power only through deception, through a *produced* ignorance. For some people, this ignorance is a *willful* ignorance. They really do not want to know that the fallen beings exist because they do not want to change their lives.

There is a relatively small percentage of the people on earth (and with that I mean less than ten percent) who are in what we might call an unconscious alliance with the fallen beings. They are not themselves fallen beings, but they gain an advantage from obeying the fallen beings. They gain a sense of power, a sense of privilege, or in some cases even the advantage that they are allowed to kill, hurt, torture or control other human beings. They gain a sense of power from doing this. These people do not want to know what is really going on, yet they are only a minority. The eighty percent of the general population would free themselves from the fallen beings if they knew what was really happening.

The top ten percent of the most spiritual people are the ones who are more open, but some of them have been diverted by the fallen beings into what I talked about, namely the idea that "it's all good" and that they don't need to do anything other than send out positive vibrations. In a sense, we could say that there are some among the top ten percent who also have a willful ignorance. They want to keep believing that they can continue doing what they are doing and that they do not need to change their lifestyle or their outlook on life by acknowledging the presence of dark forces.

You are not in opposition to the fallen beings

It is no easy task for the ascended masters to enlighten humankind to the reality of this planet. That is why we need those of you who are open to our teachings to make the calls. We can then open up pathways in the collective consciousness where more and more people can begin to awaken. They can awaken without being taken into these extremes of fanaticism that you often see as a result of people studying the many conspiracy theories and other extremist views that are out there.

I know well that there are those who will say that what I am presenting in this book and what we are presenting in other books is an extremist view. Why do I know this? Because I have studied the fallen beings for a long time, and I can tell you that there is nothing new in the fallen mindset. It is very predictable how they will respond whenever we seek to enlighten humankind.

What I wish to talk about next is the need for the spiritual people on earth to stop seeing themselves as being in opposition to the fallen beings. You are *not* the opponents of the fallen beings. There is a very fine and delicate balance to be found as you awaken yourself from the collective state of sleep concerning the fallen beings. You do not go into rebelling against them or fighting them. This we have explained in great detail in the book, *Warrior of Peace,* so I will not repeat it here. I do wish to emphasize that it is extremely important for you that you do not go into the blind alley of thinking that you have to fight the fallen beings. Also, do not go into feeling overwhelmed.

Removing war is a fully doable task

There is no reason to feel overwhelmed because, as I have explained before, the fallen beings have limited power. We of the ascended masters have *unlimited* power and can consume and deal with anything that the fallen beings can come up with, as long as you give us the authority to do so. The whole idea of this book is to get a critical mass of people to give us the authority and to invoke the energy that will allow us to remove these fallen beings and the completely unconscious demons and entities from this planet.

There is absolutely nothing hopeless about the task we are facing. There is no reason to feel overwhelmed at all. It is a perfectly doable task. It is perfectly doable for you to live a relatively normal lifestyle and to give the invocations and decrees that will give us the authority to use our power to remove the fallen beings. It is a doable task. Had it not been a doable task, we would not have given it to you because we have no desire to overwhelm our students. Unfortunately, our students do not always understand this, and they overwhelm themselves when they come in contact with our teachings.

18 | The Need to Clean Up the Astral Plane

This is the danger of giving an outer teaching that can be read on the Internet or in books. We cannot quite control who will find this teaching. It is possible that people can find it while they are ready at inner levels but not ready at the level of the outer mind. This is what causes some students to go into what I would almost call a state of fanaticism because of our teachings. They become so "fired up" about fighting the fallen beings by giving decrees and invocations that they overdo it and become unbalanced in their zeal just like you see so many other people who, for religious or political reasons or even other reasons, can become so zealous that it is not healthy. This I have no desire to encourage, and that is why I again emphasize that what we are giving you is a doable task.

Your worldview and the fallen worldview

I have earlier described what happens on a battlefield when you can see the entities and demons on the astral plane and the fallen beings in the mental and identity realms. I wish to speak again about this from a slightly different perspective. I wish to speak about it from the perspective of what the fallen beings or the demons get out of war.

This will help you understand why there is such a difference between the causes of war presented by the official worldview and then the deeper causes of war I am presenting to you. Many of the more spiritual people have been fooled by the official view of war. They have been fooled because they do not understand the fundamental difference between how you yourself look at life and how the fallen beings look at life.

It is very common for human beings to have an almost unconscious assumption that everybody else is like them and thinks, feels and looks at life the same way. If you are a spiritual person, you see that war is not desirable, and you assume that most people want to stop war. You may fall prey to the common misconception, promoted by the official worldview, that there are only a very few extreme people who deliberately want to create war.

You have all been taught about Hitler and other such extremists. You have been taught that they were particularly evil people and that was why they created war. You may have been taught about certain economic factors or political factors that cause people to go to war without really wanting to, but they feel they have to because they are threatened by some enemy outside themselves. You tend to think that it should be possible to stop war through rational means. Many of you have grown up with this sense that war is wrong, war should be avoided, and you assume that most people want to avoid it.

What I am seeking to show you here is that it is true that most people have a drive in their psychology that drives them towards wanting to avoid war. This I have explained, even as the programming of the body-mind for self-preservation and the preservation of the species. There is also your spiritual connection. There is within most human beings this desire, this drive, to stop war.

What you have not been given through the official worldview is the understanding that this drive can be set aside or overridden when people's minds are taken over and controlled by beings in the emotional, mental and identity realms. What I want you to see in this discourse is that these beings in the three higher realms, as well as some fallen beings in embodiment, have no drive to stop war.

18 | The Need to Clean Up the Astral Plane

The official world view is inadequate

The fallen beings want war because it serves a deeper agenda. This is an agenda that goes far beyond what you have been presented as the causes of war in the official worldview. Some religions do talk about a devil or hell, but they still give a very inadequate understanding of what this truly means. The Western world has been heavily influenced by the materialistic worldview, which denies the existence of both heaven and hell. Can you see how incredibly inadequate it is to have a worldview that denies both the existence of the forces that want to drag you down and keep you trapped in an endless state of war and conflict and at the same time also denies the existence of the ascended masters who are the only beings who can pull humankind beyond the struggle?

It is truly incredible that the so-called modern, developed world can pride itself on being the most sophisticated civilization ever to grace the face of this planet, while at the same time maintain such a one-sided, one-dimensional worldview. I can assure you that in a century or two, people will look back at your time and see that the official worldview, that you take such pride in today, was as primitive as the belief that the earth was flat. This worldview exists only because no one has dared to speak out and say: "But the emperor has nothing on." Or rather, some people have dared, but they have not yet been heard by a sufficient number among the population.

How the beings in the astral plane create war

Let us begin by looking at the emotional octave or the astral plane. In this realm, you find certain demons and entities that were not created as self-aware beings. They were created, as I have explained, by the self-aware co-creators, including those who had fallen into the duality consciousness. They were created from the duality consciousness, meaning that, from the very beginning, they were created with a built-in sense of conflict. They see themselves in opposition to someone or something. They were also not created with self-awareness, which means what? It means they cannot receive energy from the spiritual realm.

Everything in the world is energy and all beings need energy in order to exist and do anything. These beings can sustain themselves only by stealing energy from the material realm, which means they must steal it from human beings, from the co-creators who do have a connection to the spiritual realm.

Do you see how this plays into the causes of war? The beings in the astral plane cannot create war on earth directly. They can do it only by taking over the minds of people in embodiment. When they have done so, then those people will be as unable to respond to rational reasons as the demons and entities themselves.

You have a sense that it should be possible to come up with rational reasons to get people to stop war. What you need to see is that this simply cannot happen when people have had their minds taken over by these demons and entities. The demons cannot reason rationally. They are like computers who are programmed to do one thing: they are programmed to perpetuate the very conflict out of which they were created.

If you are swimming in the ocean and you are attacked by a big shark, would it do you any good to try to reason with the shark? Nay, it would not. You should be able to see that you cannot reason with the demons and entities in the astral plane and you cannot reason with the people whose minds are taken over by them. You will know that there are certain groups in the Middle East who have posted videos on the Internet of them beheading hostages they have taken. These people are examples of those who have allowed their minds to be completely taken over by demons in the astral plane. You cannot reason with these people because you cannot reason with the demons who are ruling their minds.

This you need to understand. I am not giving you this understanding in order to make you feel hopeless but in order to help you see that the only way to deal with such people is to make the calls that allow the ascended masters to bind and consume the demons and entities in the astral plane. This will give the people in embodiment a freedom that they have not known before. They still have free will. They can continue their behavior and their aggression, but now they have been given a choice. Since their minds are no longer taken over by the demons, then, if they still choose aggression, it becomes their judgment.

How beings can be removed from embodiment

There is a very complicated equation for how people can be taken out of embodiment before their natural time. You may have heard certain spiritual teachings that say that, when you come into embodiment, your days are numbered. There is already a certain time that is your time in this lifetime, but this can vary in both directions. You may live longer or shorter depending on your own behavior.

It is possible that the people who are committing aggression can be taken out of embodiment earlier. If not, there are many cases where – when they judge themselves by choosing to continue aggression – then the full weight of their karma will be returned to them. This may incapacitate them physically through illness or even mental illness. There is a positive physical effect that can be brought about by you, but you do not bring it about by fighting these people or by trying to reason with them. You bring it about by making the calls so that the ascended masters can step in and set these people free from the demons and entities in the astral plane.

It may sound ominous that these demons and entities have to be bound and consumed, but you need to realize that they have no self-awareness. You should not allow yourself to feel any kind of pity or sympathy for these beings. There are people in embodiment who feel sympathy for the devil, as you even find in a famous rock song. This is because these people have had their minds taken over by beings in the astral plane. Or it is because they are fallen beings in embodiment who feel sympathy for the demons that they have created in past lifetimes. Some of them are proud of having created such powerful demons that can take over the minds of other people. Even through their music, they have created and perpetuated such demons. They take pride in it, and they want other people to feel sympathy for the demons that they have created so that they will feed them their energy.

What you need to recognize is that the demons and the entities that do not have self-awareness can never be free from their aggression. They were created out of aggression, and they will continue for as long as they have opportunity. A being with self-awareness has a certain opportunity. Even a fallen being is a being with self-awareness who has simply gone into the duality consciousness. It has opportunity, it has a certain time, to turn around and start the upward path. A demon and entity has no such opportunity; therefore, there is no spiritual law that extends a certain opportunity or time to these demons. As long as they are in existence, they will continue doing what they are doing. They will remain in existence until someone in embodiment makes the calls and gives the authority to the ascended masters so we can bind and consume them.

How demons have been created

You need to understand that these demons and entities have a very simple agenda. They will continue to carry out that agenda until they are bound and consumed by us. Their agenda can be described as having two elements. One is to steal energy from human beings. This I have already explained sufficiently. They can only survive by stealing energy, and they will continue to do so as long as they are allowed to do so. They will steal as much energy as possible because it makes them more powerful.

Beyond this, you need to understand that these demons were created out of conflict. They were created by fallen beings, and I will later talk about the agenda of the fallen beings. When it comes to the demons, you need to recognize that they are programmed to destroy human beings. They are programmed for destruction. They are not capable of doing anything else because they have no self-awareness. They do not even think in terms of right and wrong. You cannot reason with them and tell them that what they are doing is wrong. They cannot see it. *They cannot see it.* They are programmed for destruction, and they will continue to do everything they can to get human beings to destroy each other, to destroy nature and the planet upon which you live. This is all they *can* or *will* ever do. You cannot even say that this is all they ever *will* do because they have no will. They only have programming.

There is only one way to deal with them and that is to give the ascended masters the authority to bind and consume them. When I say bind, I mean that Archangel Michael, or one of the other Archangels, sends legions of angels into the astral plane to literally neutralize these demons. They can bind them almost with a net spun of threads of light. This instantly neutralizes the demon so it cannot then affect human beings in embodiment or even those discarnate souls trapped in the astral plane. Then, it takes a little more time for the angels to consume the negative energy or to free the energy from the negative matrix, and then the demon is dissolved permanently.

Can fallen beings take embodiment?

We will look at some of the fallen beings who have become trapped in the astral plane. I have earlier talked about how you can call these demons, in the sense that they have almost lost the self-awareness that makes it possible to reason with them. Some of these demons truly are beyond reason. In their very core, they do have a Conscious You, a conscious self, but it is totally surrounded by such a dense shell of negative energy that you cannot reach it. The Conscious You really does not have a realistic opportunity to become conscious, as long as it is trapped behind this shell.

This is one of the criteria that determines whether a certain lifestream will be allowed to embody physically or whether it will be confined to the astral plane. If there is no practical probability that the Conscious You could step outside of its normal state of awareness, then it will not be allowed to embody. If there is just some opportunity, then that being may be allowed to take physical embodiment.

Even though this being did start out as a co-creator or an angel and does have free will and does have self awareness, it is for all practical purposes unreachable. Again, you cannot reason with them, you cannot reach through. What you *can* do is to make the calls for the ascended masters to step in. What we will do in many cases is that we will bind such a being so that it cannot continue to influence human beings. This has a double purpose. It frees the human beings in embodiment from this influence or it frees the discarnate souls who are trapped in the astral plane. It also frees the fallen being itself in the sense that it is not making more karma, and it is not reinforcing the shell around the Conscious You.

Over time, we can reduce that shell and re-qualify the energy so that the being now has more of a potential for seeing beyond its state of consciousness and choosing a higher way. If it will not choose the higher, then, as I have said before, it can be permanently removed from the earth and taken to another planet. If its time and opportunity is up, it will be taken to what we have called the final judgment and the second death, whereby the Conscious You is effectively dissolved as if it never existed.

Freeing yourself from the ties to the fallen beings

You need to avoid having sympathy for such beings. There are people in embodiment on earth who followed certain powerful fallen beings when they rebelled against God. This could have happened in any of the previous spheres, beginning with the fourth sphere. There are people, even spiritual people, who still have a certain sense of loyalty towards these leaders whom they admired. You did not follow the fallen beings because you chose the evil. You followed them out of loyalty. You followed them because you believed that the fallen beings were working for a benign cause. If you sense this in yourself, you need to make an all-out effort to clarify what it is you feel and why you feel this way. What is the belief behind it? You have an opportunity to ask us to help you with this so that you can free yourself from this tie. I can assure you that for a spiritual person to maintain a tie to a fallen being will make it impossible for you to make your ascension and to make serious progress on the higher stages of the path.

You will simply come to a point where you are stopped because it is like you have a chain tied to this fallen being. You cannot go higher on the path than a certain level, which is the level at which the fallen being fell. You need to be very sensitive to this if you feel any kind of hesitancy or sympathy for why these fallen beings should not be judged, should not be bound or should not be dissolved in the second death.

The second death is not a punishment. When a fallen being falls, it is given a very, very long time span to turn around. There are beings who have refused to turn around for so long that their time has run out. This is not a punishment from God. It is simply that the being itself has chosen selfishness and duality so many times that it is beyond reason to allow it to continue to make this choice. The I AM Presence of such a being does not want the Conscious You to be given any more opportunity because it is clear that the Conscious You is not willing or able to make use of this opportunity.

Instead of the Conscious You merging back into the I AM Presence voluntarily through the ascension, the I AM Presence can choose to call back the extension of itself that it has sent into the unascended sphere. You need to respect the free will of the I AM Presence of a fallen being. You need to choose to let go of any attachment, any sympathy, for this fallen being or the fallen beings in general. Otherwise, you will be tied to these beings in the astral plane, and it will not take you beyond a certain level of your path.

What happens in the astral plane

If you could see what is really going on in the astral plane, you would be deeply, deeply shocked. I have talked about how even the modern movies with their computer generated images cannot fully depict the ugliness and the horror that takes place there. What you would see in the astral plane was that there are many souls that are trapped there. Why are they trapped there? Because it allows the fallen beings and the demons to milk them of their energy.

I want you to realize that the existence of the fallen beings and their choice to rebel against God is not a threat to God or to God's plan for the universe. There is a way to deal with everything that the fallen beings could possibly do. There is a way to get everything back in an upward spiral. There is nothing that could be created by the fallen beings that is permanent or that can destroy or oppose God's plan. It is only a matter of how long it takes and how many twists and turns individual beings create on their own path before they find their way back to their source.

From an overall perspective, there is nothing in the astral plane that could be permanent. From the perspective of an individual lifestream and soul, the astral plane can become a trap that can keep you imprisoned for a very long time. It can possibly get you into this downward spiral that you cannot get yourself out of. It becomes, so to speak, a catch-22, and it becomes a catch-22 because the Conscious You is so imprisoned in this shell of fear-based energy that it cannot have a mystical experience. It cannot directly experience that there is anything outside of its own outer state of consciousness. When you cannot even envision that there could be something outside the prison you are in, how can you then ask for help to get out of the prison? This shows you the extreme workings of free will. There are souls trapped in the astral plane. We of the ascended masters could instantly step in and help them in various ways, but we are not allowed to do so before they ask us. If they are so trapped in fear-based energy that they cannot ask because they cannot even believe in our existence or the potential that they could ever escape their situation, then we are at an impasse, so to speak. *They* are at an impasse. These souls have been deliberately trapped there by the fallen beings and the demons so they can continue to milk them for their energy.

What can help these souls become free? What I am talking about here is not only fallen souls. There are many people who have not deliberately fallen into duality by rebelling against God. They have been fooled into gradually going into duality. What can be done to help these souls? Again, you who are in embodiment have the authority to make the calls that we of the ascended masters cut free these souls from the astral plane. This is your right. This is your opportunity to give service.

If you feel empathy or sympathy, then I am asking you to *not* direct it towards the demons and the entities that are beyond help and not to direct it towards the fallen beings who are also for practical purposes beyond help. I am asking you to direct your sympathy towards the souls who have become trapped in the astral plane but who would free themselves and who would engage in an upward path if they were set free from this trap.

How a soul becomes stuck in the astral plane

How does a soul get stuck in the astral plane? It does so through a very complicated process. I will give you just a brief description of it. You know that your physical body is a fragile contraption. You know very well that when a solider goes to war, it is possible that the body can be hurt in a variety of ways. You can have holes shot through the body. You can have the body blown up so that fragments of it are scattered all over the battlefield. You can have limbs cut off. You can have fragments of metal stuck in the body that can move around in the body for a long time, possibly coming out in various places after some time. You can have poison. You can have the body burned. What you see on the physical battlefield is very parallel to what happens to the emotional body of soldiers in war.

What happens to the physical body of a soldier will be erased when that body dies, but what happens to the emotional body of the soldier will not be erased. There are emotional wounds that can be carried from one lifetime to another. When you look back at recorded history and see how many wars and conflicts there have been on this planet, you can see that it is quite possible that there could be certain souls who have embodied lifetime after lifetime in warring cultures so that they have been in many physical battles. A certain soul may have experienced being wounded or killed many times over. Each time the emotional body received wounds. It can even happen that the emotional body becomes fragmented.

When you realize that the battles seen in known history are only a small fragment of all the battles that have taken place on this earth, you can see that there are some souls who could have been wounded in war through so many lifetimes that their emotional bodies have become so hurt that they cannot actually take physical embodiment. There are literally souls that are stuck in the astral plane, not because their consciousness is too dark, self-centered or evil for them to be allowed to take embodiment, but because their emotional bodies have become so wounded that they do not have enough emotional substance to operate a physical body. I have explained to you that you are receiving energy from your I AM Presence that descends into the identity, then the mental, then the emotional, then the physical bodies. For this process to work, there needs to be a certain amount of, what we might call, body mass or substance in each of the four bodies. If a soul has been hurt during so many lifetimes that its emotional body has been wounded beyond the critical level, then it does not have enough body mass in the emotional body to integrate with and operate a physical body.

The effects of a fragmented soul parts

What can happen to the physical body is just an illustration of what can happen to the emotional body. When you are in a physical battle and go through extreme trauma, or even when you go through other forms of trauma, then pieces of your emotional body can be separated from the whole. They can be blown off, or they can be cut off. These pieces can then become stuck in various places. They can become stuck in the physical plane or, rather, the level of the emotional octave that is very close to the physical.

This means that there are soul parts that can be stuck in physical locations where they are in the astral plane right above the vibration of the physical octave. It is so close to the physical that the soul part is stuck in that physical location. This can be a battlefield or a place that you have lived in a past lifetime. There are also other levels of the astral plane where a soul part can become stuck. If enough soul parts have been taken off from the whole, then you can get to this point where you do not have enough mass in the emotional body so that you can integrate with and operate a physical body.

18 | The Need to Clean Up the Astral Plane

Some people have such severe mental illnesses that they cannot function. They are barely conscious. In some cases (not in all cases, mind you, but in some cases) this can be caused by the soul having had its emotional body so scattered that it can take embodiment, but it cannot fully operate a physical body. There are also many people in embodiment who have other severe emotional problems, and this is in many cases caused by the scattering of the emotional body. Parts of that emotional body are stuck in various levels of the astral plane. Another possibility is that you can have a toxin come into the emotional body. You can have shrapnel of emotional energies come into your emotional body. This can be almost like a hook with a hose tied to the demons and the entities whereby they can suck out your energy. There are many, many souls attached to planet earth who are stuck in various levels of the astral plane.

How to free souls from the astral plane

Once a soul has become stuck in the astral plane as it currently is on planet earth, the soul cannot free itself. When you are in physical embodiment, you have an opportunity that you do not have when you are stuck in the astral pane. You can physically find knowledge. You can find a physical book that gives you spiritual knowledge that helps you awaken. This helps you start a process of healing yourself, but this you cannot do when you are stuck in the astral plane.

Souls who are stuck in the astral plane can become free only when they are given assistance by the ascended masters. They can receive this assistance only if they ask for it, which I have explained is very difficult for them to do. The only other possibility is that someone in embodiment makes the calls for them. This involves binding and consuming the demons and entities, binding and removing the fallen beings, who are keeping these souls and soul parts stuck there.

The emotional body of planet earth has this level that we call the astral plane. It does have higher levels, but it has thirty-three levels of the astral plane, which take up most of the emotional body on earth. This is a very dark, very chaotic and very messy place. It is clearly something that most people, especially most spiritual people, do not want to know about and do not want to put their attention upon. I am not asking you to put your attention upon it in the sense that you become overwhelmed, that you tie yourself to it or that you give it your energy. I am asking you to be aware that this exists and that as long as the emotional octave, the astral plane, has not been cleared, there is absolutely no chance of removing war from planet earth.

I am not hereby saying that the clearing of the emotional realm is the only thing that needs to happen in order to remove war. There are other things, which I will address in a coming discourse. What I *am* saying is that the biggest hindrance to the removal of war from planet earth is, indeed, the astral plane. It is essential for bringing peace to earth that a critical mass of spiritual people become willing to acknowledge the existence and the nature of the astral plane. They need to gain the determination to make the calls so that the ascended masters can step in and use our power to deal with the astral plane and the beings there.

You cannot, with your own power, remove war

If this is not done, then all of the flowery talk about bringing peace and making love not war is simply *that:* talk. As you know, talk is cheap. If enough spiritual people would stop talking about making peace and would use their voices to give our invocations, then you would begin to see change. You would be surprised at how quickly things could change if enough people would give these invocations. It may sound so simple. It may sound beyond belief that this could have such an effect, but ask yourself this: "Have not spiritual people, at least since the 1960's, been talking about making love, not war? Have not quite a few of them made a lot of love, but has it removed war from this planet?"

Perhaps, it is time to remember Albert Einstein who said: "If you keep doing the same thing and expect different results, you are insane." If what you have been doing for so long has not produced the results you desire to see, perhaps it is time to do something different. Perhaps, it is time to recognize that, regardless of your good intentions, you (the spiritual people in embodiment) cannot by your own power remove war from this planet. Perhaps, it is time to recognize that thinking that you alone can remove war is a manipulation of the fallen beings. It is the essence of the fallen mindset that you think you are a god who can know good and evil and who can do something on earth.

Contributing more than good intentions

There is a very subtle and almost completely unrecognized spiritual pride that infuses the New Age movement, most spiritual movements and most religions on earth. If you are honest you will look at many spiritual movements and religions, and you will see that the people believe that they themselves (in their group, however large or small it is) are the truly spiritual people who have the power to do something for this planet. You need to remember that Jesus said he could of himself do nothing; it is the Father within who is doing the work. He also said that with men, this is impossible, but not with God, for with God, all things are possible.

Regardless of how good your intentions are, how many positive vibrations you produce and how advanced you think you are spiritually, you do not have the power to remove war from the earth. Not even all the spiritual people taken together have that power. You do not have the power. We of the ascended masters have the power. What you have is the authority. If you stop thinking that you have the power and, instead, focus on giving us the authority, then we can use our power to remove war from the earth. We will not do it based on your romantic notions of how this should be done. We will do it based on our knowledge of the reality of this planet.

We have before talked about the fact, and this messenger has talked about the fact, that many spiritual people have a correct vision of *what* should happen, namely, that war should be removed, but they do not have the correct vision of *how* this can, must and should be done. This is indeed true for many of the spiritual people in the top ten percent. You are the ones who have the biggest potential to respond to the teachings of the ascended masters and make the calls, but too many times you are dragged into various beliefs created by the fallen beings. These beliefs keep you trapped in blind alleys where you are not having the maximum impact.

You cannot clean up a mess by ignoring it

I know well that many spiritual people do not want to hear about the astral plane and the demons, the discarnates and the entities, but you cannot clean the bathroom without acknowledging that the toilet is dirty. This does not mean that you have to let the dirt affect you or cling to you. It does mean you need to put your mind on it for the time that it takes to clean it up because ignoring it will not make it go away. The astral plane is literally the toilet of planet earth. It needs to be cleaned up before there will be any positive change. Someone on earth needs to look at it, acknowledge what needs to be done, acknowledge how it can be done, and then make the calls for the ascended masters to step in and clean it up. We are the Mr. Clean of the universe, my beloved. We *will* clean up the mess on this planet, but someone needs to make the calls before we can do so.

Will you count yourself among those someone? Or will you continue to believe it can happen some other way that seems more convenient to you? Convenience is not the hallmark of those who make a difference. Those who make a difference are those who are willing to acknowledge that, on a planet as dense as earth, there are situations where things are simply so messy that you have to roll up your sleeves and clean out the mess. You cannot always tiptoe around and avoid getting dirt under your fingernails, but we have given you the tools so that you can do the clean-up and also clean up the dirt under your fingernails. It may be inconvenient. You may indeed feel a certain burden of energy when you start making calls for the astral plane to be cleared, but you have the tools to clean this up. It is a doable task.

Are you one of those who will do the task without thinking you are the doer but allowing yourself to know that you are a co-doer, a co-creator, with the ascended masters? Then, I truly welcome you into my heart where I will gladly give you as much love as you can receive. I will also be the firm mother who says: "Now, go clean up your room. Then, we can have fun afterwards." You chose to come into embodiment at this time because you wanted to help clean up this earth. It is time to roll up your sleeves and then we will have fun afterwards, either in this lifetime or after you ascend.

As this messenger once realized, it is not really the purpose of his embodiment to seek spiritual experiences. He is here to perform a certain task, and then, after he ascends, he has eternity to pursue spiritual experiences. You chose to come into embodiment to perform a task, to be part of cleaning up this earth. There are many enjoyable things you can do on earth. I am not saying you need to stop doing anything enjoyable while you are making calls for the clearing up of the astral plane. You can still live a relatively normal lifestyle. You need to do *something,* whatever you *can* do, depending on your personal situation, to fulfill the task that you set for yourself before you took embodiment.

Do I sound like a strict mother? Nay, I am simply immovable because I hold the vision for you that I held for Jesus, and that is that you fulfill your highest potential for this lifetime, as Jesus fulfilled his. Would you really want me to do anything else? Mother Mary I AM.

19 | CLEARING THE ASTRAL PLANE

In the name of the I AM THAT I AM, Jesus Christ, I call upon Mother Mary, Shiva and Astrea for the clearing of the emotional octave, the astral plane, from all demons, entities and fallen beings who are helping to start wars or preventing people from stopping war and conflict. Awaken people to the reality that we are spiritual beings and that we can co-create a new future by working with the ascended masters. I especially call for …

[Make your own calls here.]

Part 1

1. Beloved Shiva, cut all spiritual people free from the sense that stopping war is impossible or too overwhelming. Help them see that when we work with the ascended masters, stopping war is a doable task.

O Shiva, God of Sacred Fire,
It's time to let the past expire,
I want to rise above the old,
a golden future to unfold.

O Shiva, clear the energy,
O Shiva, bring the synergy,
O Shiva, make all demons flee,
O Shiva, bring back peace to me.

2. Beloved Shiva, cut all people free to see that the fallen beings see war as a tool for accomplishing certain goals. Cut people free from the illusion that it is possible to stop war through rational reasoning.

O Shiva, come and set me free,
from forces that do limit me,
with fire consume all that is less,
paving way for my success.

O Shiva, clear the energy,
O Shiva, bring the synergy,
O Shiva, make all demons flee,
O Shiva, bring back peace to me.

3. Beloved Shiva, cut free all people to see that whereas most people have a drive to stop war, there are beings in the three higher realms, as well as some fallen beings in embodiment, who have no drive to stop war.

> O Shiva, Maya's veil disperse,
> clear my private universe,
> dispel the consciousness of death,
> consume it with your Sacred Breath.
>
> **O Shiva, clear the energy,**
> **O Shiva, bring the synergy,**
> **O Shiva, make all demons flee,**
> **O Shiva, bring back peace to me.**

4. Beloved Shiva, cut free all people to see that the official worldview is inadequate and does not give people knowledge of the spiritual causes of war.

> O Shiva, I hereby let go,
> of all attachments here below,
> addictive entities consume,
> the upward path I do resume.
>
> **O Shiva, clear the energy,**
> **O Shiva, bring the synergy,**
> **O Shiva, make all demons flee,**
> **O Shiva, bring back peace to me.**

5. Beloved Shiva, cut the spiritual people free from all illusions of thinking we have to fight the people who perpetuate war and conflict.

> O Shiva, I recite your name,
> come banish fear and doubt and shame,
> with fire expose within my mind,
> what ego seeks to hide behind.

O Shiva, clear the energy,
O Shiva, bring the synergy,
O Shiva, make all demons flee,
O Shiva, bring back peace to me.

6. Beloved Shiva, I call for the ascended masters to bind and consume the demons in the astral plane, so that people in embodiment can have a free choice to either stop their aggression or bring about their own judgment.

O Shiva, I am not afraid,
my karmic debt hereby is paid,
the past no longer owns my choice,
in breath of Shiva I rejoice.

O Shiva, clear the energy,
O Shiva, bring the synergy,
O Shiva, make all demons flee,
O Shiva, bring back peace to me.

7. Beloved Shiva, cut free the people in embodiment who are in an, often unconscious, alliance with the fallen beings, and who benefit from supporting those who create war and conflict.

O Shiva, show me spirit pairs,
that keep me trapped in their affairs,
I choose to see within my mind,
the spirits that you surely bind.

O Shiva, clear the energy,
O Shiva, bring the synergy,
O Shiva, make all demons flee,
O Shiva, bring back peace to me.

8. Beloved Shiva, I call forth the judgment of Christ upon all people in embodiment who perpetuate war and conflict. I call for the ascended masters to set these people free from the demons and entities in the astral plane.

> O Shiva, naked I now stand,
> my mind in freedom does expand,
> as all my ghosts I do release,
> surrender is the key to peace.
>
> **O Shiva, clear the energy,**
> **O Shiva, bring the synergy,**
> **O Shiva, make all demons flee,**
> **O Shiva, bring back peace to me.**

9. Beloved Shiva, I call forth the judgment of Christ upon all people in embodiment who perpetuate war and conflict. In accordance with the vision of Christ, I call for the ascended masters to return their karma to them so they are unable to perpetuate war and conflict.

> O Shiva, all-consuming fire,
> with Parvati raise me higher,
> when I am raised your light to see,
> all men I will draw onto me.
>
> **O Shiva, clear the energy,**
> **O Shiva, bring the synergy,**
> **O Shiva, make all demons flee,**
> **O Shiva, bring back peace to me.**

Part 2

1. Beloved Astrea, I call forth the judgment of Christ upon all people in embodiment who perpetuate war and conflict. I call for the ascended masters to take them out of embodiment in accordance with the vision of Christ.

> Astrea, loving Being white,
> your Presence is my pure delight,
> your sword and circle white and blue,
> the astral plane is cutting through.
>
> **Astrea, come accelerate,**
> **with purity I do vibrate,**
> **release the fire so blue and white,**
> **my aura filled with vibrant light.**

2. Beloved Astrea, cut free all people in embodiment whose minds have been taken over by the astral plane, causing them to feel sympathy for the devil or other dark forces.

> Astrea, calm the raging storm,
> so purity will be the norm,
> my aura filled with blue and white,
> with shining armor, like a knight.
>
> **Astrea, come accelerate,**
> **with purity I do vibrate,**
> **release the fire so blue and white,**
> **my aura filled with vibrant light.**

3. Beloved Astrea, bind the fallen beings in embodiment who feel sympathy for the demons they have created in past lifetimes, either through music or in other ways.

> Astrea, come and cut me free,
> from every binding entity,
> let astral forces all be bound,
> true freedom I have surely found.

> **Astrea, come accelerate,**
> **with purity I do vibrate,**
> **release the fire so blue and white,**
> **my aura filled with vibrant light.**

4. Beloved Astrea, I hereby use my free will to decide that: "Enough is enough." The demons and entities in the astral plane have had sufficient opportunity to influence this earth, and by the authority of the Christ within me, I demand that they be stopped instantly and that the astral plane be cleared.

> Astrea, I sincerely urge,
> from demons all, do me purge,
> consume them all and take me higher,
> I will endure your cleansing fire.

> **Astrea, come accelerate,**
> **with purity I do vibrate,**
> **release the fire so blue and white,**
> **my aura filled with vibrant light.**

5. Beloved Astrea, bind and consume all demons in the astral plane who are stealing energy from human beings in embodiment or from souls trapped in the astral plane.

Astrea, do all spirits bind,
so that I am no longer blind,
I see the spirit and its twin,
the victory of Christ I win.

Astrea, come accelerate,
with purity I do vibrate,
release the fire so blue and white,
my aura filled with vibrant light.

6. Beloved Astrea, bind and consume the demons who were created out of conflict and who are programmed to perpetuate conflict indefinitely.

Astrea, clear my every cell,
from energies of death and hell,
my body is now free to grow,
each cell emits an inner glow.

Astrea, come accelerate,
with purity I do vibrate,
release the fire so blue and white,
my aura filled with vibrant light.

7. Beloved Astrea, bind the demons who are programmed for destruction, and who will continue to do everything they can to get human beings to destroy each other, to destroy nature and the planet upon which we live.

Astrea, clear my feeling mind,
in purity my peace I find,
with higher feeling you release,
I co-create in perfect peace.

**Astrea, come accelerate,
with purity I do vibrate,
release the fire so blue and white,
my aura filled with vibrant light.**

8. Beloved Astrea, I hereby authorize you and the seven Archangels to bind all demons programmed for war and destruction in the astral plane. Bind them with a net of light.

Astrea, clear my mental realm,
my Christ self always at the helm,
I see now how to manifest,
the matrix that for all is best.

**Astrea, come accelerate,
with purity I do vibrate,
release the fire so blue and white,
my aura filled with vibrant light.**

9. Beloved Astrea, I hereby authorize you and the seven Archangels to consume the negative energy or to free the energy from the negative matrix, so that the demons are dissolved permanently.

Astrea, with great clarity,
I claim a new identity,
etheric blueprint I now see,
I co-create more consciously.

**Astrea, come accelerate,
with purity I do vibrate,
release the fire so blue and white,
my aura filled with vibrant light.**

Part 3

1. Beloved Shiva, I hereby authorize you and all ascended masters to step in and bind the fallen beings trapped in the astral plane. Consume the shell around their conscious selves so they again have an opportunity to make free choices.

> O Shiva, God of Sacred Fire,
> It's time to let the past expire,
> I want to rise above the old,
> a golden future to unfold.
>
> **O Shiva, clear the energy,**
> **O Shiva, bring the synergy,**
> **O Shiva, make all demons flee,**
> **O Shiva, bring back peace to me.**

2. Beloved Shiva, cut free all discarnate souls who are stuck in the astral plane, so they can again have an opportunity to take physical embodiment on earth or be taken to another planet.

> O Shiva, come and set me free,
> from forces that do limit me,
> with fire consume all that is less,
> paving way for my success.
>
> **O Shiva, clear the energy,**
> **O Shiva, bring the synergy,**
> **O Shiva, make all demons flee,**
> **O Shiva, bring back peace to me.**

3. Beloved Shiva, cut free myself and all spiritual people from any ties of loyalty to the fallen beings and any sympathy for the fallen beings or the demons they have created.

> O Shiva, Maya's veil disperse,
> clear my private universe,
> dispel the consciousness of death,
> consume it with your Sacred Breath.
>
> **O Shiva, clear the energy,**
> **O Shiva, bring the synergy,**
> **O Shiva, make all demons flee,**
> **O Shiva, bring back peace to me.**

4. Beloved Shiva, bind and consume the fallen beings and demons who are exploiting such ties in order to steal the energy of spiritual people or prevent them from fulfilling their Divine plans.

> O Shiva, I hereby let go,
> of all attachments here below,
> addictive entities consume,
> the upward path I do resume.
>
> **O Shiva, clear the energy,**
> **O Shiva, bring the synergy,**
> **O Shiva, make all demons flee,**
> **O Shiva, bring back peace to me.**

5. Beloved Shiva, bind all fallen beings in the astral plane for whom it is time to go to the second death. Take them to the Lake of Sacred Fire for their final judgment so the earth can be free of the downward pull of these lifestreams.

O Shiva, I recite your name,
come banish fear and doubt and shame,
with fire expose within my mind,
what ego seeks to hide behind.

O Shiva, clear the energy,
O Shiva, bring the synergy,
O Shiva, make all demons flee,
O Shiva, bring back peace to me.

6. Beloved Shiva, bind and consume the fallen beings in the astral plane who are stealing the energy of the souls stuck in the astral plane or people in embodiment.

O Shiva, I am not afraid,
my karmic debt hereby is paid,
the past no longer owns my choice,
in breath of Shiva I rejoice.

O Shiva, clear the energy,
O Shiva, bring the synergy,
O Shiva, make all demons flee,
O Shiva, bring back peace to me.

7. Beloved Shiva, I hereby authorize you and all ascended masters to cut free and heal all souls from the emotional wounds caused by trauma from past lifetimes.

O Shiva, show me spirit pairs,
that keep me trapped in their affairs,
I choose to see within my mind,
the spirits that you surely bind.

**O Shiva, clear the energy,
O Shiva, bring the synergy,
O Shiva, make all demons flee,
O Shiva, bring back peace to me.**

8. Beloved Shiva, heal all souls whose emotional bodies have become so fragmented that they cannot take embodiment.

O Shiva, naked I now stand,
my mind in freedom does expand,
as all my ghosts I do release,
surrender is the key to peace.

**O Shiva, clear the energy,
O Shiva, bring the synergy,
O Shiva, make all demons flee,
O Shiva, bring back peace to me.**

9. Beloved Shiva, cut these souls and their soul parts free from the astral plane so they can be whole and move on in their spiritual unfoldment.

O Shiva, all-consuming fire,
with Parvati raise me higher,
when I am raised your light to see,
all men I will draw onto me.

**O Shiva, clear the energy,
O Shiva, bring the synergy,
O Shiva, make all demons flee,
O Shiva, bring back peace to me.**

Part 4

1. Beloved Astrea, set free all souls who have soul parts stuck in certain physical locations, such as battlefields. Return those soul parts so the people can again integrate fully with their physical bodies.

> Astrea, loving Being white,
> your Presence is my pure delight,
> your sword and circle white and blue,
> the astral plane is cutting through.
>
> **Astrea, come accelerate,**
> **with purity I do vibrate,**
> **release the fire so blue and white,**
> **my aura filled with vibrant light.**

2. Beloved Astrea, set free all souls who have mental illnesses because their emotional bodies are so scattered that they cannot fully operate a physical body. Heal them so they can function naturally.

> Astrea, calm the raging storm,
> so purity will be the norm,
> my aura filled with blue and white,
> with shining armor, like a knight.
>
> **Astrea, come accelerate,**
> **with purity I do vibrate,**
> **release the fire so blue and white,**
> **my aura filled with vibrant light.**

3. Beloved Astrea, set free all souls who have emotional problems caused by a scattering of the emotional body. Cut free all parts of their emotional bodies stuck in all levels of the astral plane.

> Astrea, come and cut me free,
> from every binding entity,
> let astral forces all be bound,
> true freedom I have surely found.
>
> **Astrea, come accelerate,**
> **with purity I do vibrate,**
> **release the fire so blue and white,**
> **my aura filled with vibrant light.**

4. Beloved Astrea, cut free all souls from any toxins that have come into their emotional bodies. Consume the toxic energies with your circle and sword of fire.

> Astrea, I sincerely urge,
> from demons all, do me purge,
> consume them all and take me higher,
> I will endure your cleansing fire.
>
> **Astrea, come accelerate,**
> **with purity I do vibrate,**
> **release the fire so blue and white,**
> **my aura filled with vibrant light.**

5. Beloved Astrea, cut free all souls from any "shrapnel" that form hooks in their emotional bodies and keep them tied to demons and entities in the astral plane. Bind and consume those demons and entities.

Astrea, do all spirits bind,
so that I am no longer blind,
I see the spirit and its twin,
the victory of Christ I win.

**Astrea, come accelerate,
with purity I do vibrate,
release the fire so blue and white,
my aura filled with vibrant light.**

6. Beloved Astrea, I hereby authorize you and all ascended masters to go into the 33 levels of the astral plane and cut free all souls who are stuck there and cannot even ask for assistance to become free.

Astrea, clear my every cell,
from energies of death and hell,
my body is now free to grow,
each cell emits an inner glow.

**Astrea, come accelerate,
with purity I do vibrate,
release the fire so blue and white,
my aura filled with vibrant light.**

7. Beloved Astrea, cut free all spiritual people from the willful ignorance that makes them unwilling to recognize the existence and condition of the astral plane. Help them rediscover their determination to make the calls and authorize the ascended masters to clean up the astral plane.

> Astrea, clear my feeling mind,
> in purity my peace I find,
> with higher feeling you release,
> I co-create in perfect peace.
>
> **Astrea, come accelerate,
> with purity I do vibrate,
> release the fire so blue and white,
> my aura filled with vibrant light.**

8. Beloved Astrea, cut free the top ten percent from the spiritual pride that infuses the New Age movement, most spiritual movements and most religions on earth, namely the sense that people in embodiment have the power to change the earth without working with the ascended masters.

> Astrea, clear my mental realm,
> my Christ self always at the helm,
> I see now how to manifest,
> the matrix that for all is best.
>
> **Astrea, come accelerate,
> with purity I do vibrate,
> release the fire so blue and white,
> my aura filled with vibrant light.**

9. Beloved Astrea, cut free all of the spiritual people who chose to come into embodiment in order to help clean up the astral plane in this age. Awaken them to reconnect to the choices they made so they can find their place as co-creators with the ascended masters.

Astrea, with great clarity,
I claim a new identity,
etheric blueprint I now see,
I co-create more consciously.

**Astrea, come accelerate,
with purity I do vibrate,
release the fire so blue and white,
my aura filled with vibrant light.**

Sealing

In the name of the I AM THAT I AM, I accept that Archangel Michael, Astrea and Shiva form an impenetrable shield around myself and all constructive people, sealing us from all fear-based energies in all four octaves. I accept that the Light of God is consuming and transforming all fear-based energies that make up the forces behind war!

20 | DECEPTIONS IN THE MENTAL REALM

I am the Ascended Master Mother Mary. I come to discourse with you on what is happening in the mental realm, the mental octave, and how it relates to the creation of war.

In the astral plane, things are dominated by what I have called demons, entities or even the fallen beings who appear to be demons. Their primary goal is to steal energy to sustain themselves because they are constantly at a deficit. They are constantly in danger of running out of energy. Their secondary goal is to destroy everything that can possibly be destroyed.

The fallen beings in the mental realm

In the mental realm, you do not find what you will call demons in the same way as you find it in the astral plane. You do find beings that have been created by fallen beings and that are just like the computer programs that I have said form the core of the demons in the astral plane. The beings in the mental realm do not appear as demons because they are not outwardly angry. They are programmed to promote ideas and beliefs that appear to be benign, and they can be quite deceptive. There are many, many people in the world whose minds are taken over or dominated to some extent by these entities in the mental realm, and they do not realize this.

There are also many fallen beings in the mental realm, and they seek to control or dominate human beings in embodiment. The entities in the mental realm do what they are programmed to do and have no self-awareness. The fallen beings do have self-awareness, and they have a higher level of self-awareness than those in the astral plane. The primary goal of the fallen beings in the mental realm is to control human beings, and their primary means for attaining this control is to make human beings believe in ideas.

The ideas of the fallen beings in the mental realm

There are many types of ideas promoted by the fallen beings in the mental realm. There are the more obvious ones, such as a particular religion, philosophy, branch of science or political ideology. There are also some very subtle ideas that are not generally recognized as a particular philosophy. The most subtle idea promoted by the fallen beings in the mental realm is the concept that the ends can justify the means.

The fallen beings have defined what I have called the epic struggle between good and evil, in whatever form good and evil are presented by a particular thought system. It follows from this that there is an overall end that needs to be achieved. This might be the establishment of an ideal society through a particular political ideology or even an economic philosophy.

It may also be the establishment of God's kingdom, either here on earth or in a higher realm, where all people have been saved and have entered that realm, rather than going to hell. Whatever the particular form may be, the idea is that the establishment of this ideal condition is more important than the individual human being.

There is an overall, collective goal that is more important than the individual human being. In its extreme form, this means that it is acceptable to kill individual human beings in order to achieve the collective goal. In more milder forms, you see societies that use various forms of force or control on individuals in order to achieve the collective goal.

There are many who will say: "But is it not necessary to keep the individual within the boundaries of the collective?" Well, yes and no, my beloved. What have I said before? The fallen beings create a condition, and then they present themselves and their ideas as the savior that can save people from the condition they have created. It is true that the human ego and the separate self can create chaos that makes it impossible to maintain a society. It is often portrayed by various philosophies that you only have two options: either you have a controlled society, or you have the total chaos of anarchy. These are *not* the only two options. They *are* the only two options in a dualistic system defined by the fallen beings, but they are not the only options.

The whole is more than the sum of its parts

Whenever you have two people together, a whole is created that is more than the sum of the parts. This is a basic idea that it is important to understand. You are created as an individual being. You have a divine, spiritual individuality anchored in your I AM Presence and you have individual free will right now focused in the Conscious You. You have an outer self, your four lower bodies, that may have a personality that differs from the individuality in your I AM Presence.

The whole idea of co-creation is that you are not a separate being. You are a co-creator. This has two aspects: the Alpha, the Omega, the vertical and the horizontal. The Alpha is that you are a co-creator with your I AM Presence and with the ascended masters who created the earth; the Omega is that you are a co-creator with other co-creators. You have individual, co-creative abilities. You can reach up to your I AM Presence and allow your I AM Presence to express itself through you. You can be the open door for the Presence, and thereby you can co-create alone. Two people can create more together than any of the two could create alone. More importantly, what two people can create together is more than double what they could create alone. What three people could create together is more than triple what they could create alone.

Vertical and horizontal oneness

"Whenever two or three are gathered in my name, there I am in the midst of them." These words were spoken by Jesus, but they are really an expression of the universal Christ mind, the universal Christ mind that multiplies everything. When two co-creators come together in harmony (because each of them has a certain connection to the I AM Presence), then the Christ mind will multiply their creative efforts beyond what they can bring forth directly from their I AM Presences. For this to happen, there must be a certain harmony between two or more people. This is why you get the consideration of the individual balanced with the collective.

20 | Deceptions in the Mental Realm

In the original design, the harmony between two or more people is not achieved horizontally; it is achieved vertically. If you have established a certain connection to your I AM Presence, then you know that you are not a separate individual. You are part of a larger whole. If your partner in co-creation has also established that connection, then the two of you will know and experience a certain oneness between you.

The horizontal harmony and oneness between you will be a natural effect of the vertical oneness. You will both be open doors for the flow of the universal Christ mind and the Holy Spirit. This flow of the Spirit, this River of Life, will ensure that there is balance between the individual and the collective. Once you have the vertical oneness, you do not have to use force to establish horizontal oneness or harmony.

This is something that the fallen beings cannot do because they do not have the vertical oneness, the connection to the I AM Presence. They have blocked that oneness, and their only way of achieving any kind of harmony is to achieve it horizontally. Of course, the fallen beings are separate beings. This means they can never come together with each other as equals. They are always playing the game of establishing a rank. There always has to be someone who is the leader, who is on top, who is the most powerful.

This is a safety mechanism that makes sure that the fallen beings could never take ultimate control over the earth. Whenever one dictator gains power, there is sure to be another who will oppose that first one so they can never really come together. You will see, for example, that even though Mao and Stalin were contemporaries and both claimed to be working for the spread of communism, they could not cooperate. This is the way it has always been with the fallen beings.

There may be temporary alliances where each believes they are getting something and each believes they are manipulating the other. This is not the kind of oneness that activates the flow of the Spirit and the multiplication of the Christ mind. Even when the fallen beings manage to cooperate, they can still only make use of the energies that are already in the material spectrum. They cannot activate the multiplication of the Law of the Holy Spirit.

Seeing through the perversions of the fallen beings

The fallen beings are not necessarily creating completely false ideas. They are often observing how things work, and then they are perverting them. Thereby, it becomes easier for them to fool the people on earth, especially those who have some spiritual understanding and connection. As a spiritual person, it is relatively easy for you to see through a completely false idea. It is much more difficult to see through an idea that is a perversion of a true principle.

You may have an inner, intuitive sense of the true principle, but your outer mind is not quite able to see how it has been perverted slightly by the fallen beings. As a spiritual person, you have a deep, inner belief and knowing that it is constructive and necessary for you to come together with others. You have a deep belief in the collective and the need to establish some collective body on earth. You are relatively easily deceived by ideas that say that the interests of the collective should override the interests of the individual.

As a spiritual being, you are often willing to come into a spiritual movement and follow a spiritual teacher or leader. You can often see that, in order to achieve a goal (for example, removing war from the earth), you need to set aside some of your personal interests in order to have time to study this book and give the invocations. This is natural and normal for you. What the fallen beings are doing is a perversion of this inner knowing where they seek to *force* people to come together. This is not done with respect for your divine individuality. The whole idea of the fallen beings is to get you to shut off the creative flow through you so that you are not freely expressing the energies from your I AM Presence. You are only expressing energies in a perverted form. They have been lowered so that they are no longer vibrating at the level of love but now vibrating at the level of fear.

When you are connected to your I AM Presence, you have no need to force, you have no need to suppress your individuality. You may still, as a spiritual person walking the path, need to suppress certain aspects of the outer personality, the outer self, the separate self, but you do not need to suppress your divine individuality. The fallen beings want you to suppress that divine individuality. In some cases, they want you to also suppress the human individuality, but in other cases they actually encourage people, at least some people, to express that human individuality. This depends on what they are seeking to achieve.

The whole idea of the fallen beings is that in order to achieve a collective end, you need to suppress your divine individuality because you need to live up to a standard that they have defined. You have an inner, intuitive sense that it is necessary to come together with others in a state of harmony. The fallen beings use this intuitive sense, but they pervert it by saying that you have to submit to this outer organization or thought system. They are seeking to force people to come into a state of "harmony" through sameness.

How the fallen beings seek control through sameness

Sameness is not a goal of God or the ascended masters. Each co-creator, each self-aware being, is created with a unique individuality. You are meant to expand upon that individuality and continue to do so until you reach the full God consciousness. You do not reach God consciousness by suppressing or destroying your individuality. It is not correct, as some spiritual teachings say, that the goal of life is to walk this difficult path until you reach nirvana, and then the self disappears and there is nothing left of you. This is not the goal of life. The goal of life is that you multiply what you have been given and expand upon that individuality until you reach the full God consciousness. You can then express that individuality in full measure.

It is the fallen beings who want you to believe that the goal of life is to destroy what you have been given by God. A few may believe this because they have an intuitive knowing that it is necessary for them to overcome the ego and the separate self, but that is not the same. The fallen beings want you to believe that if all human beings entered nirvana, they would all be the same. The reality is that you would all be different, beautiful facets of the diamond of the mind of God, each shining with its own sparkle and radiance.

The fallen beings want people to become the same because then they are easier to control. If everybody is the same, then it is relatively easy to predict how everyone will behave and this is the basis for control. It is not that beings in the astral plane do not seek to control people. They do, but for them the purpose of controlling people is to either steal their energy or get them to destroy themselves and each other. In the mental realm, the fallen beings seek to control people because it gives them a sense of power. They are addicted to having power. This is because you descend to the mental realm from the identity realm by lowering your consciousness.

Why the power of the fallen beings is limited

As you lower your consciousness, it is inevitable that you feel disempowered. This is one of the reasons the demons and fallen beings in the astral plane have such anger because they constantly feel disempowered. They constantly feel at a deficit. Of course, when you go into the emotional octave, your consciousness is lowered even more than in the mental. That is why the beings in the emotional realm are so angry. They are angry because they have accepted that there is nothing they can ever really do to go beyond a certain level of power. They can seek to steal energy from human beings, but they know that they cannot rise beyond the vibrations of the emotional realm.

The fallen beings in the mental realm have not quite gotten to that point of accepting the limitations of their power. They are so deceived by the intellect, and its ability to reason for or against any idea, that they believe they can manipulate the universe into functioning according to their ideas. The beings in the emotional realm have given up this belief. They realize that there are certain things they cannot change so they seek to achieve power within the boundaries that they know are immovable.

In the mental realm, the fallen beings do not believe there are any boundaries that are immovable, any laws of nature that they cannot manipulate. They think everything is susceptible to being argued about, to being argued against. They think that if they can define the right idea, they can force the universe to comply with that idea. This is why they are willing to go to such lengths to force people to conform to ideas. It is why they have come up with the notion that establishing the dominance of a certain idea or thought system is so important that it justifies the killing of almost any number of human beings.

I say "almost" any number of human beings because the fallen beings do realize that if they kill *all* human beings on earth, they will have no one to control and then they will have no sense of power. The fallen beings in the mental realm do realize this. The fallen beings in the emotional realm and the demons there do not realize this, and they have no limit to how many people they will kill. It is only a matter of what they can get people in embodiment to do.

The fallen beings in the mental realm do have a limitation, and that is why you will see that their goal is to establish the dominance of a certain thought system without going into the completely uncontrollable killing of human beings. Whereas the beings in the emotional realm will kill without reflecting upon it, the beings in the mental realm do have a desire, a philosophy or a goal to limit the human population.

It is impossible to achieve total control

The beings in the mental realm are, first of all, concerned about controlling human beings. They walk a very uneasy balance because they face certain challenges to them establishing control. On the one hand, the more people that are in embodiment, the more people they can potentially control. This will give them a greater sense of power. On the other hand, they have experienced that the more people there are in embodiment, the more difficult it becomes to control them. There is always one or a few individuals who refuse to submit to their control. They are facing this constant challenge of how to control as many people as possible, while at the same time keeping the population at the level that they can control given their current power, which is to some degree dependent upon technology.

They believe that with the advent of modern technology, they will have much better means for controlling a larger population. The mass media has been largely taken over by the fallen beings, and they use it as a means for control. The educational establishments of the world have been taken over by the fallen beings, and they use them as a platform for introducing the ideas that they think will allow them to control people. Whenever you go into duality, you can create an idea, but someone else will create an opposite idea. You now have two groups of fallen beings who each believe that they are promoting the only true idea and that it is their job to destroy those who promote the opposing idea.

Right there, you see how it is impossible for the fallen beings to ever achieve the control that they are seeking to achieve. They, of course, do not understand this, and you would not be able to explain it to them. You *will* be able to understand it for yourself, and you will be able to explain it to other spiritual people who have some intuitive knowing. They just need to be given the right teachings in order to see the fallacy of the reasoning of the fallen beings and the futility of their efforts to establish the ideal society through control. Control, truly, can never establish a permanent society on earth.

In the past, you have seen certain empires that achieved a high degree of control for a time. You will also see that, for example, the Roman Empire was in a constant state of struggle. The same was true for the Soviet Union, and the same can be said to be true for the modern so-called capitalist societies. Communism was a thought system defined by the fallen beings but so was capitalism.

These are not the only two options for developing an economic theory. This should be seen by the fact that they are both elitist in nature. In a capitalist system, the established capitalists can control the economy and keep others down. In a communist system, this has simply been taken to the ultimate level where the state controls the economy. The small elite that controls the state controls society. The alternative is, of course, to have a critical mass of people who have established a connection to their I AM Presences and can serve as the open doors for bringing forth the ideas and the flow of energy through the Spirit. It is the one, indivisible Holy Spirit that is in control of the economy, and that way you will have sustained growth in a society.

I have mentioned before that the Roman Empire faced a very difficult, or rather insurmountable, problem because they could only sustain themselves by continuing to expand their territory. There came a point where they could not expand any more, given the technology of the time. I have also explained that the size of the earth is adapted to making it impossible for the fallen beings to take complete control here. No matter what technology you develop and how good communications technology you have, you will not be able to control the entire earth. Through the Holy Spirit, you do not need to control from a horizontal level because you have oneness at a vertical level, which makes control unnecessary.

Doing what is best for you

You do not need to control people if they know that what they are doing together is what is best for them individually. People will do what is best for them. As the ascended masters say: "If people knew better, they would do better." When they know what is best for them, they will do it.

The essential problem of the fallen beings is that they do not want people to do what is best for them. They want them to do less than what is best for them so they can take advantage of them. Right there, you have the central dynamic faced by the fallen beings in the mental realm. They need to fool people in order to maintain control. Therefore, they need to keep coming up with ideas that can fool people.

The problem they face is that when an idea is implemented, (as, for example, you saw with communism), all of a sudden it faces the test: "Can it create a sustainable society?" If the idea is out of touch with the oneness of the Holy Spirit, then the society cannot be sustainable, as you saw with communism, as you saw with the Roman Empire, as you have seen with other dictatorships. You will also see this with the modern democracies with their so-called capitalist free-market economy, which is not free.

There will be limitations. The second law of thermodynamics will do its work and break down all structures in closed systems. A closed system is one that does not have the flow of the Holy Spirit. *Any* system created by the fallen beings cannot, by definition, have a flow of the Holy Spirit.

How can a system be sustained over time? Only if you can manage to get people who still have some flow of energy from their I AM Presences to believe in the system. When these people believe in the system and see it as a benign goal, they will feed their energy to the system. This can uphold the system for some time.

Exposing the deceptions of the fallen beings

That is why it is important for you to use the teachings of the ascended masters to free yourself so that you do not believe in any of the ideas and systems created by the fallen beings. You do not give your energy to sustaining them. It is also extremely important for you to make the calls for other spiritual people and the general population to be cut free from the lies and deceptions of the fallen beings. It is important for you to make the calls for the entities in the mental realm to be bound, consumed and taken from the earth.

It is important for you to make the calls for the judgment of the fallen beings in the mental realm so that they can be taken from the earth, and the earth can be freed from the weight of these beings. It is also important for you to make the calls for the judgment of those human beings in embodiment who are completely taken over by the fallen beings in the mental realm and will not let go of this. There are people who need to be taken out of embodiment in order for the earth to rise to a higher level. Making calls for this is lawful according to the Law of Free Will when your calls are based on the vision of Christ and not the vision of your outer self.

It is also important for you to make the calls for the exposure of the lies and ideas presented by the fallen beings and also for the exposure of the institutions that have become dominated by the fallen beings. The media establishments all over the world are largely dominated by the fallen beings and their ideas. This does not mean that the media is not "free" in the sense that it is independent of political parties or political ideologies. In many parts of the world, there are some very subtle ideas that are dominating the thinking of people in the media world. I am not here promoting a conspiracy theory. Of course, you can look at who owns the mass media and see that there are a few people who own the media in the so-called free world, but I am not talking about a small group of people who can control everything.

This is where there is a problem with most conspiracy theories. There is a limit to how much physical control you can establish, and the fallen beings in the mental realm realize this. That is why they are seeking to control people through ideas, and this can be very effective. For example, there are many of the nations in Europe where, not so long ago, most journalists were educated in institutions that were dominated by a dialectical mindset. This was not necessarily openly communist or Marxist, but it was based on a certain mindset of needing to always be critical of everything and to only accept what could be proven with material means. This neutralized the intuition of these journalists.

The limitations of the intellect

Do you understand what this means, my beloved? You do not, most likely, because very few people on this planet understand this. Very few people have understood the nature and the limitations of the human intellect. Rest assured, that the fallen beings in the mental realm have understood this. They have understood how to take advantage of it when it comes to controlling human beings. They have *not* understood how their own intellects are controlling themselves, and you could not make them understand this.

The intellect is a relative faculty. You can come up with an argument with the intellect, but you can always come up with a counter-argument. How do you then get anywhere? How do you know what to do, how to act? There are people (and some of them are sitting in educational institutions around the world, being the intellectuals and the scientists) who are paralyzed by their intellects. They are so good at arguing for or against, arguing both sides of the issue, that they do not know what to believe, or what is true. They are paralyzed and can do nothing. The question is: "How can you actually get anything done in a society dominated by the intellect?"

You *can* when you have an overriding idea that people have been programmed not to question. This creates a filter so that the people say: "But this we know is real so this we do not need to argue against with the intellect. The arguments that go against what we know is real, we can push aside and ignore." What does this do? It gives an incredible control to those who have defined the standard for evaluating ideas, the standard that you use to say what we need to question and what we do not need to question. Who do you think has managed to define these standards around the world? Well, the fallen beings, of course. How could you ever free yourself from the influence of the fallen beings once you have gotten into this system? You could do so only by questioning what you have been programmed not to question.

Many people are not able to do this, but if you got the idea that you needed to question the establishment, then how would you really do so? You could easily go into the closed circle of the intellect and just come up with arguments without having anything decisive. This is partly what happened to the youth movement, the protest movement, in the 1960s. They were based on the idea that they needed to overthrow the old authoritarian control of educational institutions. Once they started dismissing some of the old established ideas, they came up with so many different counter-ideas that they did not know what to believe, what to accept or what to act upon.

Escaping the quicksand of the intellect

What is the only way out of this closed circle of the intellect? It is to use your intuitive faculties to establish a connection to the I AM Presence and the ascended masters. When you have a direct mystical experience, you experience that there is something that is real. You may very well experience that there is a state of consciousness that is more real than your normal state of consciousness. That is how you know there is something that cannot be controlled by the intellect and the fallen beings. There is a reality beyond the mental level. Only by connecting to the reality that is beyond the mental level, will you be able to free yourself from the control at the mental level. Is this not obvious, my beloved?

If it is not, then consider what happens if you fall into a hole of quicksand. You are floating in the sand. There is absolutely no firm point that you can hold on to and pull yourself out of the sand. The more you struggle, the deeper you sink. The only way out is that someone outside the quicksand throws you a rope so that you have a firm point to hold on to, which then allows you to pull yourself beyond the quicksand. If you do not have that, you cannot escape the quicksand of the intellect. It has never been done, even by the biggest intellects on the planet who, in most cases, have been fallen beings. It is only through a mystical experience that connects you to your I AM Presence and to the ascended masters that you can escape the quicksand created by the fallen beings in the mental realm.

There is no other way. You may feel something in you that says: "But there *must* be another way. There *must* be a way to come up with an ultimate argument." Here is where you need to be very careful, my beloved. I have said that you have an intuitive sense and that the fallen beings will pervert it in order to trap you. You have an intuitive sense, as a spiritual being, that there is *something* that is real. As I have said, once you have an experience that there is something beyond your normal state of consciousness and that this something is more real, then you have a rope that you can use to pull yourself up. What the fallen beings will do is to pervert this sense that there is something that is real by saying: "There must be an ultimate argument that can convince all people that this idea is right."

I understand very well the difficulty you face when you are in embodiment. I have been in embodiment myself and faced this difficulty. You could even say that by giving you teachings expressed in words, we are almost confirming the idea that there must be an ultimate argument. The purpose of giving you teachings in words is, of course, to give you a teaching that can explain something that cannot be explained by traditional religions or materialistic philosophies. Take note that we have never actually claimed that the teachings we give you in words are the ultimate truth or the absolute truth. We have consistently told you that you need to never turn these teachings into an end in themselves. You use them as a springboard for gaining the direct, inner, mystical experience.

Our outer teachings are not an end in themselves; they are a ladder that you can climb until you have a direct experience of our presences, of our beings. If you allow the teachings to become a substitute for the direct experience of us, you have abused the teaching and done exactly what the fallen beings in the mental realm want you to do: Turning them into an end in themselves. The whole idea of taking the ascended master teachings and turning them into a religion and then going out using them as a weapon to fight other religions, is not coming from the ascended masters. It is coming from the fallen beings.

Our outer teachings represent the rope that we are throwing down to you. You can grab on to it and use it to pull yourself beyond the quicksand of the mental realm. You can pull yourself beyond the lies and the deceptions promoted by the fallen beings. This is the only way that human beings can escape the deception and control at the mental realm. I am not saying that the particular teachings given through this messenger are the only way to escape this. The only way to escape it is to find some teaching that helps you attain the inner, mystical experience that there is a reality that cannot be manipulated by the fallen beings at the mental level.

Do not use the teachings to argue

This is the deeper awareness that we seek to spread with our teachings. We need you to be extensions of ourselves so that you can also spread this awareness. You can also make the calls for people to be cut free to actually awaken and accept this awareness. There is literally nothing that can be gained by using the teachings of the ascended masters to go out and argue with other people at the level of the intellect. Any teaching expressed in words can be argued against.

Surely, people can come up with arguments against everything I have said in this book. Perhaps, if the book ever becomes known beyond a certain limit, then people *will* argue against it. You can rest assured that the fallen beings will seek to counter our teachings if our teachings ever seem to be a threat to them. Right now, there are, of course, fallen beings who see our teachings as a threat. They would like to shut down the flow of teachings from the ascended masters. They would like to prevent anyone from becoming an open door, a messenger, for our teachings.

They would also like to prevent anyone from accepting these teachings and from following them. Right now, we have not achieved the number of people who are studying our teachings that they have become an obvious threat to the people in embodiment who either are fallen beings or are controlled by them. That is why you have not seen an official reaction, but you might well see this if the teachings ever became known beyond a certain level.

This, of course, can also be counteracted if enough people make the calls for those who oppose the teachings of the ascended masters to be judged and taken from the earth, from the physical level, the emotional level, the mental level and the identity level. This is perfectly lawful to do, based on the vision of the Christ mind and not your outer vision. It is perfectly necessary for you to make the calls for the cleaning up of the media establishments of the world and the educational establishments of the world.

Going beyond a materialistic explanation

It is certainly a hindrance to the growth of this planet and the removal of war on this planet that there are so many of the most intelligent people who, during their education in universities around the world, have been programmed to accept certain fallen ideas without ever questioning them. One of the most important lies spread by the fallen beings over the last couple of hundred years is the idea of finding a materialistic explanation for everything and accepting only what can be proven through material means. Just look at how many scientists and educators are caught up in this idea and dare not question it.

An offspring of it is the idea that science does not need to seriously investigate the human mind, to investigate consciousness. This has been invalidated by quantum physics, which has proven that consciousness plays a role in the very fundamental processes that create the matter world. Despite this discovery by quantum physicists, scientists at large have not accepted the consequences and accepted that it is essential to study consciousness in order to reach a new level of scientific inquiry. The fallen beings have managed to keep the educational establishments around the world trapped at a certain level. Scientific inquiry cannot rise beyond a certain point because it is held back by this idea that consciousness can only be subjective and that only materialistic proof can be objective.

First of all, nothing will ever be objective if it involves a human mind when that mind is trapped in duality. You can achieve objectivity through the Christ mind, but it must be noted that even this objectivity will be individualized. This is not a problem because your divine individuality is a facet in the diamond mind of God. God has created innumerable self-aware extensions of itself. They each have a unique individuality, but they do not clash or cancel out each other.

This may seem almost impossible to fathom to the human mind. A crude illustration is that you have billions of stars in the physical universe and that they can engage in the complicated dance of galaxies without destroying each other or the universe. You do see stars that merge. You see stars that enter a new phase. Consider that you do not see conflict at the cosmic level because there is enough space in the universe for all of the stars to co-exist. I know this is a crude illustration and you can argue against it, but those who are willing can see the greater point. Divine individuality does not create conflict between individuals. It is only the separate self that creates conflict. When people attain a measure of Christ consciousness, they can work together in harmony without becoming the same, without having to control each other or to conform to a standard established by the fallen beings. What do you see if you look at the educational establishments of the entire world? What are they, really? Many want to believe that they are institutions for spreading knowledge. You are supposed to go to a university, and you attain knowledge that gives you a foundation so that, when you become a scientist or researcher, you can take science higher. You can take scientific inquiry to a new level.

If you look at what is happening in the field of science and technology, you will see an almost exponential growth in knowledge. You will see the development of new technology, new methods. If you step further back, you see that this growth in knowledge and technology happens within certain strict boundaries. These boundaries are the effect of the fact that the educational establishments of the world are not institutions for *spreading* knowledge but for *filtering* knowledge. The educational establishments of the world are based on the very subtle notion that there is a standard for what is valid knowledge and what is invalid knowledge and that this standard has to be defined in materialistic terms.

How materialistic science is fundamentally flawed

What have I told you throughout this book, and what have we told you in many of our books? The flow of the universe starts in the spiritual realm, then goes into the identity octave, then the mental, then the emotional, then the physical. If you have a scientific and educational establishment based on the idea that only what is proven with materialistic means can give you valid knowledge, then is it not obvious that this science has limited itself in a fundamental way? Only when energies have come into the physical frequency spectrum can they be detected by materialistic instruments. Science in its current form has limited itself to explaining everything that happens in the material world based on observing what has already come into the material frequency spectrum.

This would be comparable to scientists studying and seeking to explain the content of a movie by only studying the movie screen. They would refuse to consider that the images on the movie screen could be projected from somewhere else. They would refuse to go to the projection room and look at the film strip. They would refuse to go even further back and look at the director and the script writer who came up with the idea for the movie. Is it not obvious that this is a tremendous limitation of the potential of science?

What have I said throughout this book? You cannot understand the cause of war by looking only at the physical level. The causes of war start at the identity level, take a more concrete form at the mental and an even more concrete form in the emotional. Only then do they break through to the physical. The same happens with disease, the same happens with bringing forth abundance. If you want to cure disease, you need to look at all of the four lower bodies of a human being. If you want to bring forth greater abundance and eradicate poverty, you need to start researching the flow of energy through all four levels and finding ways to make better use of it in order to bring more energy into the physical spectrum.

There is a limit to how much abundance can be brought forth through technology, material technology. There will come a point where the only way to bring forth more abundance is to bring more energy into the physical spectrum. This can be done only through the minds of human beings, not through a technological, mechanical device. The only way to increase the level of abundance on earth is that a critical mass of human beings in embodiment raise their consciousness so they can become the open doors for the flow of creative energy.

How the fallen beings act as substitute teachers

These are the illusions that need to be punctured so that people in the scientific and educational establishments can awaken and cry out: "But the emperor has nothing on. The emperor of materialism has nothing on." These are the things that you need to be aware of, that you need speak out about and that you need to make the calls about. Then we of the ascended masters can step in and bind, consume and remove the energies, the entities and the fallen beings in the mental realm. We also need to remove certain human beings in embodiment who have had sufficient opportunity, but this can happen only when a critical mass of people transcend the consciousness that these people have embodied. Right now, they are there as substitute teachers, and they cannot be removed until they are no longer needed because a critical mass of people have learned the lesson in a positive way.

Do you understand this equation, my beloved? There are fallen beings in embodiment. Let us, again, use the obvious example, even though I know some of you are tired of hearing it, of Adolf Hitler. He was in essence a substitute teacher. He was meant to act out a certain state of consciousness to such an extreme that people could finally see that this was too much. How could such a person be removed from embodiment? Only when a critical mass of people in embodiment had learned the lesson so that they could speak out against and explain the fallacy of that state of consciousness through a positive awareness. If people do not have a positive awareness that a certain state of consciousness needs to be transcended, then the substitute teacher comes in to act out that state of consciousness to such an extreme that people can see it that way. When enough people internalize the lesson and now can expose that state of consciousness through a positive awareness, then the substitute teacher is no longer needed.

This is the reality faced by the ascended masters. We have so many situations where we see that humankind needs to come up to a higher level in some area. We are always watching the balance here. Is there a critical mass of people who are willing to learn the lesson and internalize the lesson into their consciousness? If there is not, then we must stand by and watch how the fallen beings in the three higher octaves manage to take over the mind of some person in embodiment so that the person becomes the substitute teacher who can act out that state of consciousness to an absolute extreme, thereby making it – hopefully – visible for more people.

Learning through the school of hard knocks

We would love for people to learn in a less dramatic and painful way. We would love to have avoided the pain and wounds created by Nazism. We had a plan that was able to achieve this, but there were not enough people in the 1920's and 1930's who responded to our teachings. Therefore, this could not be avoided. We are hoping that this will begin to change in this age so that a critical mass of people will respond to our teaching. Then we can avoid a third world war that could otherwise become a very painful substitute teacher for humankind.

We have the plans for this to be achieved. This book is part of that plan, but the success of this plan will depend on one thing only: what human beings in embodiment do with it.

We can only give teachings and then allow free will to do its work. Then, we must stand by and allow human beings to learn the way they need to learn, be it through our teachings or the School of Hard Knocks.

The School of Hard Knocks is a very effective teacher. If you do not get the lesson the first time, the second knock will become harder, and the third will become even harder. There will come a point where the knocks become so hard that very few people can ignore them. Those who *can* ignore them can no longer remain in embodiment but will become trapped in the astral plane.

Once again, I am not seeking to make you feel overwhelmed or depressed. I do need to give you a dose of reality, and I will also give you the hope that, by you responding positively to this book, you have taken an important step. By you hopefully speaking out about these teachings to others, you will contribute to creating a snowball effect that will roll around the planet. Then, a critical mass of people will abandon the old consciousness and make the calls so that we of the ascended masters can prevent not only a third world war but also many other wars that could otherwise come to pass.

If enough people make the calls, we will also be able to stop the conflicts you see today, even those that have been going on for years and seem to have no obvious solution. As I have said before: "With men, this is impossible, but not with God, for with God, all things are possible." When human beings in embodiment give the authority to the ascended masters, then all things are possible, including the removal of war from this planet. If a critical mass of people respond, we can remove war on a permanent basis. Within a couple of decades, war can be effectively ruled out as a possibility on this planet.

This is the vision I hold. I know that you hold it also in your identity body. It is my hope that this book and giving the invocations will help you consciously connect to what you already know to be a reality that is more real than anything in the physical octave. I AM more real than anything in the physical octave. I am the Ascended Master Mother Mary!

21 | CLEARING THE MENTAL REALM

In the name of the I AM THAT I AM, Jesus Christ, I call upon Mother Mary and Gautama Buddha to remove space from the demons, entities and fallen beings in the mental realm who are helping to start wars or preventing people from stopping war and conflict. Awaken people to the reality that we are spiritual beings and that we can co-create a new future by working with the ascended masters. I especially call for ...

[Make your own calls here.]

Part 1

1. Gautama Buddha, remove space from the fallen beings in the mental realm who seek to control or dominate human beings by making them believe in ideas.

Gautama, show my mental state
that does give rise to love and hate,
your exposé I do endure,
so my perception will be pure.

**Gautama, Flame of Cosmic Peace,
unruly thoughts do hereby cease,
we radiate from you and me
the peace to still Samsara's Sea.**

2. Gautama Buddha, remove space from the fallen beings in the mental realm who promote the idea that the ends can justify the means through a particular religion, philosophy, branch of science or political ideology.

Gautama, in your Flame of Peace,
the struggling self I now release,
the Buddha Nature I now see,
it is the core of you and me.

**Gautama, Flame of Cosmic Peace,
unruly thoughts do hereby cease,
we radiate from you and me
the peace to still Samsara's Sea.**

3. Gautama Buddha, remove space from the fallen beings in the mental realm who promote the idea that the goal of winning an epic struggle or establishing an ideal society justifies war and the killing of human beings.

Gautama, I am one with thee,
Mara's demons do now flee,
your Presence like a soothing balm,
my mind and senses ever calm.

**Gautama, Flame of Cosmic Peace,
unruly thoughts do hereby cease,
we radiate from you and me
the peace to still Samsara's Sea.**

4. Gautama Buddha, remove space from the fallen beings in the mental realm who promote the idea that an overall, collective goal is more important than the freedom and life of an individual human being.

Gautama, I now take the vow,
to live in the eternal now,
with you I do transcend all time,
to live in present so sublime.

**Gautama, Flame of Cosmic Peace,
unruly thoughts do hereby cease,
we radiate from you and me
the peace to still Samsara's Sea.**

5. Gautama Buddha, awaken all spiritual people so they can see through the subtle ideas created by the fallen beings through a perversion of a true principle. Help them see that the interests of the collective should never override the spiritual growth of the individual.

> Gautama, I have no desire,
> to nothing earthly I aspire,
> in non-attachment I now rest,
> passing Mara's subtle test.
>
> **Gautama, Flame of Cosmic Peace,**
> **unruly thoughts do hereby cease,**
> **we radiate from you and me**
> **the peace to still Samsara's Sea.**

6. Gautama Buddha, remove space from the fallen beings in the mental realm who seek to force people to come together and shut off their individuality and creative flow.

> Gautama, I melt into you,
> my mind is one, no longer two,
> immersed in your resplendent glow,
> Nirvana is all that I know.
>
> **Gautama, Flame of Cosmic Peace,**
> **unruly thoughts do hereby cease,**
> **we radiate from you and me**
> **the peace to still Samsara's Sea.**

7. Gautama Buddha, remove space from the fallen beings in the mental realm who promote the idea that in order to achieve a collective end, we need to suppress our divine individuality because we need to live up to a standard that they have defined.

> Gautama, in your timeless space,
> I am immersed in Cosmic Grace,
> I know the God beyond all form,
> to world I will no more conform.

**Gautama, Flame of Cosmic Peace,
unruly thoughts do hereby cease,
we radiate from you and me
the peace to still Samsara's Sea.**

8. Gautama Buddha, remove space from the fallen beings in the mental realm who promote the idea that we need to come into a state of "harmony" through sameness by suppressing the individuality given to us by God.

> Gautama, I am now awake,
> I clearly see what is at stake,
> and thus I claim my sacred right
> to be on earth the Buddhic Light.

**Gautama, Flame of Cosmic Peace,
unruly thoughts do hereby cease,
we radiate from you and me
the peace to still Samsara's Sea.**

9. Gautama Buddha, remove space from the fallen beings in the mental realm who promote ideas of sameness in order to make it easier for them to control us by making us more predictable.

> Gautama, with your thunderbolt,
> we give the earth a mighty jolt,
> I know that some will understand,
> and join the Buddha's timeless band.

**Gautama, Flame of Cosmic Peace,
unruly thoughts do hereby cease,
we radiate from you and me
the peace to still Samsara's Sea.**

Part 2

1. Gautama Buddha, remove space from the fallen beings in the mental realm who seek to control people because it gives them a sense of power.

> Gautama, show my mental state
> that does give rise to love and hate,
> your exposé I do endure,
> so my perception will be pure.

> **Gautama, Flame of Cosmic Peace,
> unruly thoughts do hereby cease,
> we radiate from you and me
> the peace to still Samsara's Sea.**

2. Gautama Buddha, remove space from the fallen beings in the mental realm who are not accepting the limitations of their power because they are deceived by the intellect and believe they can manipulate the universe into functioning according to their ideas.

> Gautama, in your Flame of Peace,
> the struggling self I now release,
> the Buddha Nature I now see,
> it is the core of you and me.

**Gautama, Flame of Cosmic Peace,
unruly thoughts do hereby cease,
we radiate from you and me
the peace to still Samsara's Sea.**

3. Gautama Buddha, remove space from the fallen beings in the mental realm who do not believe there are any boundaries that are immovable, and who think that if they can define the right idea, they can force the universe to comply with that idea.

Gautama, I am one with thee,
Mara's demons do now flee,
your Presence like a soothing balm,
my mind and senses ever calm.

**Gautama, Flame of Cosmic Peace,
unruly thoughts do hereby cease,
we radiate from you and me
the peace to still Samsara's Sea.**

4. Gautama Buddha, remove space from the fallen beings in the mental realm who are willing to take any measures in order to force people to conform to ideas.

Gautama, I now take the vow,
to live in the eternal now,
with you I do transcend all time,
to live in present so sublime.

**Gautama, Flame of Cosmic Peace,
unruly thoughts do hereby cease,
we radiate from you and me
the peace to still Samsara's Sea.**

5. Gautama Buddha, remove space from the fallen beings in the mental realm who promote the idea that establishing the dominance of a certain idea or thought system is so important that it justifies the killing of almost any number of human beings.

> Gautama, I have no desire,
> to nothing earthly I aspire,
> in non-attachment I now rest,
> passing Mara's subtle test.
>
> **Gautama, Flame of Cosmic Peace,**
> **unruly thoughts do hereby cease,**
> **we radiate from you and me**
> **the peace to still Samsara's Sea.**

6. Gautama Buddha, remove space from the fallen beings in the mental realm who want to limit the human population because they think that the more people there are in embodiment, the more difficult it becomes to control them.

> Gautama, I melt into you,
> my mind is one, no longer two,
> immersed in your resplendent glow,
> Nirvana is all that I know.
>
> **Gautama, Flame of Cosmic Peace,**
> **unruly thoughts do hereby cease,**
> **we radiate from you and me**
> **the peace to still Samsara's Sea.**

7. Gautama Buddha, remove space from the fallen beings in the mental realm who believe that with the advent of modern technology, they will have much better means for controlling a larger population.

> Gautama, in your timeless space,
> I am immersed in Cosmic Grace,
> I know the God beyond all form,
> to world I will no more conform.

> **Gautama, Flame of Cosmic Peace,**
> **unruly thoughts do hereby cease,**
> **we radiate from you and me**
> **the peace to still Samsara's Sea.**

8. Gautama Buddha, remove space from the fallen beings in the mental realm who have taken over the mass media and use it as a means for control.

> Gautama, I am now awake,
> I clearly see what is at stake,
> and thus I claim my sacred right
> to be on earth the Buddhic Light.

> **Gautama, Flame of Cosmic Peace,**
> **unruly thoughts do hereby cease,**
> **we radiate from you and me**
> **the peace to still Samsara's Sea.**

9. Gautama Buddha, remove space from the fallen beings in the mental realm who have taken over the educational establishments of the world and use them as a platform for introducing the ideas that they think will allow them to control people.

Gautama, with your thunderbolt,
we give the earth a mighty jolt,
I know that some will understand,
and join the Buddha's timeless band.

**Gautama, Flame of Cosmic Peace,
unruly thoughts do hereby cease,
we radiate from you and me
the peace to still Samsara's Sea.**

Part 3

1. Gautama Buddha, remove space from the fallen beings in the mental realm who form two groups that promote opposing ideas and who each believe they are promoting the only true idea and that it is their job to destroy those who promote the opposing idea.

Gautama, show my mental state
that does give rise to love and hate,
your exposé I do endure,
so my perception will be pure.

**Gautama, Flame of Cosmic Peace,
unruly thoughts do hereby cease,
we radiate from you and me
the peace to still Samsara's Sea.**

21 | Clearing the Mental Realm

2. Gautama Buddha, awaken all spiritual people to see the fallacy of this dualistic approach and how it is impossible for the fallen beings to establish the ideal society through control. Control can never establish a permanent society on earth.

> Gautama, in your Flame of Peace,
> the struggling self I now release,
> the Buddha Nature I now see,
> it is the core of you and me.
>
> **Gautama, Flame of Cosmic Peace,**
> **unruly thoughts do hereby cease,**
> **we radiate from you and me**
> **the peace to still Samsara's Sea.**

3. Gautama Buddha, remove space from the fallen beings in the mental realm who are promoting the ideas behind both communism and capitalism.

> Gautama, I am one with thee,
> Mara's demons do now flee,
> your Presence like a soothing balm,
> my mind and senses ever calm.
>
> **Gautama, Flame of Cosmic Peace,**
> **unruly thoughts do hereby cease,**
> **we radiate from you and me**
> **the peace to still Samsara's Sea.**

4. Gautama Buddha, awaken the spiritual people to see that the alternative to the fallen beings and their ideas is that we establish a direct contact with the ascended masters and bring forth ideas that will allow us to create a sustainable society.

> Gautama, I now take the vow,
> to live in the eternal now,
> with you I do transcend all time,
> to live in present so sublime.
>
> **Gautama, Flame of Cosmic Peace,**
> **unruly thoughts do hereby cease,**
> **we radiate from you and me**
> **the peace to still Samsara's Sea.**

5. Gautama Buddha, remove space from the fallen beings in the mental realm who do not want people to do what is best for them. They want them to do less than what is best for them so they can take advantage of them.

> Gautama, I have no desire,
> to nothing earthly I aspire,
> in non-attachment I now rest,
> passing Mara's subtle test.
>
> **Gautama, Flame of Cosmic Peace,**
> **unruly thoughts do hereby cease,**
> **we radiate from you and me**
> **the peace to still Samsara's Sea.**

6. Gautama Buddha, remove space from the fallen beings in the mental realm who know they need to fool people in order to maintain control, and who keep coming up with ideas that can fool people.

21 | Clearing the Mental Realm

Gautama, I melt into you,
my mind is one, no longer two,
immersed in your resplendent glow,
Nirvana is all that I know.

**Gautama, Flame of Cosmic Peace,
unruly thoughts do hereby cease,
we radiate from you and me
the peace to still Samsara's Sea.**

7. Gautama Buddha, remove space from the fallen beings in the mental realm who seek to maintain flawed systems by getting spiritual people to believe in them and thereby give their energies to upholding the system.

Gautama, in your timeless space,
I am immersed in Cosmic Grace,
I know the God beyond all form,
to world I will no more conform.

**Gautama, Flame of Cosmic Peace,
unruly thoughts do hereby cease,
we radiate from you and me
the peace to still Samsara's Sea.**

8. Gautama Buddha, remove space from the entities and demons in the mental realm and cut free the spiritual people and the general population from the lies and deceptions of the fallen beings.

Gautama, I am now awake,
I clearly see what is at stake,
and thus I claim my sacred right
to be on earth the Buddhic Light.

**Gautama, Flame of Cosmic Peace,
unruly thoughts do hereby cease,
we radiate from you and me
the peace to still Samsara's Sea.**

9. Gautama Buddha, remove space from the fallen beings in the mental realm who control intellectual people. Remove space from those human beings in embodiment who are completely taken over by the fallen beings in the mental realm and will not let go of the sense of superiority it gives them.

Gautama, with your thunderbolt,
we give the earth a mighty jolt,
I know that some will understand,
and join the Buddha's timeless band.

**Gautama, Flame of Cosmic Peace,
unruly thoughts do hereby cease,
we radiate from you and me
the peace to still Samsara's Sea.**

Part 4

1. Gautama Buddha, expose the lies and ideas presented by the fallen beings, and expose the institutions that have become dominated by the fallen beings.

> Gautama, show my mental state
> that does give rise to love and hate,
> your exposé I do endure,
> so my perception will be pure.
>
> **Gautama, Flame of Cosmic Peace,**
> **unruly thoughts do hereby cease,**
> **we radiate from you and me**
> **the peace to still Samsara's Sea.**

2. Gautama Buddha, remove space from the fallen beings in the mental realm who have understood the nature and the limitations of the human intellect and who have understood how to take advantage of it when it comes to controlling human beings.

> Gautama, in your Flame of Peace,
> the struggling self I now release,
> the Buddha Nature I now see,
> it is the core of you and me.
>
> **Gautama, Flame of Cosmic Peace,**
> **unruly thoughts do hereby cease,**
> **we radiate from you and me**
> **the peace to still Samsara's Sea.**

3. Gautama Buddha, remove space from the fallen beings and demons at the physical level, the emotional level, the mental level and the identity level who oppose the teachings of the ascended masters.

Gautama, I am one with thee,
Mara's demons do now flee,
your Presence like a soothing balm,
my mind and senses ever calm.

**Gautama, Flame of Cosmic Peace,
unruly thoughts do hereby cease,
we radiate from you and me
the peace to still Samsara's Sea.**

4. Gautama Buddha, remove space from the fallen beings in the mental realm who promote the idea that there must be a materialistic explanation for everything and society should accept only what can be proven through material means.

Gautama, I now take the vow,
to live in the eternal now,
with you I do transcend all time,
to live in present so sublime.

**Gautama, Flame of Cosmic Peace,
unruly thoughts do hereby cease,
we radiate from you and me
the peace to still Samsara's Sea.**

5. Gautama Buddha, remove space from the fallen beings in the mental realm who promote the very subtle ideas that prevent people from questioning the establishment in all areas of society.

21 | Clearing the Mental Realm

> Gautama, I have no desire,
> to nothing earthly I aspire,
> in non-attachment I now rest,
> passing Mara's subtle test.
>
> **Gautama, Flame of Cosmic Peace,**
> **unruly thoughts do hereby cease,**
> **we radiate from you and me**
> **the peace to still Samsara's Sea.**

6. Gautama Buddha, remove space from the fallen beings in the mental realm who promote the idea that science does not need to seriously investigate the human mind or consciousness.

> Gautama, I melt into you,
> my mind is one, no longer two,
> immersed in your resplendent glow,
> Nirvana is all that I know.
>
> **Gautama, Flame of Cosmic Peace,**
> **unruly thoughts do hereby cease,**
> **we radiate from you and me**
> **the peace to still Samsara's Sea.**

7. Gautama Buddha, remove space from the fallen beings in the mental realm who promote the idea that consciousness can only be subjective and that only materialistic proof can be objective.

> Gautama, in your timeless space,
> I am immersed in Cosmic Grace,
> I know the God beyond all form,
> to world I will no more conform.

> Gautama, Flame of Cosmic Peace,
> unruly thoughts do hereby cease,
> we radiate from you and me
> the peace to still Samsara's Sea.

8. Gautama Buddha, remove space from the fallen beings in the mental realm who use the educational establishments of the world to promote the idea that there is a standard for what is valid knowledge and what is invalid knowledge and that this standard has to be defined in materialistic terms.

> Gautama, I am now awake,
> I clearly see what is at stake,
> and thus I claim my sacred right
> to be on earth the Buddhic Light.

> Gautama, Flame of Cosmic Peace,
> unruly thoughts do hereby cease,
> we radiate from you and me
> the peace to still Samsara's Sea.

9. Gautama Buddha, by the Christ within me, I hereby give authority to the ascended masters to step in and bind, consume and remove the energies, the entities and the fallen beings in the mental realm so that this planet can be set free from the limitations of materialism.

> Gautama, with your thunderbolt,
> we give the earth a mighty jolt,
> I know that some will understand,
> and join the Buddha's timeless band.

**Gautama, Flame of Cosmic Peace,
unruly thoughts do hereby cease,
we radiate from you and me
the peace to still Samsara's Sea.**

Sealing

In the name of the I AM THAT I AM, I accept that Archangel Michael, Astrea and Shiva form an impenetrable shield around myself and all constructive people, sealing us from all fear-based energies in all four octaves. I accept that the Light of God is consuming and transforming all fear-based energies that make up the forces behind war!

22 | ILLUSIONS OF IDENTITY

I am the Ascended Master Mother Mary! Consider for a moment the question: "What is war?" War can be said to be the antithesis of life. Then, what is life? Life is an opportunity to expand self-awareness.

When you look at a human life, one physical body, it may seem insignificant when you consider the amount of people that are in embodiment right now, the amount of people that have been in embodiment in the past and have died, and how easily people can die, how easily many people can die, how easily millions of people can die in a war. From a cosmic perspective, one life is not insignificant because that life represents a unique opportunity for that particular lifestream to expand its self-awareness. Given that this lifestream is a part of the whole, then that one life is significant for the whole.

The whole can be said to be what? Ultimately, it is God, and then it is all beings in the spiritual realm who form the hierarchal structure, the pyramid of life, out of which you are a part. You are one individual lifestream, and you are, so to speak, at the lowest level of the pyramid of life. You have volunteered and have decided to descend into the most dense sphere because you realize that the density of this sphere affords you an opportunity for growth, and thereby you are helping the whole to grow. This means that a physical life on planet earth has a cosmic significance because it is an opportunity for the whole to grow.

Thou shalt not kill

This is the real reason why the command was given: "Thou shall not kill." This is the real reason why it is an unconditional command. This is the real reason why God or the ascended masters never defined any conditions based on which it becomes acceptable or even desirable to kill other human beings.

We realize that free will must be allowed to outplay itself. There are many things you can do to interfere with or force the free will of other human beings. I am not saying they are lawful. What I *am* saying is that the one thing that you definitely are not allowed to do according to the law is to take the life of a human being in embodiment. This not only interferes with free will but it also cuts off the opportunity to exercise free will for what would have been the remainder of that lifetime.

It is not that it is lawful to force others, but as long as they are in embodiment, they still have the opportunity to make certain choices that they will no longer have once the physical body dies. The soul and the lifestream lives on, of course, and it can still grow even though it is not in a body. It can still make choices based on that embodiment, even based on the way it died, but it is not the same opportunity as it would have been to remain in embodiment.

I am fully aware that hardly anyone on this planet has grown up with an awareness of what I have just told you. Most religions do not even give you this awareness and this understanding of the value of life, the purpose of life. Certainly, materialist philosophies of any persuasion cannot do so. This is why so many human beings on earth are susceptible to the lies, the deceptions, the manipulations of the fallen beings in the identity realm. These beings rarely work directly with human beings because most human beings are attuned to either the astral plane or the mental realm. There have been a few people in embodiment who have been able to attune to the fallen beings in the identity realm. They have received ideas directly from these beings in the identity realm, and they have been incorporated into various philosophies both political, religious and so-called scientific philosophies.

Ideas from fallen beings in the identity realm

There have been many of these. I will mention but a few. Christianity, of course, started with the teachings of Jesus. He had attained a very high level of Christhood and was able to receive pure teachings. The problem was that, because of the technology of the time, not everything that Jesus said was passed on accurately before it was written down. There were many things that Jesus could not say because of the limited awareness of the people at the time.

Nevertheless, Christianity did start out with a pure foundation, but that foundation was severely distorted after the formation of the Catholic Church. St. Augustine, who is considered one of the primary church fathers, was an example of a person who was able to tune in to the fallen beings in the identity realm. Other church fathers were able to do so to a lesser extent. The whole idea of original sin was not invented by Augustine but was channeled by Augustine, as we might say with a modern expression, by him tuning in to the fallen beings in the identity realm.

They were the ones who came up with the idea that human beings are fundamentally flawed because they were created that way by God. This is an idea that could not originate with God or with the ascended masters because we know the reality that I started out telling you. You are an extension of the entire hierarchy of self-aware beings that reaches all the way back to the Creator. Therefore, you cannot be created in a way that is fundamentally different from the rest of this hierarchy, and certainly the entire hierarchy is not made of flawed beings. We know that we were not created as sinners. Therefore, we also know that human beings are not created as sinners. You *are* created with free will and with a point-like sense of self-awareness, which you can then expand upon.

You understand that, in the original pure state and in the original vision of God, you would never descend into a state of consciousness where you could even entertain the idea that there was something wrong with you. It is entirely possible to start with a point-like self-awareness and expand it to the full God consciousness without ever going into the negatives of seeing yourself as wrong, flawed or a sinner. You can grow to full God consciousness by having an entirely positive experience. You start out with a certain self-awareness and you expand upon it, build on to it and spiral upwards without ever seeing yourself as having failed, as having made a mistake, as having sinned.

Consider rationally the reasoning of the fallen beings

There is no necessity for going into this negativity, my beloved. This is a complete invention of the fallen beings. It was invented in a previous sphere, but for earth it is focused in the beings in the identity realm. They are the ones who have come up with the even more subtle idea that something has gone wrong with God's creation. This is their very operational idea, as we might say, their modus operandi. This is their primary idea. They truly, at least some of them, believe that there is a flaw in God's design, that God somehow made a mistake. They also believe that someone needs to correct that mistake, and that someone is, of course, *them*.

Let me ask you to consider this logically and rationally, even though I realize there are some limitations to logic and reason. When you understand what the fallen beings are saying, you understand that the core of their argument relates to free will. The mistake that God made was to give self-aware beings free will. Beings with free will have the option to go against the growth process of the entire cosmos. They can choose to rebel against self-transcendence and the growth in consciousness. By giving beings free will, God gave them the potential to go into the duality consciousness and see themselves as separate beings, rather than connected to the whole. This is what the fallen beings say is the flaw in God's design.

Now use a little bit of reason and logic here. Free will is *free*. The fallen beings are not disputing, at least not at the identity level, that you have free will. They are saying that it is the problem. If free will is truly free, as they do acknowledge, how can there be a mistake on God's part? Yes, it is a potential that you can go into duality, but it is not a *necessity*. What God has truly done by giving you free will is that God has said: "The goal of life is to expand your self-awareness, but *you* decide how you do this." We might say that, ultimately, the goal is to walk a path that leads from a point-like sense of self to an omnipresent sense of self. God has given you complete freedom as to how you walk that path, how you define your own path. Yes, you can choose to go into separation and duality. Yes, there are certain consequences of doing this. It becomes a self-reinforcing, closed circle. It is much more difficult to get out of it once you have gone into it, but you *can* get out of it. You can never quite lose the ability to step outside of your state of consciousness and attain pure awareness.

I have talked about the fallen beings who become almost completely trapped in a downward spiral. We of the ascended masters are not trapped in that downward spiral. We can confront them with the reality that there is something outside of their own spiral, and this gives them the opportunity to step out of it and to, thereby, walk the path back to oneness.

God does not distinguish fallen and not fallen

There are those who will say that once you have fallen, you have fallen and there is no way back. This is not the case from God's perspective. What I am giving you here is the idea of beings who have fallen and beings who have not fallen. This is not even considered by God. It is not that what I am saying to you is not true or correct. It is just that what I am giving you is a perspective based on the fact that you live on a planet that is so heavily dominated by the fallen consciousness, by the duality consciousness. I am giving you a contrast between the fallen consciousness and the Christ consciousness, between those who have fallen and those who have not. From God's overall perspective, God does not even see this.

God only sees that the fallen beings have chosen a certain path. It does not really matter to God in which direction they are going, whether they are going *with* the flow of the entire cosmos or *against* that flow. If they awaken, they can still come back to oneness, and now they have what you all have, a certain individualized perspective. Yes, certainly, on a planet like earth, the fallen ones have created tremendous suffering for others and for themselves. Certainly, it is not necessarily the path that God would have envisioned or that the ascended masters would have envisioned for any lifestream. It is still a path that can lead you back to oneness—once you awaken from it.

Why is this so? It is so because whether you take the upward path or the downward path, what are you doing? You are starting out with a point-like sense of self. You then define a wider self, and you define a wider self and a wider self. Each time you go from one sense of self to another, the former self dies. Whether you are conscious of this or not, you are saying: "I am not this." Do you see the essential realization here? Growth, life, self-transcendence is a process whereby you look at your present self, and you say: "I am not this." It does not really matter what your present self is. You still grow in only one way, by coming to the realization: "I am not this." You may be a saint, you may be a sinner, but the way to transcend and go beyond is still to say: "I am not this."

We have before hinted at the fact that there can be those who consider themselves very spiritual and religious people and who have built a spiritual sense of self, and this may actually prevent them from ascending. They are so attached to this spiritual self that they think they have to take it with them into heaven, and they will not let go of it. Even if you have qualified for your ascension, there still comes that point where you have to look at the self that brought you to that point, and then you have to say once more: "I am not this." *Then,* you can rise to the ascended state.

There is no condition whatsoever that could ever exist in an unascended sphere, even in the deepest levels of hell, that could prevent a lifestream from transcending that condition. Yes, I have said that the fallen consciousness becomes a self-reinforcing downward spiral. Yes, I have said you cannot pull yourself out of it by your own power, but this does not mean you cannot transcend it by coming to see that this is just a self and that you are not this.

You are not a sinner or an animal

This is important for spiritual people to understand because it allows you to see through some of the illusions projected on humankind by the fallen beings in the identity realm. There is, of course, the illusion that you are a sinner, that you are somehow flawed by nature because God has created you that way. This is, we might say, the Alpha illusion. The Omega aspect of the same illusion is that you are nothing more than an evolved animal, that you really are an animal, that you are an entirely material being. Your personality, your sense of self-awareness, your consciousness is a product of mechanical processes in the physical brain and will be extinguished when the brain ceases to function. When somebody flips the switch and turns off the light in the brain, then you are supposedly gone.

Consider how much this has limited people and is still limiting people today. Consider how many people grow up feeling they are sinners. Their entire lives are revolving around compensating for this condition that God has supposedly put upon them from the very beginning. What good and perfect God would come up with the idea to create you as sinners who are fundamentally flawed by design and, therefore, condemned to suffering until God's son supposedly comes down and has mercy upon you, saves you and takes you to heaven? What would be the purpose of this? How could this help you grow in self-awareness?

Why the fallen beings don't talk about separation

Then, there is the deeper sense that you are not only a sinner or a material being, but you are a *separate* being. This people readily believe because it is an effect of going into the duality consciousness. You start seeing yourself as a separate being when you step into duality. The fallen beings do not even need to come up with a philosophy that defines this. In fact, they have not done so. You will notice that there is hardly a philosophy on earth that talks about you being "separate beings," as something that is unavoidable. It is only the ascended masters who talk about the idea that you are a separate being.

Why do the fallen beings not talk about this? Because they do not want to even put the idea in people's minds that you are separate beings. Why not? Because when you say that you are a separate being, you are at the same time saying that there is an alternative, namely that you could be a not-separate being, a connected being. The fallen beings at the identity level do not even want you to know this as an option. They do not want you to even be able to question separation, and that is why they do not have any philosophies that define separation as unavoidable, necessary or beneficial.

Do you see how subtle the fallen beings can be, how manipulative, how calculating? What they are really trying to say with various philosophies is that you are not a spiritual being. Even many religions portray you as not being a spiritual being by saying that you are a sinner or that you are flawed or limited in other ways.

Even many modern so-called New Age movements are centered around a guru who supposedly has special qualities. This is, again, an idea created by the fallen beings. There is one person who has special qualities, therefore, you should follow that guru because he or she is so special. In defining this, you are also automatically putting yourself down as not having the same inherent qualities as the guru. Are not all men and women created equal? Are not all self-aware beings created with a point-like self and the opportunity to rise in awareness? How can one guru be so fundamentally different from you? How can thinking that the guru is fundamentally different from you help your growth in self-awareness?

It cannot, but it can help you follow the fallen beings. Of course, if this is the experience that you need to have on your way back to God, then by all means pursue it. What I am seeking is those who have had enough of pursuing that experience and who are ready to step up to a higher level and say: "I do not want one of these fallen gurus. I want an ascended master as my guide, as my teacher, as my guru."

Denying your Christ potential

The fallen beings will deny the reality that you are an extension of the Creator's being, that you are an extension of an ascended Master, that you are a spiritual being, that you are a son or daughter of God. They want you to deny, first of all, your Christ potential.

What is the Christ? The Christ is basically a state of mind. It is the one mind, the indivisible mind. The mind that always knows that, regardless of appearances on a dense planet like earth, the underlying reality is that all life is one. God is everywhere. Nothing can be separated from God's creation.

This is what the fallen beings do not want you to realize for yourself. It is okay that you are following a guru who supposedly has Christ consciousness, but you are not allowed to claim it for yourself. That is why they defined these false gurus who do not have Christ consciousness but who may claim to do so or to have some other superior state of consciousness, be it enlightenment or whatever it is.

There are many false gurus in the world, and there have been many false gurus throughout time. Some of them have, indeed, been able to tune in to the fallen beings in the identity realm. They have fulfilled the function of leading those astray who may be close to having the potential to manifest personal Christhood. By following one of these false gurus, you deny that potential because you are always looking to the guru as being the only one who could attain that superior state. Jesus, when he was in embodiment, met an Indian guru who was such a false guru. The guru did everything he could possibly think of to get Jesus to deny his own Christ potential. This was a necessary initiation for Jesus. He had to pass that test and still be willing to claim his Christhood. It was a difficult test for Jesus, I can assure you, as it will be for everyone.

We have said: "When the student is ready, the teacher appears." Many of you will know from your own personal experience that when you do discover a true teaching or a true teacher, you are often presented with a false teaching and a false teacher at the same time. Many of you have had to follow a false teaching or false teacher for some time. You needed that contrast, that perspective, so that you could see the difference between the higher and the lower, the true and the false, between that which is based on duality and separation and that which is based on oneness. You could see the difference between that which is based on raising the individual from an ego-perspective so you are raised to superiority, or raising the individual based on the Christ perspective where you are raised into oneness.

How the fallen beings create a false path

The fallen beings in the identity realm have been very clever at creating a false path. They know, as Abraham Lincoln said, that: "You cannot fool all of the people all of the time." From time to time, someone begins to awaken, and then they do everything they can to lead that someone onto the false path. This leads that person to seek to raise up the separate self to a state of perfection where it supposedly becomes acceptable to God. Therefore, God is almost forced to allow him to come into heaven.

This is what some of the fallen beings in the identity realm are believing about themselves. They honestly believe that if they can get enough people on earth to follow their false ideas, then God will be forced to acknowledge their superiority and allow them not only to enter heaven but to also have power over the unascended lifestreams on earth and other planets. Some of them have dreams of being the master of the entire universe. That is why some of them have a certain anger against the people on earth who will not comply, who will not follow them blindly, and support their dream of being the undisputed masters of this planet.

Fallen beings in the mental realm and identity realm

The fallen beings in the identity realm have done everything they can to distort people's identity. The purpose is to prevent you from claiming your Christhood while you are in embodiment. They want to do everything possible to prevent you from following the example of Jesus, as we explained in several other books. The last thing they want is for ten-thousand Christed beings to step forward, to claim their Christhood and express it publicly. What will they do to prevent this? Absolutely anything in their power.

The fallen beings in the identity realm have a very high degree of control over the fallen beings in the mental realm. They have a somewhat lesser degree but still a high degree of control over the fallen beings and the demons in the astral plane. Some of these demons are so far out into anger and destructivity that no one can really control them, but it does not matter because the destruction they are into actually supports the agenda of the fallen beings in the identity realm, at least to some degree.

As I said about the fallen beings in the mental realm, they do face a certain challenge. They want to control people so there must be people in embodiment to control. They cannot kill them all in a war. This is faced also by the fallen beings in the identity realm, and that is why they do sometimes look at the demons in the astral plane as being beyond their control. They look at this as a threat because their goal is not necessarily to kill all people on earth. Their goal is to control them but, if they cannot be controlled, then they are perfectly willing to kill them, even kill all of them. This is a subtle difference between the fallen beings in the identity realm and those in the mental realm. Those in the mental realm do not want to kill all people because that would defeat their desire for control. The beings in the identity realm are not driven primarily by a desire to control people on earth. They are driven by a desire to control God. This, of course, is impossible, but they cannot see this, and you could not explain it to them. I can assure you from personal experience of having tried.

The fallen beings cannot be reasoned with

Even after we qualify for our ascension, we have to go through a learning process before we actually qualify to serve in a capacity such as what I am serving, holding the office of the Divine Mother for earth. We have to go through a testing where we are allowed to attempt to persuade the fallen beings with the perspective we have as ascended masters.

We need to have the direct experience that even we as ascended masters cannot persuade the fallen beings of the errors of their ways. This helps us serve the unascended brothers and sisters on earth by understanding what you are going through when you are in embodiment. We understand that there are certain tasks on earth where you cannot use reason, logic or even the Christ mind. You cannot persuade people, and that is why the only way to raise a planet is to remove certain beings so that the state of consciousness they represent, that they have embodied, can also be removed from the earth.

Instead of focusing on persuading the fallen beings, we are focusing on persuading and awakening the spiritual beings who are still in embodiment. They can use their authority to make the calls so that we can step in and remove some of the fallen beings and the state of consciousness they embody from the earth. This is how we can raise the earth, not by working with the fallen beings but by working with the spiritual beings in embodiment who have come to the point where they have had enough of seeing the havoc wreaked by the fallen beings on earth.

The authority rests with people in embodiment

In this book, the central question for you has been: "Have I had enough of war on earth?" Have you come to the point where you look at war and you say: "It is absolutely unacceptable and intolerable to me that war continues to happen on this planet. I will no longer accept war on planet earth." This is the determination I have attempted to bring you to through various steps. The fallen beings will do everything they can to prevent you from coming to that point because they also know that you who are in embodiment have the authority.

The fallen beings in the identity realm are in a certain sense feeling high and mighty because they feel they have immense power, knowledge, insight and ability to control. They have a mastery of controlling and deceiving, and this makes them feel very powerful. On the other hand, they also know the reality of the law that they do not have any authority over planet earth because that authority rests with the lifestreams who are in physical embodiment. They may be able to control, manipulate and deceive you, but they also know that if you were to free yourself from that control, then you have the authority to call for them to be bound and taken from the earth. We of the ascended masters would instantly execute that authority given to us by you.

They know they are walking a fine line. They are walking on a knife's edge. They even know that, by seeking to deceive you, they are actually increasing the opportunity that you will awaken. The more they go to extremes in order to keep up their deception, the more visible their deception becomes. As I have said, Hitler, Stalin and Mao were allowed to go to such extremes because they became substitute teachers. Whatever the fallen beings do, they must go to greater and greater extremes, and this makes their deception and its consequences more visible.

What you need to understand about the fallen beings in the identity realm is that on the one hand they might appear to be very benign, very advanced, very masterful, very powerful. Certainly, they *are* very skilled at using the intellect and coming up with reasoning and ideas. You would not necessarily look at these fallen beings, if you could see them, and see them as the typical warmongers who are out to create war. You might very well think that they are peaceful. You might think that they are actually seeking to create an ideal society on earth by promoting a false Christianity.

Look at how, for over a thousand years, the Catholic Church held the Western world in an iron grip with its doctrines and dogmas. What was the claim? It was that this is the only true way to salvation and that, therefore, the Catholic Church was promoting the eternal salvation of people on earth. The Catholic Church was almost entirely the brainchild of the fallen beings in the identity realm so how could it be fulfilling that purpose? Yet, it was making the claim, was it not?

Then look at another brainchild of the fallen beings in the identity realm, that of Marxism, Communism. Again, it was claiming to establish an ideal society on earth. Another offshoot was Darwin's theory of evolution in its original form, the idea that you are an evolved animal and then the idea of the survival of the fittest. The entire materialistic mindset that followed it was also the brainchild of the fallen beings, claiming to liberate the minds of human beings from the dogmas and doctrines of the Catholic Church. Who created the dogmas and doctrines of the Catholic Church? Oh yes, was that not the fallen beings in the identity realm? Who is now claiming that they want to liberate you from those dogmas and doctrines by giving you materialism? Oh yes, that is also the fallen beings in the identity realm.

Seeing through the smokescreen of a benign cause

Have you had enough of being like a bull with a ring in your nose, being pulled around by these fallen beings? Have you had enough of this, my beloved? Then, I am offering you, in this book and in our other teachings, the path to freedom from the fallen beings, the fallen mindset and the consciousness of duality and separation. This is what we have been giving you through this messenger: A systematic path that can take most spiritual people on earth to a state of freedom from duality and freedom from the fallen beings.

In this book, I am also seeking to take you to the point where you are not only pursuing your personal freedom. You are also seeing that you, by raising your consciousness to a certain level, can claim the authority to make the calls and set other people free as well. You have the potential to be one of the forerunners for removing war from the earth. You need to understand that in order to really, truly remove war from the earth, we have to remove the fallen beings and the consciousness behind war.

That is why you need to step up and look at the fallen beings in the identity realm. You need to see that, even though they are putting on a facade of working for a benign, beneficial cause, this is all lies. This is all a smokescreen. I have said that the fallen beings in the mental realm would not kill all people on earth. I have said that the fallen beings in the identity realm would, indeed, kill all people on earth if they could not control them. Why is this so? Because the fallen beings in the identity realm have the overall agenda of wanting to prove God wrong. How do you ultimately prove God wrong? You do so by proving free will wrong, by proving that free will leads to disastrous consequences.

Fallen beings are insensitive to human beings

The fallen beings think that, if they can get all human beings on earth to enter a completely self-destructive spiral, then they will have ultimately proven that free will has such drastic consequences that it must be a mistake. I have attempted to explain to you why this can never work, but the fallen beings cannot and will not see this. The fallen beings in the identity realm, who otherwise appear benign, benevolent and masterful, still have such anger against God that they are ultimately willing to kill all human beings on earth. They are willing to have them kill each other and even to destroy the entire planet in order to prove their point.

If you look at the fallen beings – beginning with those in embodiment, those in the astral plane, those in the mental plane and those in the identity level – you can see a very strange, almost contradictory phenomenon. I have told you that you cannot reason with someone like Hitler because their minds are closed. I have told you that the demons in the astral plane are so trapped in anger that there is no reasoning capability there. I have told you that the beings in the mental realm are so trapped in the intellect that you cannot cut through.

In a sense you could say that Hitler was insensitive to the suffering of those he considered expendable, such as the Jews. The fallen beings in the astral plane are also insensitive because they are so trapped in anger. They have no consideration for human beings. The fallen beings in the mental realm are so trapped in their intellectual, spiritual pride that they also are very insensitive. Even though the fallen beings in the identity realm may appear to be the most sophisticated, the most masterful, and may appear to be working for a benign cause, they are actually the ones who have the most extreme insensitivity towards human beings.

They have no consideration whatsoever for human beings. They are just pawns in the game. They are just tools. They are just pieces they can move around on the battlefield. They are willing to destroy the entire planet in order to prove God wrong. Their first agenda is to control everything, but if they cannot control, they are willing to destroy. You need to look at this as a spiritual being. You need to realize that this is the reality. The fallen beings are absolutely unbending. They are completely insensitive to you, to all human beings and to any argument or reasoning you could ever come up with.

Being reasonable when dealing with the fallen beings

I am not telling you this because I want you to become angry at the fallen beings. I am telling you this because you have an intuitive sense of the oneness of all life. You tend to believe that it should be possible to turn any being around, that it should be possible to make everything good. I realize that even what I am telling you here can be used in your mind to reason like this. I have told you that there is no fallen being who is beyond redemption, that they can always awaken. You have to realize that the fallen beings in the identity realm, who are attached to planet earth, cannot be awakened *from below*. They cannot be awakened by any being on earth. There is nothing you could do or say that could awaken them. They have reached a point where, if they have not already been awakened by being associated with the earth, then they cannot be awakened by remaining with the earth. They must go somewhere else and receive a new opportunity. It truly does not matter where they go. This is not essential for the progression of the earth.

What I want you to see here is that you need to make a decision. Where is your loyalty? Where is your interest. Where is your attachment? Where is your desire, your vision? Do you want to try and save the fallen beings in the identity realm, or do you want to make an effort to raise the earth? You have free will. If you are attached to the fallen beings, then by all means follow them, but then you are beyond the tools and teachings I give you in this book. If you know in your heart that you came into embodiment in order to raise the earth, then I am asking you to step up and realize that this can happen only in one way: The fallen beings *must* be removed from the earth!

I am not asking you to be angry or negative towards them, but I am asking you to be absolutely realistic in seeing that these fallen beings in the identity realm have had a very long time with this planet. They have had a very long time with other planets. It is time for them to go so that the earth can move forward. If you feel this determination, then you can make the calls and give us the authority to remove these fallen beings so that the earth can become lighter. More people can wake up and start seeing the false ideas that program them towards war.

Seeing the fallacy of fallen ideas

All of the ideas spread by the fallen beings in the identity realm can so easily be turned into a justification for war. You can see how the Catholic Church justified war in the crusades and in the wars against the Protestants and how communism justified war and how materialism, even though it may not directly justify war, certainly becomes an indirect justification for war. The idea of survival of the fittest appealed very much to Hitler and was part of his intellectual reasoning for the superiority of the German people and their right to forcefully suppress other people and to forcefully kill those Jews who were unfit, according to their ideology.

People need to wake up and see the fallacy of these ideas. The most important step in that direction is to remove the fallen beings in the identity realm. The next step is to make the calls for the energies and for all of the structure that is below the fallen beings in the identity realm to be consumed. You understand that for each fallen being in the identity realm, there is an entire structure below them, a false pyramid, a pyramid of death. There are beings in the mental realm that are directly tied to or controlled by the fallen beings in the identity realm. There are demons in the astral plane, entities who are controlled by them, and there are people in embodiment.

All of these levels need to be judged, bound, taken, consumed and removed from the earth. *We* can do this. We can do this in the blink of an eye when we have the authority. Only *you* can give us that authority—you and a critical mass of other people. You do not need to worry about the critical mass. You need to worry about yourself. *You* make the choice. *You* make the call. *You* give us the authority, and you will have done what you came here to do. You have done all you *can* do, and I am not asking you to do any more.

23 | CLEARING THE IDENTITY OCTAVE

In the name of the I AM THAT I AM, Jesus Christ, I call upon Mother Mary, Alpha and Omega for the clearing of the identity realm from all demons, entities and fallen beings who are helping to start wars or preventing people from stopping war and conflict. Awaken people to the reality that we are spiritual beings and that we can co-create a new future by working with the ascended masters. I especially call for …

[Make your own calls here.]

Part 1

1. Beloved Alpha, I call forth your judgment upon the fallen beings in the identity realm who have taken the unconditional command "Thou shall not kill" and turned it into a relative statement where killing is acceptable based on their conditions.

> Beloved Alpha, God's great plan,
> in Central Sun it all began,
> what wondrous vision of a world,
> the cosmic spheres were then unfurled.
>
> **Beloved Alpha, in your light,**
> **I now see God with inner sight,**
> **as man I will no longer live,**
> **my life to God I fully give.**

2. Beloved Alpha, I call forth your judgment upon the people in embodiment who have been able to attune to the fallen beings in the identity realm.

> Beloved Alpha, serve the All,
> this is Creator's timeless call,
> from out Creator's perfect whole,
> sprang lifestreams with a sacred goal.
>
> **Beloved Alpha, in your light,**
> **I now see God with inner sight,**
> **as man I will no longer live,**
> **my life to God I fully give.**

3. Beloved Alpha, I call forth your judgment upon the fallen beings in the identity realm who used St. Augustine and other church fathers to bring forth the false ideas behind the Catholic Church.

> Beloved Alpha, all was one,
> as we were sent from Central Sun,
> to you we shall in time return,
> for cosmic union we do yearn.
>
> **Beloved Alpha, in your light,**
> **I now see God with inner sight,**
> **as man I will no longer live,**
> **my life to God I fully give.**

4. Beloved Alpha, I call forth your judgment upon the fallen beings in the identity realm who promote the idea that human beings are fundamentally flawed because they were created that way by God.

> Beloved Alpha, I now see,
> you with Omega form the key,
> it was from your polarity,
> that I received identity.
>
> **Beloved Alpha, in your light,**
> **I now see God with inner sight,**
> **as man I will no longer live,**
> **my life to God I fully give.**

5. Beloved Alpha, I call forth your judgment upon the fallen beings in the identity realm who promote the idea that something has gone wrong with God's creation, that there is a flaw in God's design.

> Beloved Alpha, cosmic gate,
> the nexus of your figure-eight,
> I sprang from Cosmic Cube so bright,
> I am at heart a spark of light.
>
> **Beloved Alpha, in your light,**
> **I now see God with inner sight,**
> **as man I will no longer live,**
> **my life to God I fully give.**

6. Beloved Alpha, I call forth your judgment upon the fallen beings in the identity realm who promote the idea that God made a mistake and that someone needs to correct that mistake, namely themselves.

> Beloved Alpha, from your womb,
> I did descend to matter's tomb,
> but buried I will be no more,
> my inner vision you restore.
>
> **Beloved Alpha, in your light,**
> **I now see God with inner sight,**
> **as man I will no longer live,**
> **my life to God I fully give.**

7. Beloved Alpha, I call forth your judgment upon the fallen beings in the identity realm who promote the idea that God made a mistake by giving self-aware beings free will and the option to go against the growth process of the cosmos.

> Beloved Alpha, I now know,
> the love you did on me bestow,
> a co-creator, I will bring,
> the light to make all matter sing.

> **Beloved Alpha, in your light,**
> **I now see God with inner sight,**
> **as man I will no longer live,**
> **my life to God I fully give.**

8. Beloved Alpha, I call forth your judgment upon the fallen beings in the identity realm who promote the idea that we are nothing more than evolved animals, that our sense of self-awareness and consciousness is a product of mechanical processes in the physical brain.

> Beloved Alpha, on this earth,
> a new age we are giving birth,
> for we are here to bring the love,
> that you are sending from Above.

> **Beloved Alpha, in your light,**
> **I now see God with inner sight,**
> **as man I will no longer live,**
> **my life to God I fully give.**

9. Beloved Alpha, I call forth your judgment upon the fallen beings in the identity realm who promote the idea that we are not only sinners or material beings, but we are separate beings.

> Beloved Alpha, you and me,
> we form a true polarity,
> as up Above, so here below,
> with life's own river I do flow.
>
> **Beloved Alpha, in your light,**
> **I now see God with inner sight,**
> **as man I will no longer live,**
> **my life to God I fully give.**

Part 2

1. Beloved Omega, I call forth your judgment upon the fallen beings in the identity realm who promote the idea that a guru has special qualities and we should follow that guru because he or she is so special.

> Omega, I now meditate,
> upon your throne in cosmic gate.
> I'm born out of the figure-eight,
> that Alpha and you co-create.
>
> **O Song of Life, you vitalize,**
> **all hearts you truly synchronize.**
> **O Sacred Sound, you alchemize,**
> **turn earth into a paradise.**

2. Beloved Omega, awaken all spiritual people from the tendency to follow the false gurus of the fallen beings, so they can say: "I do not want one of these fallen gurus. I want an ascended master as my guide, as my teacher, as my guru."

> Omega, in your sacred space,
> my cosmic parents I embrace.
> I see that it is such a grace,
> that I take part in cosmic race.
>
> **O Song of Life, you vitalize,**
> **all hearts you truly synchronize.**
> **O Sacred Sound, you alchemize,**
> **turn earth into a paradise.**

3. Beloved Omega, I call forth your judgment upon the fallen beings in the identity realm who deny the reality that we are extensions of the Creator's being, that we are extensions of the ascended masters, that we are spiritual beings, that we are sons or daughters of God.

> Omega in the Central Sun,
> you show me life is cosmic fun.
> And thus a victory is won,
> my homeward journey has begun.
>
> **O Song of Life, you vitalize,**
> **all hearts you truly synchronize.**
> **O Sacred Sound, you alchemize,**
> **turn earth into a paradise.**

4. Beloved Omega, I call forth your judgment upon the fallen beings in the identity realm who want us to deny our Christ potential, our potential to know the underlying reality that all life is one, that God is everywhere, that nothing can be separated from God's creation.

> Omega, femininity
> is doorway to infinity.
> With you I have affinity,
> to know my own divinity.
>
> **O Song of Life, you vitalize,**
> **all hearts you truly synchronize.**
> **O Sacred Sound, you alchemize,**
> **turn earth into a paradise.**

5. Beloved Omega, I call forth your judgment upon the fallen beings in the identity realm who control the false gurus in the world. I call forth your judgment upon the false gurus who are able to tune in to the fallen beings in the identity realm and who are leading those astray who have the potential to manifest personal Christhood.

> Omega, in your cosmic flow,
> my plan divine I clearly know.
> My heart is now a lamp aglow,
> as love on all I do bestow.
>
> **O Song of Life, you vitalize,**
> **all hearts you truly synchronize.**
> **O Sacred Sound, you alchemize,**
> **turn earth into a paradise.**

6. Beloved Omega, I call forth your judgment upon the fallen beings in the identity realm and the false gurus in embodiment who promote the idea that we can perfect the separate self and force God to allow it into the ascended realm.

> Omega, cosmic Mother Flame,
> this is the light from which I came.
> As I take part in cosmic game,
> Christ victory I do proclaim.

> **O Song of Life, you vitalize,**
> **all hearts you truly synchronize.**
> **O Sacred Sound, you alchemize,**
> **turn earth into a paradise.**

7. Beloved Omega, I call forth your judgment upon the fallen beings in the identity realm and the false gurus in embodiment who seek to lead those who begin to awaken onto the false path, so they seek to raise up the separate self instead of letting it die.

> Omega, I now comprehend,
> why I did to earth descend.
> And thus I fully do intend,
> to help this planet to ascend.

> **O Song of Life, you vitalize,**
> **all hearts you truly synchronize.**
> **O Sacred Sound, you alchemize,**
> **turn earth into a paradise.**

8. Beloved Omega, I call forth your judgment upon the fallen beings in the identity realm who believe that if they can get enough people on earth to follow their false ideas, then God will be forced to acknowledge their superiority and allow them not only to enter heaven but to also have power over the unascended lifestreams on earth and other planets.

> Omega, I do now aspire,
> to join the ranks of cosmic choir.
> My heart burns with a Christic fire,
> that is this planet's sanctifier.

> **O Song of Life, you vitalize,**
> **all hearts you truly synchronize.**
> **O Sacred Sound, you alchemize,**
> **turn earth into a paradise.**

9. Beloved Omega, I call forth your judgment upon the fallen beings in the identity realm who dream of being the masters of the entire universe, those who have anger against the people on earth who will not follow them blindly.

> Omega, my heart is ablaze,
> my life is in an upward phase.
> Come teach me now the secret phrase,
> so that I can this planet raise.

> **O Song of Life, you vitalize,**
> **all hearts you truly synchronize.**
> **O Sacred Sound, you alchemize,**
> **turn earth into a paradise.**

Part 3

1. Beloved Alpha, I call forth your judgment upon the fallen beings in the identity realm who do everything they can to distort people's sense of identity, to prevent us from claiming our Christhood while we are in embodiment.

> Beloved Alpha, God's great plan,
> in Central Sun it all began,
> what wondrous vision of a world,
> the cosmic spheres were then unfurled.
>
> **Beloved Alpha, in your light,**
> **I now see God with inner sight,**
> **as man I will no longer live,**
> **my life to God I fully give.**

2. Beloved Alpha, I call forth your judgment upon the fallen beings in the identity realm who seek to control all people on earth, but who are willing to kill all those who cannot be controlled.

> Beloved Alpha, serve the All,
> this is Creator's timeless call,
> from out Creator's perfect whole,
> sprang lifestreams with a sacred goal.
>
> **Beloved Alpha, in your light,**
> **I now see God with inner sight,**
> **as man I will no longer live,**
> **my life to God I fully give.**

3. Beloved Alpha, I call forth your judgment upon the fallen beings in the identity realm who are not driven primarily by a desire to control people on earth, but by a desire to control God.

> Beloved Alpha, all was one,
> as we were sent from Central Sun,
> to you we shall in time return,
> for cosmic union we do yearn.
>
> **Beloved Alpha, in your light,**
> **I now see God with inner sight,**
> **as man I will no longer live,**
> **my life to God I fully give.**

4. Beloved Alpha, I call forth your judgment upon the fallen beings in the identity realm who are feeling high and mighty because they feel they have immense power, knowledge, insight and ability to deceive and control.

> Beloved Alpha, I now see,
> you with Omega form the key,
> it was from your polarity,
> that I received identity.
>
> **Beloved Alpha, in your light,**
> **I now see God with inner sight,**
> **as man I will no longer live,**
> **my life to God I fully give.**

5. Beloved Alpha, I call forth your judgment upon the fallen beings in the identity realm who know the reality of the law that they do not have any authority over planet earth because that authority rests with the lifestreams who are in physical embodiment.

> Beloved Alpha, cosmic gate,
> the nexus of your figure-eight,
> I sprang from Cosmic Cube so bright,
> I am at heart a spark of light.
>
> **Beloved Alpha, in your light,**
> **I now see God with inner sight,**
> **as man I will no longer live,**
> **my life to God I fully give.**

6. Beloved Alpha, I call forth your judgment upon the fallen beings in the identity realm who appear benign, advanced, masterful and powerful because they are very skilled at using the intellect and coming up with reasoning and ideas.

> Beloved Alpha, from your womb,
> I did descend to matter's tomb,
> but buried I will be no more,
> my inner vision you restore.
>
> **Beloved Alpha, in your light,**
> **I now see God with inner sight,**
> **as man I will no longer live,**
> **my life to God I fully give.**

7. Beloved Alpha, I call forth your judgment upon the fallen beings in the identity realm who promote the idea that the Catholic Church is the only means to salvation, thereby promoting an external salvation.

> Beloved Alpha, I now know,
> the love you did on me bestow,
> a co-creator, I will bring,
> the light to make all matter sing.
>
> **Beloved Alpha, in your light,**
> **I now see God with inner sight,**
> **as man I will no longer live,**
> **my life to God I fully give.**

8. Beloved Alpha, I call forth your judgment upon the fallen beings in the identity realm who promote the ideas behind Marxism and Communism on one side and Capitalism on the other side.

> Beloved Alpha, on this earth,
> a new age we are giving birth,
> for we are here to bring the love,
> that you are sending from Above.
>
> **Beloved Alpha, in your light,**
> **I now see God with inner sight,**
> **as man I will no longer live,**
> **my life to God I fully give.**

9. Beloved Alpha, I call forth your judgment upon the fallen beings in the identity realm who promote the ideas behind Darwin's theory of evolution, the idea that we are evolved animals and the idea of the survival of the fittest.

> Beloved Alpha, you and me,
> we form a true polarity,
> as up Above, so here below,
> with life's own river I do flow.
>
> **Beloved Alpha, in your light,**
> **I now see God with inner sight,**
> **as man I will no longer live,**
> **my life to God I fully give.**

Part 4

1. Beloved Omega, I call forth your judgment upon the fallen beings in the identity realm who promote the materialistic mindset, claiming to liberate the minds of human beings from the dogmas and doctrines of the Catholic Church, the dogmas they themselves had created.

> Omega, I now meditate,
> upon your throne in cosmic gate.
> I'm born out of the figure-eight,
> that Alpha and you co-create.

> O Song of Life, you vitalize,
> all hearts you truly synchronize.
> O Sacred Sound, you alchemize,
> turn earth into a paradise.

2. Beloved Omega, I call forth your judgment upon the fallen beings in the identity realm who are putting on a facade of working for a benign, beneficial cause, but they would kill all people on earth if they could not control them.

> Omega, in your sacred space,
> my cosmic parents I embrace.
> I see that it is such a grace,
> that I take part in cosmic race.

> **O Song of Life, you vitalize,**
> **all hearts you truly synchronize.**
> **O Sacred Sound, you alchemize,**
> **turn earth into a paradise.**

3. Beloved Omega, I call forth your judgment upon the fallen beings in the identity realm who have the overall agenda of wanting to prove God wrong by proving free will wrong, by proving that free will leads to disastrous consequences.

> Omega in the Central Sun,
> you show me life is cosmic fun.
> And thus a victory is won,
> my homeward journey has begun.

**O Song of Life, you vitalize,
all hearts you truly synchronize.
O Sacred Sound, you alchemize,
turn earth into a paradise.**

4. Beloved Omega, I call forth your judgment upon the fallen beings in the identity realm who think that, if they can get all human beings on earth to enter a completely self-destructive spiral, then they will have ultimately proven that free will has such drastic consequences that it must be a mistake.

> Omega, femininity
> is doorway to infinity.
> With you I have affinity,
> to know my own divinity.

**O Song of Life, you vitalize,
all hearts you truly synchronize.
O Sacred Sound, you alchemize,
turn earth into a paradise.**

5. Beloved Omega, I call forth your judgment upon the fallen beings in the identity realm who appear benign, benevolent and masterful, but still have such anger against God that they are ultimately willing to kill all human beings on earth. They are willing to have them kill each other and even to destroy the entire planet in order to prove their point.

> Omega, in your cosmic flow,
> my plan divine I clearly know.
> My heart is now a lamp aglow,
> as love on all I do bestow.

> O Song of Life, you vitalize,
> all hearts you truly synchronize.
> O Sacred Sound, you alchemize,
> turn earth into a paradise.

6. Beloved Omega, I call forth your judgment upon the fallen beings in the identity realm who appear to be sophisticated and masterful, but who have the most extreme insensitivity towards human beings.

> Omega, cosmic Mother Flame,
> this is the light from which I came.
> As I take part in cosmic game,
> Christ victory I do proclaim.

> **O Song of Life, you vitalize,**
> **all hearts you truly synchronize.**
> **O Sacred Sound, you alchemize,**
> **turn earth into a paradise.**

7. Beloved Omega, I call forth your judgment upon the fallen beings in the identity realm who look upon human beings as tools, and who are willing to destroy what they cannot control.

> Omega, I now comprehend,
> why I did to earth descend.
> And thus I fully do intend,
> to help this planet to ascend.

> **O Song of Life, you vitalize,**
> **all hearts you truly synchronize.**
> **O Sacred Sound, you alchemize,**
> **turn earth into a paradise.**

8. Beloved Omega, I call forth your judgment upon the fallen beings in the identity realm and the entire structure below them, the false pyramid, the pyramid of death. I call forth your judgment upon the beings in the mental realm, the beings in the astral plane and the people in embodiment who are controlled by the fallen beings in the identity realm.

> Omega, I do now aspire,
> to join the ranks of cosmic choir.
> My heart burns with a Christic fire,
> that is this planet's sanctifier.
>
> **O Song of Life, you vitalize,**
> **all hearts you truly synchronize.**
> **O Sacred Sound, you alchemize,**
> **turn earth into a paradise.**

9. Beloved Omega, I hereby use the authority of Christ within me to declare: "I have had enough of war on earth. It is absolutely unacceptable and intolerable to me that war continues to happen on this planet. I will no longer accept war on planet earth."

> Omega, my heart is ablaze,
> my life is in an upward phase.
> Come teach me now the secret phrase,
> so that I can this planet raise.
>
> **O Song of Life, you vitalize,**
> **all hearts you truly synchronize.**
> **O Sacred Sound, you alchemize,**
> **turn earth into a paradise.**

Sealing

In the name of the I AM THAT I AM, I accept that Archangel Michael, Astrea and Shiva form an impenetrable shield around myself and all constructive people, sealing us from all fear-based energies in all four octaves. I accept that the Light of God is consuming and transforming all fear-based energies that make up the forces behind war!

24 | PROTECTING YOURSELF FROM THE FALLEN BEINGS

I know very well that our teachings can encourage some students to become unbalanced. You become so fired up, so to speak, about doing what you came here to do. Some people feel that they have wasted a big part of their lives by not having found the teachings. When they finally find the teachings, they want to compensate for this by throwing themselves at it and making calls all day and neglecting other parts of life. I am not asking you to do this.

I know that war is an extreme condition on earth. I know that when you are a soldier in war, you are in a very extreme state. I am not asking you, as an ascended master student, to go into a warlike mindset and put other aspects of your life aside and think that now you have to live some unbalanced, extreme lifestyle in order to bring the judgment of the fallen beings. I am asking you to live a balanced spiritual life, but to still find time to make the calls and give us the authority and the energy to multiply so that we can do our work.

Yes, war is an extreme condition. Yes, it needs to be removed, but do you not see that what the fallen beings are doing by creating war is that they are forcing human beings in embodiment to go towards greater and greater extremes to defeat the enemy?

Do you not also see, as I have been explaining over and over again, that for everything that happens in the physical, there is a parallel in consciousness? When you see people take extreme physical actions, you know that they have gone into a parallel extreme in their emotional, mental and identity bodies. Do you not also see that it is this unbalance in the three higher bodies that leads to the imbalance at the physical level? Why would you think that you going into an imbalanced state would help remove war from the earth?

You would actually contribute to the imbalance on earth, even though you are a spiritual student following a spiritual teaching. There are ascended master students who have found our teachings, given in past dispensations, and who have used them to become so unbalanced that they have actually contributed to the survival of war on earth through their imbalance. They have also become so angry with the fallen beings, or with certain human beings from another political system, that they have contributed to the misqualified energy that feeds the entire war machine. This I am asking you to *not* do.

I am asking you to take our teachings, and the many other teachings we have given about balance, and to walk a balanced path, to live a balanced life. I am not asking you to go to war against war. I am asking you to fight war by finding your own personal inner balance, by finding your personal inner peace and, from that state of peace, making the calls that give us the authority to go in and do the dirty work, so to speak, of cleaning up the astral pit and the mental and identity realms. This is *our* job. This is *our* task. This is *our* joy. We are perfectly capable of doing this without going into a state of imbalance. Archangel Michael is absolutely unbending when he is dealing with the fallen beings, but he is not angry with them. He is not in his mind fighting a battle against them. He is simply doing his work, being completely centered in the peace of God.

There is more to be said about war

You will notice that in this book I have talked a lot about war but very little about peace. Of course, I want you to find the peace that will make you the most efficient warrior against war. You do not remove war by fighting it but by transcending the consciousness behind it.

For you to be most efficient in making the calls for the removing of the forces of war, you need to transcend the consciousness that you want to see removed. This we have given you the tools to do, both in this book and in our other books. I would consider it important for those who are using this book in order to make the calls that you also study the book *Warrior of Peace* and other of our books that talk about the duality consciousness. Certainly, you should be familiar with the teachings given by Maitreya, and you may find them in a concentrated form in the book *Cosmology of Evil*.

My beloved, I have said many things in this book about war, but I do not want you to think that this is the end-all or be-all of war. Much more can be said. Perhaps, more *will* be said if a critical mass of people take the teachings we are giving in this book and make use them. What I *will* say is that if a critical mass of people take this book, take the tools and teachings, and make use of them, then we can make an incredibly significant step towards removing war from this planet. Even though there is more to be said about war, what I have given you here is complete in itself. If a critical mass of people took and used the tools and teachings I have given in this book, then we could start a process that would quickly become irreversible and would lead to the complete removal of war from planet earth.

It is possible that, within a few decades, people would look back and would scarcely be able to understand that such dramatic changes could happen in such a short time. They would look at the specter of war as it has been hanging over humankind for thousands of years and they would say: "How could it disappear so quickly?" Probably, official society would never recognize the importance of spiritual people making the calls. If a critical mass of people would embrace the teachings and tools in this book, then I can assure you that war could become an impossibility in the lifetimes of many of you.

Would this not be a great joy to your heart? Would it not give you a sense that you have fulfilled an important part of your purpose for coming to this planet? Would it not make you feel that it was worthwhile, even though this is such a difficult and dense planet upon which to embody?

I know many of you have gone through many hardships, many sufferings, but if you could feel that you had made an important contribution to the removal of war, would it not all have been worth it? Would you not feel this connection to the River of Life and a sense that, even though one human lifetime may seem insignificant, it can still be part of the cosmic purpose, the cosmic upward movement that is the River of Life?

Overcoming the recoil from the fallen beings

I know that if you start making the calls on war, you will go through a period where you will feel very burdened by the

24 | Protecting Yourself from the Fallen Beings

energies you are dealing with. You should be able to realize by now that, when you start using the tools in this book, the fallen beings will throw everything they have at you in all four levels. They will attempt to manipulate you. They will attempt to burden you in all ways. They might even attempt to do this with the people in your circle of influence. That is why you need to make the calls for the protection not only of yourself but of all people around you.

Again, I am not asking you to go into a state of fear or a sense of being at war or fighting the fallen beings. I am just asking you to make the calls so that we can do the work of protecting you. I am also asking you to be aware that when you feel burdened, when you feel you are under attack, it is because there is something, some illusion, in your consciousness that the fallen beings are using to burden you. I am asking you to look at that beam in your own eye and to use our teachings and tools to remove it so that you can transcend it and become even more efficient.

What I am telling you here is this: If you make the decision to seriously start using the tools and teachings in this book, you will go through an initial period where you will feel, perhaps, even more burdened than you feel today. You will feel you are being attacked. You should know that this is the fallen beings throwing everything at you in order to discourage you from doing the work that will lead to their removal from the earth. With all I have told you about the fallen beings, you should not be surprised that they would do this. They will do absolutely anything they can to prevent anyone from using the teachings and tools of the ascended masters because it will lead to their own removal from the earth. For them, it is seen as a life-and-death battle.

I am asking you to *not* see it this way but to simply be aware of what is happening and what will be happening. Then make the calls for it. Then look at yourself and overcome the illusion that gives them an inroad into your consciousness. If you do this knowingly, you will be surprised at how quickly you can work through this period. You will come out the other side feeling that you have now raised yourself to a point where the fallen beings cannot reach you as they used to be able to do. You have accelerated yourself. You have accelerated your consciousness beyond the reach of those fallen beings who were attacking you in the past. This is a great sense of freedom, a great sense of inner knowing.

You cannot awaken by remaining blind

My beloved, do you begin to see here that even though they say "ignorance is bliss," ignorance is *not* bliss? I have talked about the spiritual people who feel that all they need to do is to be positive and send out positive vibrations. There are those who say that you should not put your mind on anything dark or evil because even by making the calls or the invocations I am giving you, you are, they say, giving your energy to the dark forces. I can assure you that these invocations are designed in such a way that they will not give your energy to the dark forces, unless you give them from a state of extreme imbalance. If you give them with non-attachment, centered in peace, knowing that *we* will do the work, then you will not give your energies to the dark forces.

What I am pointing out to you is that the spiritual path is a path of awakening. You do not awaken by remaining blind. There are spiritual people who refuse to look at the existence of dark forces, and they think they can still walk the spiritual path, but you cannot walk the path beyond a certain level. The real path is that, as you begin to awaken yourself, you must look at the planet you are on. You must look at what is going on here. You must acknowledge the presence of fallen beings because they are such an intricate part of planet earth and have been for so long. You cannot walk the spiritual path on a planet like earth without becoming aware of the fallen beings. I am not asking you to fight them or give them energy. I am not asking you to be afraid of them. I am asking you to be aware.

Do you understand what I am saying? You cannot walk the spiritual path towards a higher state of consciousness by remaining unaware. You cannot walk the path by refusing to look at something just because it is inconvenient or unpleasant to you. You walk the path by being willing to look at *everything*.

First, you must look at the fallen beings. Then you will be disturbed when you begin to acknowledge the things I have told you in this book. As you keep rising, you will come to a point where you have now transcended the fallen beings. Now you can look at them and acknowledge their existence with complete non-attachment and inner peace.

Looking at darkness while maintaining harmony

Some spiritual students think that it is so important to be at peace and maintain their inner harmony that they will not look at anything that might disturb that harmony. As long as there is *anything* that can disturb your inner harmony, you have not reached a high level of spiritual attainment. You have only created the outer impression of having spiritual attainment because you are supposedly always able to maintain this state of inner harmony and balance. This is not true spiritual attainment. This is not mastery.

The Buddha did not enter nirvana by ignoring the demons of Mara. The last test he faced was that he had to look at all the demons of Mara, and he had to allow them to do anything and everything they could think of to get him to react. He had to sit there and see it all and remain non-attached so that he did not react. Then, he could enter nirvana. You cannot enter your own personal nirvana until you are able and willing to look at everything the fallen beings can throw at you and simply look at it all and say: "I am not this."

You cannot walk the spiritual path by being unaware of what is happening on the planet where you have taken embodiment. You must see everything, and then you must see beyond it. You see that, behind all the demons of Mara, everything is still the Buddha nature. Everything is still one. You look at everything here on earth and you say: "I am not this." Then, you look at the oneness of the spiritual realm and you say: "I AM this. I am that 'I AM' up there, not the separate 'I am' down here." Then you can enter nirvana.

Be here Below all that You are Above

I will be the first to greet you. I am asking you to consider that your goal for taking embodiment on earth in this lifetime was not primarily to enter nirvana. It was to do some work while you are in embodiment on this planet. You came here to make a difference because you saw how critical this time is for the evolution of the earth. You set aside your personal entering of nirvana in order to do the work of raising the earth and setting free the billions of lifestreams that embody upon it.

With this, I simply want to welcome you into the ranks of those who consider themselves not only ascended master students but who are also beginning to consider themselves the extensions of the ascended masters on earth.

24 | Protecting Yourself from the Fallen Beings

You are among those who are beginning to realize that the highest potential of earth is to be "as Above, so below." This will happen only when you become as Above, so below. Will you become here below all that you already are Above? I AM Mother Mary Above. Will *you* be Mother Mary below?

25 | PROTECTION FROM DARK FORCES

In the name of the I AM THAT I AM, Jesus Christ, I call upon Mother Mary, Archangel Michael, Astrea and Saint Germain to help us accelerate ourselves beyond the reach of the dark forces. Awaken people to the reality that we are spiritual beings and that we can co-create a new future by working with the ascended masters. I especially call for …

[Make your own calls here.]

Part 1

1. Archangel Michael, I accept your total protection for myself and all people in my circle of influence from any backlash from the fallen beings in the form of physical accidents, mishaps or acts of violence.

Archangel Michael, light so blue,
my heart has room for only you.
My mind is one, no longer two,
your love for me is ever true.

Archangel Michael, you are here,
your light consumes all doubt and fear.
Your Presence is forever near,
you are to me so very dear.

2. Archangel Michael, I accept your total protection for myself and all people in my circle of influence from any backlash from the fallen beings in the form of disease or problems with the physical body.

Archangel Michael, I will be,
all one with your reality.
No fear can hold me as I see,
this world no power has o'er me.

Archangel Michael, you are here,
your light consumes all doubt and fear.
Your Presence is forever near,
you are to me so very dear.

3. Archangel Michael, I accept your total protection for myself and all people in my circle of influence from any backlash from the fallen beings in the form of emotional projections causing erratic or insane behavior.

Archangel Michael, hold me tight,
shatter now the darkest night.
Clear my chakras with your light,
restore to me my inner sight.

**Archangel Michael, you are here,
your light consumes all doubt and fear.
Your Presence is forever near,
you are to me so very dear.**

4. Archangel Michael, I accept your total protection for myself and all people in my circle of influence from any backlash from the fallen beings in the form of emotional projections causing depression or a sense of discouragement.

Archangel Michael, now I stand,
with you the light I do command.
My heart I ever will expand,
till highest truth I understand.

**Archangel Michael, you are here,
your light consumes all doubt and fear.
Your Presence is forever near,
you are to me so very dear.**

5. Archangel Michael, I accept your total protection for myself and all people in my circle of influence from any backlash from the fallen beings in the form of mental projections causing confusion or mental instability.

Archangel Michael, in my heart,
from me you never will depart.
Of hierarchy I am a part,
I now accept a fresh new start.

**Archangel Michael, you are here,
your light consumes all doubt and fear.
Your Presence is forever near,
you are to me so very dear.**

6. Archangel Michael, I accept your total protection for myself and all people in my circle of influence from any backlash from the fallen beings in the form of mental projections causing fanaticism or closed-mindedness.

Archangel Michael, sword of blue,
all darkness you are cutting through.
My Christhood I do now pursue,
discernment shows me what is true.

**Archangel Michael, you are here,
your light consumes all doubt and fear.
Your Presence is forever near,
you are to me so very dear.**

7. Archangel Michael, I accept your total protection for myself and all people in my circle of influence from any backlash from the fallen beings in the form of identity projections causing attachments to certain belief systems.

> Archangel Michael, in your wings,
> I now let go of lesser things.
> God's homing call in my heart rings,
> my heart with yours forever sings.
>
> **Archangel Michael, you are here,**
> **your light consumes all doubt and fear.**
> **Your Presence is forever near,**
> **you are to me so very dear.**

8. Archangel Michael, I accept your total protection for myself and all people in my circle of influence from any backlash from the fallen beings in the form of identity projections causing an identity crisis or fanaticism.

> Archangel Michael, take me home,
> in higher spheres I want to roam.
> I am reborn from cosmic foam,
> my life is now a sacred poem.
>
> **Archangel Michael, you are here,**
> **your light consumes all doubt and fear.**
> **Your Presence is forever near,**
> **you are to me so very dear.**

9. Archangel Michael, I accept your total protection for myself and all people in my circle of influence from any backlash from the fallen beings in the form of any opposition to our spiritual growth.

Archangel Michael, light you are,
shining like the bluest star.
You are a cosmic avatar,
with you I will go very far.

**Archangel Michael, you are here,
your light consumes all doubt and fear.
Your Presence is forever near,
you are to me so very dear.**

Part 2

1. Beloved Astrea, I accept that you are cutting free myself and all people in my circle of influence from any fallen beings in embodiment or any people controlled by fallen beings in the three higher octaves.

Astrea, loving Being white,
your Presence is my pure delight,
your sword and circle white and blue,
the astral plane is cutting through.

**Astrea, come accelerate,
with purity I do vibrate,
release the fire so blue and white,
my aura filled with vibrant light.**

2. Beloved Astrea, I accept that you are cutting free myself and all people in my circle of influence from any fallen beings, demons or entities in the astral plane.

Astrea, calm the raging storm,
so purity will be the norm,
my aura filled with blue and white,
with shining armor, like a knight.

**Astrea, come accelerate,
with purity I do vibrate,
release the fire so blue and white,
my aura filled with vibrant light.**

3. Beloved Astrea, I accept that you are cutting free myself and all people in my circle of influence from any fallen beings or demons in the mental realm.

Astrea, come and cut me free,
from every binding entity,
let astral forces all be bound,
true freedom I have surely found.

**Astrea, come accelerate,
with purity I do vibrate,
release the fire so blue and white,
my aura filled with vibrant light.**

4. Beloved Astrea, I accept that you are cutting free myself and all people in my circle of influence from any fallen beings or demons in the identity octave.

Astrea, I sincerely urge,
from demons all, do me purge,
consume them all and take me higher,
I will endure your cleansing fire.

> **Astrea, come accelerate,**
> **with purity I do vibrate,**
> **release the fire so blue and white,**
> **my aura filled with vibrant light.**

5. Beloved Astrea, I accept that you are binding and consuming the demons and fallen beings in the astral plane who are attacking myself or any people in my circle of influence as an act of revenge for me making the calls for putting a stop to war.

> Astrea, do all spirits bind,
> so that I am no longer blind,
> I see the spirit and its twin,
> the victory of Christ I win.

> **Astrea, come accelerate,**
> **with purity I do vibrate,**
> **release the fire so blue and white,**
> **my aura filled with vibrant light.**

6. Beloved Astrea, I accept that you are binding and consuming the demons and fallen beings in the mental realm who are attacking myself or any people in my circle of influence as an act of revenge for me making the calls for putting a stop to war.

> Astrea, clear my every cell,
> from energies of death and hell,
> my body is now free to grow,
> each cell emits an inner glow.

> Astrea, come accelerate,
> with purity I do vibrate,
> release the fire so blue and white,
> my aura filled with vibrant light.

7. Beloved Astrea, I accept that you are binding and consuming the demons and fallen beings in the identity realm who are attacking myself or any people in my circle of influence as an act of revenge for me making the calls for putting a stop to war.

> Astrea, clear my feeling mind,
> in purity my peace I find,
> with higher feeling you release,
> I co-create in perfect peace.

> Astrea, come accelerate,
> with purity I do vibrate,
> release the fire so blue and white,
> my aura filled with vibrant light.

8. Beloved Astrea, I accept that you are binding and consuming the demons and fallen beings who are aggressively seeking to discourage me from doing the work that will lead to their removal from the earth.

> Astrea, clear my mental realm,
> my Christ self always at the helm,
> I see now how to manifest,
> the matrix that for all is best.

**Astrea, come accelerate,
with purity I do vibrate,
release the fire so blue and white,
my aura filled with vibrant light.**

9. Beloved Astrea, I accept that you are binding and consuming the demons and fallen beings who are seeking to prevent anyone from using the teachings and tools of the ascended masters that will lead to their removal from the earth.

Astrea, with great clarity,
I claim a new identity,
etheric blueprint I now see,
I co-create more consciously.

**Astrea, come accelerate,
with purity I do vibrate,
release the fire so blue and white,
my aura filled with vibrant light.**

Part 3

1. Mother Mary, I accept that you are helping myself and all people in my circle of influence see and transcend all physical habits that are making us vulnerable to the attacks of the demons and fallen beings in all for octaves.

O blessed Mary, Mother mine,
there is no greater love than thine,
as we are one in heart and mind,
my place in hierarchy I find.

**O Mother Mary, generate,
the song that does accelerate,
the earth into a higher state,
all matter does now scintillate.**

2. Mother Mary, I accept that you are helping myself and all people in my circle of influence see and transcend all emotional patterns that are making us vulnerable to the attacks of the demons and fallen beings in all for octaves.

> I came to earth from heaven sent,
> as I am in embodiment,
> I use Divine authority,
> commanding you to set earth free.

**O Mother Mary, generate,
the song that does accelerate,
the earth into a higher state,
all matter does now scintillate.**

3. Mother Mary, I accept that you are helping myself and all people in my circle of influence see and transcend all mental illusions that are making us vulnerable to the attacks of the demons and fallen beings in all for octaves.

> I call now in God's sacred name,
> for you to use your Mother Flame,
> to burn all fear-based energy,
> restoring sacred harmony.

> **O Mother Mary, generate,**
> **the song that does accelerate,**
> **the earth into a higher state,**
> **all matter does now scintillate.**

4. Mother Mary, I accept that you are helping myself and all people in my circle of influence see and transcend all false sense of identity that is making us vulnerable to the attacks of the demons and fallen beings in all for octaves.

> Your sacred name I hereby praise,
> collective consciousness you raise,
> no more of fear and doubt and shame,
> consume it with your Mother Flame.

> **O Mother Mary, generate,**
> **the song that does accelerate,**
> **the earth into a higher state,**
> **all matter does now scintillate.**

5. Mother Mary, I accept that you are helping myself and all people in my circle of influence see and transcend any tendency to think we are in opposition to the fallen beings or other people.

> All darkness from the earth you purge,
> your light moves as a mighty surge,
> no force of darkness can now stop,
> the spiral that goes only up.

**O Mother Mary, generate,
the song that does accelerate,
the earth into a higher state,
all matter does now scintillate.**

Part 4

1. Saint Germain, send oceans of violet flame into the lives of myself and all people in my circle of influence. Transmute any karmic vulnerability to physical accidents, mishaps or other events that block our Divine plans.

> O Saint Germain, you do inspire,
> my vision raised forever higher,
> with you I form a figure-eight,
> your Golden Age I co-create.

> **O Saint Germain, what love you bring,
> it truly makes all matter sing,
> your violet flame does all restore,
> with you we are becoming more.**

2. Saint Germain, send oceans of violet flame into the physical bodies of myself and all people in my circle of influence. Transmute any karmic vulnerability to physical diseases or bodily imbalances that block our Divine plans.

> O Saint Germain, what Freedom Flame,
> released when we recite your name,
> acceleration is your gift,
> our planet it will surely lift.

**O Saint Germain, what love you bring,
it truly makes all matter sing,
your violet flame does all restore,
with you we are becoming more.**

3. Saint Germain, send oceans of violet flame into the emotional bodies of myself and all people in my circle of influence. Transmute any karmic ties to any beings in the emotional octave and any tendency for depression or emotional instability.

O Saint Germain, in love we claim,
our right to bring your violet flame,
from you Above, to us below,
it is an all-transforming flow.

**O Saint Germain, what love you bring,
it truly makes all matter sing,
your violet flame does all restore,
with you we are becoming more.**

4. Saint Germain, send oceans of violet flame into the mental bodies of myself and all people in my circle of influence. Transmute any karmic ties to any beings in the mental octave and any tendency for confusion or lack of clarity.

O Saint Germain, I love you so,
my aura filled with violet glow,
my chakras filled with violet fire,
I am your cosmic amplifier.

> **O Saint Germain, what love you bring,**
> **it truly makes all matter sing,**
> **your violet flame does all restore,**
> **with you we are becoming more.**

5. Saint Germain, send oceans of violet flame into the identity bodies of myself and all people in my circle of influence. Transmute any karmic ties to any beings in the identity octave and any tendency for fanaticism or closed-mindedness.

> O Saint Germain, I am now free,
> your violet flame is therapy,
> transform all hang-ups in my mind,
> as inner peace I surely find.

> **O Saint Germain, what love you bring,**
> **it truly makes all matter sing,**
> **your violet flame does all restore,**
> **with you we are becoming more.**

6. Saint Germain, send oceans of violet flame into the lives of myself and all people in my circle of influence. Transmute any karmic vulnerability that prevents us from walking a balanced path and living a balanced life.

> O Saint Germain, my body pure,
> your violet flame for all is cure,
> consume the cause of all disease,
> and therefore I am all at ease.

> O Saint Germain, what love you bring,
> it truly makes all matter sing,
> your violet flame does all restore,
> with you we are becoming more.

7. Saint Germain, send oceans of violet flame into the lives of myself and all people in my circle of influence. Transmute any karmic vulnerability that prevents us from finding the personal inner balance that allows us to make the calls that give the ascended masters the authority to remove war from the earth.

> O Saint Germain, I'm karma-free,
> the past no longer burdens me,
> a brand new opportunity,
> I am in Christic unity.

> O Saint Germain, what love you bring,
> it truly makes all matter sing,
> your violet flame does all restore,
> with you we are becoming more.

8. Saint Germain, send oceans of violet flame into the lives of myself and all people in my circle of influence. Transmute any illusion in our own consciousness that makes us vulnerable to the energies and attacks from the dark forces.

> O Saint Germain, we are now one,
> I am for you a violet sun,
> as we transform this planet earth,
> your Golden Age is given birth.

**O Mother Mary, generate,
the song that does accelerate,
the earth into a higher state,
all matter does now scintillate.**

8. Mother Mary, I accept that you are helping myself and all people in my circle of influence see and transcend the intent of the fallen beings to force us to go towards greater and greater extremes in order to defeat an enemy.

> As Mother Earth is free at last,
> disasters belong to the past,
> your Mother Light is so intense,
> that matter is now far less dense.

**O Mother Mary, generate,
the song that does accelerate,
the earth into a higher state,
all matter does now scintillate.**

9. Mother Mary, I accept that you are helping myself and all people in my circle of influence see and transcend any imbalance in the three higher bodies that leads to imbalances at the physical level.

> In Mother Light the earth is pure,
> the upward spiral will endure,
> prosperity is now the norm,
> God's vision manifest as form.

**O Mother Mary, generate,
the song that does accelerate,
the earth into a higher state,
all matter does now scintillate.**

6. Mother Mary, I accept that you are helping myself and all people in my circle of influence see and transcend any tendency to think we have to live an extremist or unbalanced lifestyle in order to fulfill our Divine plans.

> All elemental life you bless,
> removing from them man-made stress,
> the nature spirits are now free,
> outpicturing Divine decree.

**O Mother Mary, generate,
the song that does accelerate,
the earth into a higher state,
all matter does now scintillate.**

7. Mother Mary, I accept that you are helping myself and all people in my circle of influence see and transcend any tendency to go into a mindset where we produce inharmonious energies that actually feed the forces of war.

> I raise my voice and take my stand,
> a stop to war I do command,
> no more shall warring scar the earth,
> a golden age is given birth.

**O Saint Germain, what love you bring,
it truly makes all matter sing,
your violet flame does all restore,
with you we are becoming more.**

9. Saint Germain, send oceans of violet flame into the lives of myself and all people in my circle of influence. Transmute any karmic vulnerability and energies so that the fallen beings can no longer hurt us because we have accelerated our consciousness beyond their reach.

O Saint Germain, the earth is free,
from burden of duality,
in oneness we bring what is best,
your Golden Age is manifest.

**O Saint Germain, what love you bring,
it truly makes all matter sing,
your violet flame does all restore,
with you we are becoming more.**

Sealing

In the name of the I AM THAT I AM, I accept that Archangel Michael, Astrea and Shiva form an impenetrable shield around myself and all constructive people, sealing us from all fear-based energies in all four octaves. I accept that the Light of God is consuming and transforming all fear-based energies that make up the forces behind war!

www.ingramcontent.com/pod-product-compliance
Lightning Source LLC
Chambersburg PA
CBHW031720230426
43669CB00007B/187